Public Policy and Urban Crime

Public Policy and Urban Crime

Yong Hyo Cho
The University of Akron

Ballinger Publishing Company ● **Cambridge, Mass.**
A Subsidiary of J.B. Lippincott Company

Library of Congress Catalog Card Number: 74–1145

International Standard Book Number: 0–88410–201–7

Printed in the United States of America

Library of Congress Cataloging in Publication Data

Cho, Yong Hyo, 1934–
  Public policy and urban crime.

  Bibliography: p.
  1. Criminal justice, Administration of–United States. 2. Crime and criminals–United States. 3. Criminal justice, Administration of–Economic aspects–United States. I. Title.
HV8141.C45   364'.973   74–1145
ISBN 0–88410–201–7

Dedication

To My Wife Chungsoon and Our Children, Miyun and Hearn

Contents

List of Figures

List of Tables

Acknowledgments

The conceptual framework and research design for the policy impact analysis and part of the research reported in this volume were developed from the Local Financing for Criminal Justice Project for which I was the principal investigator during the 1971–1972 academic year. The project was supported by a research grant from the Ohio Department of Economic and Community Development and the Northeast Ohio Areawide Coordinating Agency (NOACA). A faculty research grant by the University of Akron during the 1971–1972 academic year enabled me to gather a part of the data incorporated here. I gratefully acknowledge the invaluable role of both research grants.

In the course of my research and preparation of this manuscript, I was indebted to many individuals whose assistance made it possible for me to bring this work to an expeditious conclusion. I would like to thank my colleagues, particularly Edward Hanten, James Richardson, William Hendon, Gerald Pyle, Frank Costa, Frank Kendrick, and Hugh F. Coyle, to name a few, for their unfailing cooperation in various ways. Many of my former and present graduate students have given me most valuable assistance in gathering the data or computer-processing them. I single out Barbara Wade, Norman Pellegrini, Allen Pearson, Tae Gun Lee, Gary Doyle, Elaine Wiggins, and Robert Reis as those to whom I express my appreciation.

As usual, this manuscript was typed by Arlene Lane and her dedicated team of student assistants, Dianne Esakov, Karen George, Beth Simonson, and Maz Troppe. I extend my thanks to each of them. Needless to say, I am alone responsible for whatever shortcomings there may be in this volume.

Public Policy and Urban Crime

Chapter One

Introduction

Suddenly, in the middle of the 1960s, the nation's cities were besieged with yet another crisis—the crisis of crime in their streets. As the rising crime rate cast its ominous shadow on the streets and neighborhoods, the public fear of crime and the public anger against the "criminals" coalisced into a powerful political pressure clamoring for "law and order." The problem of crime control policy became an all consuming political issue, and government at all levels, pressured by the public demands and dictated by the situational imperatives, strived to develop countervailing policy measures to fight back the assault of the crime wave. The main thrust of the policy responses has been directed toward the expansion of traditional programs of law enforcement and criminal justice—control policies.

Generally speaking, the public policy decisions for crime control were made without the benefit of systematic analysis of their possible effectiveness. The policy-makers, as well as the public, remained faithful to the belief that more policemen on the streets in their patrol cars and better equipment for the policemen, for example, would function as a more effective deterrent to crime. Analytic questions concerning the possible crime-reducing impact of those policy measures were not asked. It is the purpose of this book to ask such questions and seek answers to them through a most systematic analysis of empirical data. The central question raised in this book represents a newly emerging direction in comparative policy analysis. How effective is public policy in producing its intended impact?

For over one-third of a century, the question that dominated the comparative policy analysis was: What makes the outcomes of public policy different from one unit of government to another? The answer to this question was attempted by unravelling the economic, social, and political forces underlying the variance of public policy outcomes among the states or the cities in the United States.

The determinants analysis of public policy outcomes through comparative and statistical methods was initiated by Gerhard Colm in 1936.[1] A generation of economists who followed the analytical framework set forth by Colm have demonstrated that the variance in expenditure or tax policy outcomes among the states or the cities is primarily a function of variance in the economic and social conditions.[2]

In the 1960s, political scientists introduced political and governmental variables into the analysis of policy outcomes. The political science analyses of policy outcomes generated two conflicting conclusions: (1) socioeconomic determinism of policy outcomes; and (2) political-governmental determinism of policy outcomes. The socioeconomic determinism of policy outcomes has demonstrated with a set of empirical data that the variance of policy outcomes among the states or the cities is primarily determined by socioeconomic variables, not political or governmental variables.[3] Political-governmental determinism of policy outcomes does not necessarily prove that government and politics rather than economics determine the outcomes of public policy. What it has demonstrated is that political and governmental variables are important as a determinant of policy outcomes.[4]

Neither of the two conflicting conclusions (socioeconomic determinism vs. political-governmental determinism) seem to fully represent the reality of public policy determination. In view of the results of a more recent study, it is evident that the influence-mix that determines the policy outcomes varies as the policy types differ.[5] Some types of policies are highly sensitive to economic influence, while others are dominated by political influence.

The purpose of this book is not to rehash the determinants analyses of public policy outcomes; it is to test the effectiveness of policy outcomes. Thus, the specific questions we ask for this purpose are as follows: (1) Do those public policy measures that are specifically designed to function as a deterrent to crime, in fact, have a crime-reducing effect? (2) Do those policy measures that are expected to have a crime-reducing influence, though not specifically designed for crime control as such, have a crime-reducing influence as they are expected?

It is important to have these questions answered because we must know whether or not the various measures of public policy adopted for specific purposes and augmented in ensuing years actually generate the intended effect. The problem is that once a policy measure is adopted, the effectiveness of the policy measure is rarely questioned or evaluated systematically in order to justify its continuation or even its expansion. The so-called "incrementalism" in budget policy-making is the most illustrative of this phenomenon.

We must not assume that doing more of the same will better achieve the intended effect for a policy measure. The effectiveness of a policy measure must be tested systematically through empirical analysis. Empirical testing of policy effectiveness is indispensable for the attainment of governmental or social objectives and for the allocation of public resources based on empirical rationality. If an ineffective policy measure receives continuous support without being evaluated and thus without its ineffectiveness being discovered, the governmental objective for which that particular policy measure was originally formulated will remain unaccomplished. The continuous support of an ineffective policy measure is also bound to accelerate the waste of public resources since the programs implementing the policy are most likely to grow if they are not terminated.

This book consists of two parts. The first part is an eclectic introduction to develop a context for the empirical analysis of policy impact on crime. The second part reports our empirical analysis of policy impact on crime in selected cities.

Our introductory part describes and discusses a number of related issues to define the problem context of the policy impact analysis on urban crime. The nature of crime problems including the extent of crime, the trends of crime, and urban vs. rural crime are discussed in Chapter 2. The 7 categories of the FBI index crimes are used for the purpose of our analysis throughout this book. Chapter 3 deals with crime and crime policy problems as social and political issues and, more specifically, as campaign issues in recent elections. Organizational structure and administrative procedures for law enforcement and criminal justice as a part of federal system of government in America are discussed in Chapter 4. The patterns and trends of expenditures for the criminal justice system are presented for all levels of government in the United States, for state and local governments, and for local governments in the Northeast Ohio urbanized region (the jurisdiction of the Northeast Ohio Areawide Coordinating Agency covering 7 counties) in Chapters 5, 6, and 7.

We chose two categories of public policy for the measurement of their impact on city crime rates. They are control policies and social service policies. All measures of law enforcement and criminal justice policy are considered as control policies because they are the principal instrument developed for the specific purpose of crime control. Social service policies include any of the policy measures that can be defined as social welfare policies in a broad sense of the term. Their primary purpose may be to enhance the social or economic equity in the opportunity structure of the society or to improve the environmental quality of urban living. The social service policies are expected to dissipate the crime-inducive influence in the community and, thus, contribute to the reduction of crime indirectly.

To test the effectiveness of selected policy measures of both categories in reducing the crime rate, the recent experiences of two groups of cities are systematically analyzed. The two groups of cities are the 49 largest cities in the United States and the 40 largest cities in the state of Ohio. The step-wise multiple regression technique is employed for our data analysis in two separate stages: first, to identify and select the most influential social ecological variables for each crime rate variable; and second, to measure the "net" effect of each of the policy measures on the crime rate pattern while controlling for the selected ecological variables.

The research design and analytical methods and techniques are discussed in Chapter 8, and the ecological theory of crime and the ecological determinants of the city crime rates that resulted from our first-stage analysis are discussed in Chapter 9. The net impact of the selected policy measures on the crime rate computed through the second-stage regression runs while controlling for the selected ecological variables are reported in Chapters 10 and 11. The final chapter summarizes the relationships between the selected measures of public policy and the crime rates considered in our analysis and proposes some alternatives for the reordering of policy priorities to achieve a better result in reducing crime in the streets of our cities.

NOTES TO CHAPTER ONE

1. "Public Expenditures and Economic Structure in the United States," *Social Research,* Vol. 3, No. 1 (February, 1936). pp. 57–77.
2. Some of the better known works of this type include: Joseph Berolzheimer, "Influence Shaping Expenditures for Operation of State and Local Governments," *Bulletin of National Tax Association,* XXXII, Nos. 6, 7, and 8 (March, April, May, 1947), pp. 170–177, 213–219, 237–244; Solomon Fabricant, *The Trend of Government Activity in the United States Since 1900* (New York: National Bureau of Economic Research, 1952); Harvey Brazer, *City Expenditures in the United States,* Occasional Paper, No. 65 (New York; National Bureau of Economic Research, 1959); Glenn W. Fisher, "Determinants of State and Local Government Expenditures: A Preliminary Analysis," *National Tax Journal,* XIV, 4 (December, 1961), pp. 349–355; Seymour Sacks and Robert Harris, "The Determinants of State and Local Government Expenditures and Intergovernmental Flows of Funds," *National Tax Journal,* XVII, 1 (March, 1964), pp. 75–85; and Roy W. Bahl and Robert J. Saunders, "Determinants of Changes in State and Local Government Expenditures," *National Tax Journal,* XVIII, 1 (March, 1965) pp. 50–57 among others.
3. The socioeconomic determinism was popularized most by the following studies: Richard E. Dawson and James A. Robinson, "Inter-party Competition, Economic Variables and Welfare Policies in the American States," *Journal of Politics,* XXV, 2 (May, 1963), pp. 265–289; Thomas R. Dye, *Politics, Economics, and the Public: Policy Outcomes in the American States* (Chicago: Rand McNally, 1966); and Richard I. Hofferbert, "The Relation Between Public Policy and Some Structural and Environmental Variables in the American States," *American Political Science Review,* LX, 1 (March, 1966), pp. 73–82 to name a few.

4. See, for example, Brian R. Fry and Richard F. Winters, "The Politics of Redistribution," *American Political Science Review,* LXIV, 2 (June, 1970), pp. 504–522; Charles F. Cnudde and Donald J. McCrone, "Party Competition, and Welfare Policies in the American States," *American Political Science Review,* LXIII, 3 (September, 1969) pp. 858–866; and Allan G. Pulsipher and James L. Weatherby, Jr., "Malapportionment, Party Competition, and Functional Distribution of Government Expenditures," *American Political Science Review,* LXII, 4 (December, 1968), pp. 1207–1219.
5. Yong Hyo Cho and H. George Frederickson, *Determinants of Public Policy in the American States: A Model for Synthesis,* Sage Professional Paper Series on Administrative and Policy Studies (Beverly Hills, California: Sage Publications, April, 1974).

Chapter Two

The Crisis of Urban Crime

The sense of crisis is, in a way, a self-centered perception in that every generation may feel that problems that generation is to contend with are not only critical but unprecedented. The temporally magnified perception of social problems may lack complete objectivity. Be that as it may, urban America today is in crisis: the pervasiveness of crime and the fear of crime in American cities, particularly in the centers of the nation's large and old metropolitan areas, constitute a major component of "urban crisis."

The problems of crime rampant in the streets and neighborhoods of our cities have been repeatedly belabored by the governmental reports of crime statistics, mass media, various study commissions—governmental and private—and scholars of social and public affairs. For example, the President's Commission on Law Enforcement and Administration of Justice, appointed by President Lyndon B. Johnson to study the causes of crime and to search for the measures effective in controlling crime, declares in its report:

> There is much crime in America, more than ever is reported, far more than ever is solved, far too much for the health of the Nation. Every American knows that. Every American is, in a sense, a victim of crime. Violence and theft have not only injured, often irreparably, hundreds of thousands of citizens, but have indirectly affected everyone.[1]

Crime has always been a serious social problem in American cities. However, in the mid-1960s the problem of crime became an all consuming public issue that remains as one of today's most controversial and frustrating public policy matters. Crime became a crisis in American cities in the mid-1960s due to a number of important reasons. First, of course, the crime rate, particularly that of more common crimes, became higher than ever in the mid-1960s, and since that time, it has continued to increase at a rapid rate.

9

Second, the pervasiveness of crime and the ever-increasing crime rate, as they became more visible and more directly affected a vast and increasing number of citizens in the course of everyday life, besieged the minds of individual citizens with fears for both personal safety and security of property. Particularly, the incidences of violent crimes close at home—muggings and robberies in elevators and on residential streets, senseless killings in public parks, streets, and college campuses, and heinous mass slayings committed by psychopaths all sensationally headlined in the nation's mass media—intensified the fear of crime.

Third, the governmental inability to cope with the problem of crime contributed much to the sense of crisis. The 1960s marked an era of new hopes, aspirations, and expectations in American history. It was the era that America's industrial economy brought unprecedent affluence to the vast majority of Americans. It was the era that Americans put a man on the moon. It was the era that man could "borrow" a new extension of life through heart or other organic transplant. Yet, the massive machinery of government for law enforcement and administration of justice (many thousands of police agencies, courts, prisons, and prosecutorial offices) demonstrated little evidence of curbing crimes in the streets and neighborhoods of American cities.

Fourth, other social turbulences, often violent, accentuated the sense of crisis of crime, violence, and social disorder in the 1960s. Ghetto riots, beginning with those in Harlem in 1964, brought a series of "long hot summers" to nearly every major city throughout the country. The long and arduous civil rights movement with its demonstrations, sit-ins, and marches reached a tragic climax with the assassination of Dr. Martin Luther King and paved the way for black militantism, groups such as the Black Panthers, and the black power movement. Assassins' bullets cut down President John Kennedy in 1963 and Senator Robert Kennedy in 1968. The unwanted, unsupported, and unending war in Vietnam delivered a chilling wave of youth protests, campus riots, and radical movements of civil disobedience, thus obscuring the distinction between what is lawful and what is unlawful.

This social and political significance of crime as a critical and continuing problem in our urban society has compelled this author to undertake the present study with temerity.

THE EXTENT OF CRIME IN AMERICA

As the crime commission declares, we know that there is much crime in America. But there is no way of knowing exactly how much crime there is in the United States. Not all crimes committed are reported to and recorded by the police; nor can all crimes be detected by the police. Although the accuracy has been questioned, the crime statistics compiled and published by the Federal Bureau of Investigation in its *Uniform Crime Reports* are undoubtedly the best source available to measure the magnitude of crime in the United States. The FBI's

Uniform Crime Reports has its central thrust in the 7 categories of the index crimes. The index crimes are devised as a means of ascertaining the extent and the trends of criminality in American society similar to the consumer price index method of measuring the movement of prices of goods and services in the nation's economy. The index crimes include murder, forcible rape, robbery, aggravated assault, burglary, larceny, and auto theft.

These 7 categories of crimes are referred to as serious crimes and are considered as representative of the criminal tendency of the nation. As we shall discuss later, this assumption has been challenged as much as the accuracy of the actual data collected has been questioned.

The *Uniform Crime Reports* also compile data on 19 additional categories of crimes: they include other assault; arson; forgery and counterfeiting; fraud; embezzlement; stolen properties—buying, receiving, and possessing; vandalism; weapons—carrying and possessing; prostitution and commercialized vice; sex offenses other than forcible rape and prostitution; narcotic drug law violations; gambling; offenses against family and children; driving under the influence; liquor law violations; drunkenness; disorderly conduct; vagrancy; and all other offenses.[2]

Table 2–1 shows the national aggregate of the index crimes in 1971. The 7 categories totaled 5,995,211 offenses, which correspond to a crime rate of 2,907 cases of offenses per 100,000 population. This total implies that on the average 3 out of every 100 persons were victims of 1 of the 7 crimes listed. However, this average does not represent the probability of everyone in society being victimized, since criminal victimization is generally concentrated in larger cities and in the ghetto areas within these cities. If we add the number of offenses for the 19 other categories of crimes to that of the index crimes, the total number of crimes known to the police in 1971 becomes 7,839,419, and the total crime rate exceeds 4,000 per 100,000 population.

The number of criminal offenses varies greatly among the 7 categories, ranging from the high of 2,368,423 for burglaries to the low of 17,627 for

Table 2–1. The Index Crimes: The U.S. Aggregate, 1971

	Number in Total	Per 100,000 Population
All offenses	5,995,211	2,906.7
Murder	17,627	8.5
Forcible Rape	41,888	20.3
Robbery	385,908	187.1
Aggravated Assault	364,595	176.8
Burglary	2,368,423	1,148.3
Larceny	1,875,194	909.2
Auto Theft	941,576	456.5

Source: The F.B.I., *Uniform Crime Reports, 1971.*

murders (willful homicides). In general, the number of crimes against persons (murder, forcible rape, robbery, and aggravated assault) is markedly smaller than that against properties (burglary, larceny, and auto theft). However, the fact that the criminal offenses against persons are less frequent than those against properties does not suggest that personal crimes constitute a less serious problem.[3] The truth is that personal crimes have a more terrorizing effect on the victims than property crimes and the damages are incalculable, often inflicting a lasting tragedy to the victims or their relatives.[4]

THE DISTRIBUTION OF CRIME RATE

Crime rate varies from region to region and from urban to rural areas as well as from one urban area to the next. Table 2–2 shows the pattern of crime rate distribution of the index crimes among the Standard Metropolitan Statistical Areas, other smaller cities, and rural areas in the United States in 1971. In general, the crime rates are much higher in metropolitan areas than in smaller cities and rural areas in every crime category. The relation also follows between smaller cities and rural areas except that the murder rate is higher in rural areas than in smaller cities.

Columns 3 and 5 of the table show each of the crime rates in SMSA's as a percent of that in small cities and rural areas, respectively. The combined offense rate of the 7 crimes is 87.6 percent higher in metropolitan areas than in small cities and 243.6 percent higher than in rural areas. This pattern of crime rate distribution indicates that there is a positive correlation between crime rates and urbanism.

The metropolitan–small city and metropolitan–rural difference in the

Table 2–2. The Distribution of the Index Crime Rate: Metropolitan, Small Cities, and Rural Areas, 1971
(Crime per 100,000 Population)

	1 SMSA's	2 Other Cities	3 SMSA's % of Other Cities	4 Rural Areas	5 SMSA's % of Rural Areas
All Offenses	3,546.7	1,890.7	187.6	1,032.3	343.6
Murder	9.5	5.2	182.7	6.9	137.7
Forcible Rape	24.4	9.4	259.6	11.1	219.8
Robbery	255.3	34.1	748.7	14.9	1,713.4
Aggravated Assault	201.4	144.3	139.6	100.5	200.4
Burglary	1,381.8	744.5	185.6	484.9	285.0
Larceny	1,074.1	779.7	137.8	344.4	311.9
Auto Theft	600.2	173.5	345.9	69.6	862.4

Source: The F.B.I., *Uniform Crime Reports, 1971.*

crime rates shows a wide variation among the different criminal offenses. The metropolitan—small city ratio ranges from the high of 748.7 percent for robbery and 345.9 percent for auto theft to the low of 137.8 percent for larceny and 139.6 percent for aggravated assault. The metropolitan—rural ratio ranges from the high of 1,713.4 percent for robbery and 862.4 percent for auto theft to 137.7 percent for murder. What is apparent in this comparison is that robbery and auto theft are the most dominant crimes in metropolitan areas although the crime rates in metropolitan areas are higher in every category than those in small city and rural areas. On the other extreme, aggravated assault and larceny in metropolitan areas show a relatively small difference from those in small cities and particularly the murder rate in metropolitan areas shows the least difference from that in rural areas.

Big City Crime Rate

The Standard Metropolitan Statistical Areas do not entirely represent urban areas or cities. An SMSA includes a central city, its surrounding suburbs, and the rural fringe areas.[5] Furthermore, SMSA central cities range in size from a minimum of 50,000 population to New York City with some 7 million population. Therefore, the crime rates that aggregate all SMSA's do not necessarily represent the pattern of crimes in large cities. The SMSA's as a whole are a mixture of all types of communities, since they vary both in size and socio-economic characteristics.

The crime rates presented in Table 2—3 are the average of the 49 largest cities in the United States in 1970. In every category of the index crimes, the mean rate of the 49 cities is substantially higher than the aggregate crime rate of the entire SMSA's combined, as shown in column 3 of the table. When the average crime rate of the 49 cities is computed as a percent of the aggregate rate of all SMSA's combined, the percent ranges from the high of 179.5 for auto theft, 178.5 for robbery, and 177.9 for murder to the low of 125.6 for larceny and 136.1 for burglary.

This comparison further reveals that while robbery and auto theft

Table 2—3.   Crime Rates in the 49 Largest U.S. Cities, 1970

	1 *Mean*	*2* *Standard* *Deviation*	*3* *As a % of* *All SMSA's*
Willful Homicide	16.9	10.5	177.9
Forcible Rape	39.8	19.6	163.1
Robbery	455.7	361.3	178.5
Aggravated Assault	307.2	185.0	152.5
Burglary	1,881.2	697.4	136.1
Larceny	1,349.1	475.7	125.6
Auto Theft	1,077.3	491.1	179.5

Source: The F.B.I., *Uniform Crime Reports, 1970.*

are dominant in metropolitan areas in general, they are even more so in the large central cities. Larceny, however, shows a relatively small difference between the big cities and all metropolitan areas. The metropolitan—small city difference in the larceny rate was also the smallest of the 7 crimes.

Also noteworthy is that there is a high degree of inter-city variation in the crime rates. The standard deviations, shown in column 2, are uniformly high relative to the means in every crime category. The range of variation may be more illustrative of this variation pattern. For example, the murder rate ranged from the high of 48.7 in Atlanta and 42.7 in St. Louis to the low of 2.7 in San Jose and 4.0 in El Paso, with a difference of 46 between the two extremes.

The Crime Rates of Large Ohio Cities

The 40 largest Ohio cities include all those in the state with a 1970 population of 25,000 or more. The average crime rates of the 40 cities are substantially lower than those of the nation's largest cities, but they are con-siderably higher than those of the nation's small cities. However, as the standard deviations in column 2 show, the inter-city variation in the crime rates is strik-ingly high. In the case of the murder rate, the standard deviation is greater than the mean and in larceny, the standard deviation and the mean are identical.

THE RISING CRIME RATE

As a way of ascertaining the trends of crime in America, we computed the per-cent change in the crime rates for each of the 7 offense categories during the last 12 years from 1960 to 1971. These trends are computed for metropolitan areas, small cities, and rural areas. Table 2—5 shows the results. The crime rate is rising in every crime category and in each of the 3 areas. In general, the crime rate has increased the fastest in metropolitan areas, followed by small cities, then rural areas. During the 12-year period, the total crime rate has increased more than one and a half times in metropolitan areas and small cities, and slightly less than that in rural areas. The fact that the crime rate is increasing fastest in metro-

Table 2—4.   Crime Rates in the 40 Largest Ohio Cities, 1970

	Mean	Standard Deviation
Murder	6.3	7.4
Forcible Rape	16.1	12.0
Robbery	158.4	153.6
Aggravated Assault	120.8	103.6
Burglary	949.8	461.0
Larceny	980.8	980.8
Auto Theft	555.4	493.3

Source: Derived from the F.B.I., *Uniform Crime Reports, 1970.*

Table 2–5. The Trends of Crime Rates in Metropolitan, Small City, and Rural Areas, from 1960 to 1971
(Percent Change of Crime per 100,000 Population)

	SMSA's	Other Cities	Rural Areas
All Offenses	167.1	159.4	143.9
Murder	93.9	36.8	7.8
Forcible Rape	136.9	135.0	63.2
Robbery	261.1	128.9	25.2
Aggravated Assault	127.1	194.5	138.2
Burglary	142.9	106.8	129.9
Larceny	215.2	319.6	235.0
Auto Theft	146.3	55.9	65.3

Source: F.B.I., *The Uniform Crime Reports* for 1960 and 1971.

politan areas and that the crime rate is the highest in metropolitan areas indicates that the problem of crime is not only more serious in metropolitan areas than elsewhere, but also the crime problem in metropolitan areas is getting worse faster than elsewhere.[6]

Murder, forcible rape, robbery, burglary, and auto theft has increased faster in metropolitan areas than in small cities and rural areas. However, aggravated assault and larceny increased faster in small cities than in metropolitan areas or rural areas, and the increase rate in rural areas was even faster than that in metropolitan areas.

THE FBI INDEX CRIMES: THE ISSUE OF VALIDITY AND ACCURACY

The FBI reports of the index crimes have been widely used, or accepted, as the statistical basis in assessing the magnitude of crimes and crime trends in the United States. The FBI index crimes are the best available source of national crime data compiled for various geographical subdivisions of the nation. However, the painful truth is that the best is just not good enough. There have been perceptive criticisms of the FBI crime reports for a number of reasons. The major criticisms are centered on: (1) the questionable validity of the concept of a crime index; (2) incompleteness of the crime statistics; and (3) inaccuracy of the crime statistics.

The Concept of a Crime Index
Many noted criminologists including Quetelet, Mayr, Messedaglia, De Castro, and Sellin have considered the possibility of constructing a crime index from available crime statistics so as to measure the magnitude and trends

of criminality in the society.[7] The FBI index crimes are an attempt to construct an index of crime based on the 7 common and major (or serious) crimes known to the police. However, the validity of using the FBI crime statistics for the 7 offenses as a crime index has been questioned for a number of reasons.

First, the seven crimes used by the FBI for the crime index are a sample of crimes arbitrarily selected from the unknown universe of criminality. Harry M. Shulman argues that " . . . to use a sample as an index we must know the size and composition of the universe from which the sample was drawn and we must have assurances that the sample was a representative one." He continues " . . . we know that the universe of crime in our society is largely unknown, both as a whole and in its particulars, and that the police sample is likely to be unrepresentative, not only in its concentration upon certain categories of crime, but owning to the fact that those categories are unduly drawn from the offenses of certain racial and ethnic minorities and social classes."[8]

Wolfgang appears to share Shulman's apprehension of the statistical validity of using the police statistics about crime as a crime index when he writes "Unlike a cost-of-living index or an index of production, a crime index is based upon a selection of items from unknown volume—all crimes committed. Yet the underlying assumption in the use of criminal statistics for an index is that a constant ratio exists between the unknown universe and a properly selected portion of the known universe."[9] However, Wolfgang does not discourage the use of the police crime statistics for a crime index. His reasoning is based not on statistical theory but on practicality. Wolfgang writes:

> Our knowledge of "hidden" delinquency and crimes which never come to the attention of the public authorities has raised many questions about the problems of using official criminal statistics for measuring the extent of the crime problem. But, although it is obvious that some crimes are not reported to the police, adequate and proper selection, classification, and statistical analysis of offenses can overcome most of the problems and produce a reasonably valid index of crime. At least it is generally agreed that if we are to have a continuous collection of delinquency and criminal statistics, police records are the best source of official information.[10]

Elinor Ostrom challenges the validity of the FBI crime index on a somewhat different ground. First, many categories of serious crimes are not included in the index crimes such as bribery, graft, embezzlement, arson, and narcotics violation, and so forth. Second, "the index is not weighted so as to provide an indication of whether a gross increase in the index represents a real increase in the aggregate threat to individual life and property." Third, the index lacks "a consistant data base over time," particularly the number of jurisdictions reporting to the FBI.[11]

The Incompleteness of the FBI
Crime Statistics

The FBI crime data are criticized for incompleteness as a measure of the extent of crimes in American society—that is, a variety of crimes is not included in the *Uniform Crime Reports.* The criminal offenses reported in the police statistics are only those crimes that are directly within purview of the police functions. Criminal offenses and violations of the law controlled by regulatory agencies, under the jurisdictions of administrative and civil law, and other agencies of criminal justice systems are either totally excluded from the police statistics, or woefully inadequately accounted for in the police reports. For example, offenses not included in the police reports are: those in commerce and industry such as finance, securities, manufacturing, communications, and real estate; those in management—labor relations; those in industry—consumer relations; those in the area of taxation; and those in the areas of social legislation such as unemployment and industrial compensations insurance, and so forth.

Shulman, who seems to be most critical of the incompleteness of the FBI crime statistics, argues that:

> Together, the crimes and offenses committed in the areas of sex and family relationships, and by professionals, businessmen, landlords, taxpayers, employees, customers and general public probably number in the tens of millions of cases and must far outweigh in volume and monetary loss the offenses that are the subject of police action.[12]

The Inaccuracy of Reported Crimes

It has become increasingly evident that those categories of criminal offenses that are directly subject to the police function are not fully accounted for in the police statistics. Some of the major reasons attributed to the inaccurate account for the number of criminal offenses for those crime categories reported in the police statistics are: (1) underreporting by the police; (2) variations in police behavior and statutory definitions of crimes; (3) crime-reporting procedures; and (4) nonreporting of offenses by victims.

Police Underreporting. Sometimes it has been alleged that criminal offenses known to the police are not fully reported in the police statistics of crime. Some of the criminal offenses reported to the police are believed to be "canned" without being recorded in the criminal statistics, thus causing police underreporting of the criminal offenses. Some evidences of police underreporting in the earlier years were found in New York City until 1952, in Philadelphia between 1951 and 1953, and Chicago between 1928 and 1931, for example.[13]

The police underreporting of crimes is primarily attributed to the attempt of the police to maintain a public appearance of its performance efficiency. The effectiveness of the police performance is often judged by the ability of the police to arrest criminal offenders. Fewer criminal offenses reported and larger numbers of offenders arrested in proportion to the number of reported offenses results in a high arrest ratio that makes the police performance appear more effective.

Variations in Police Behavior and Statutory Definitions of Crimes. There are variations in police handling of violations of the law in different communities. The value orientation and behavior patterns of the police as well as community mores may vary from one community to another.[14] Thus, police handling of identical criminal offenses is likely to differ, when there is a difference in the degree of "professionalism" of the particular police departments and the mores of the communities, which may either favor leniency or rigidity in the enforcement of law. Undoubtedly, some degree of accuracy in police reporting is reduced by such variations.

The statutory definitions of various criminal offenses are not identical among different communities. The definitional differences create problems for maintaining the uniformity in police reporting and crime classification and compound the problem of securing accuracy in police reporting.

Reporting Procedures for the Index Crimes. When multiple offenses are involved in a criminal event, the most serious of the multiple offenses is recorded in the criminal statistics "because only the highest order of an index offense is used when there are multiple offenses committed in a single criminal event . . . "[15] For example, when an offender simultaneously commits forcible rape and robbery, only the forcible rape case is used for crime reporting purposes, while robbery is dropped from the criminal statistics.

Non-Reporting to the Police. Perhaps, the most serious problem causing inaccuracy in the police crime statistics seems to be contributed by the victims and witnesses of criminal offenses by not reporting the offenses to the police. The criminal offenses not known to the police because of non-reporting are believed to be many times more than the offenses known to the police. There are two ways through which a case of criminal offense can come to the attention of the police; one, the discovery of a criminal act in progress by the police, and the other, the information on criminal offenses reported to the police by victims or witnesses of the criminal offense. In a predominant majority of the cases, the criminal offenses are known to the police through the citizen reporting.

For the first time, some major surveys were conducted under the auspices of the President's Commission on Law Enforcement and Administration of Justice to learn not only how many criminal offenses are not reported to the police by the victims or their relatives but also the reasons for non-reporting. The National Opinion Research Center of the University of Chicago conducted a national survey of 10,000 households, and more detailed surveys were made in a number of selected precincts of Washington, D.C., Chicago, and Boston by the Bureau of Social Science Research of Washington, D.C., and the Survey Research Center of the University of Michigan. As shown in Table 2–6, the NORC survey results indicate that:

> Forcible rapes were more than three and one half times the reported rate; burglaries, three times; aggravated assaults and larcenies of $50 and over, more than double; and robbery, 50 percent greater than the reported rate. Only vehicle theft was lower and then by a small amount. (The single homicide reported is too small a number to be statistically useful.)[16]

The Reasons for Non-Reporting. The reasons for non-reporting as revealed by the NORC survey are diverse. The more important reasons include: (1) the lack of confidence in the police (2) the offenses being considered as a private matter or no desire to harm the offender. Other minor reasons include: fear of reprisal, no desire to take time, or the lack of knowledge on reporting methods. The summary of the survey results is shown in Table 2–7. Assuming that these survey results are generally reliable, the findings that criminal offenses are most often not reported to the police because the victims believe that "the police could not do anything" or because of fear of reprisal certainly raise a serious issue of public confidence in law enforcement authority. This, as indicated earlier, points to the frightening reality of governmental and political crisis in urban crime.

Table 2–6. Comparison of the NORC Survey and UCR Rates
(Per 100,000 Population)

Index Crimes	NORC Survey 1965–66 (1)	UCR Rate for Individuals 1965 (2)	UCR Rate for Individuals and Organizations 1965 (3)	1 as a % 3
Willful Homicide	3.0	5.1	5.1	58.8
Forcible Rape	42.5	11.6	11.6	366.3
Robbery	94.0	61.4	61.4	153.0
Aggravated Assault	218.3	106.6	106.6	204.7
Burglary	949.1	299.6	605.3	156.7
Larceny ($50 and over)	606.5	267.4	393.3	154.2
Motor Vehicle Theft	206.2	226.0	251.0	82.1
Total Violence	357.8	184.7	184.7	193.7
Total Property	1,761.8	793.0	1,249.6	140.9

Source: Adopted from the President's Commission on Law Enforcement and Administration of Justice, *The Challenge of Crime in a Free Society,* (Washington, D.C.: U.S. Government Printing Office, 1967), p. 21.

Table 2–7. Victim's Most Important Reasons for Not Notifying Police (in percentages)

	Percent of cases in which police not notified	Reasons for Not Notifying Police				
		Felt it was private matter or did not want to harm offender	Police could not be effective or would not want to be bothered	Did not want to take time	Too confused or did not know how to report	Fear of reprisal
Robbery	35	27	45	9	18	0
Aggravated Assault	35	50	25	4	8	13
Simple Assault	54	50	35	4	4	7
Burglary	42	30	63	4	2	2
Larceny ($50 and over)	40	23	62	7	7	0
Larceny (under $50)	63	31	58	7	3	*
Auto Theft**	11	20	60	0	0	20
Malicious Mischief	62	23	68	5	2	2
Consumer Fraud	90	50	40	0	10	0
Other Fraud (bad checks, swindling, etc.)	74	41	35	16	8	0
Sex Offenses (other than forcible rape)	49	40	50	0	5	5
Family Crimes (desertion, nonsupport, etc.)	50	65	17	10	0	7

*Less than 0.5%

**Only two instances in which auto theft was not reported

Source: The President's Commission on Law Enforcement and Administration of Justice, *The Challenge of Crime in a Free Society* (Washington, D.C.: U.S. Government Printing Office, 1967), p. 22.

SUMMARY

Crime in America is a significant part of the American urban crisis. The pervasiveness of crime and the rapid increase in crime in urban areas, as evidenced by the official statistics of crime, suggests that the problem of urban crime is compounding rather than diminishing. More importantly, the apparent inability of the governmental agencies for law enforcement and administration of justice to cope with the surging problem as well as the evidence of the lack of public confidence in the police and criminal justice agencies make the crisis of urban crime a crisis of urban governance.

The official crime statistics—the FBI index crimes—have been criticized for being invalid, incomplete, and inaccurate as an index of crime. Although such criticisms are not unreasonable, the FBI crime data are useful for understanding the magnitude of crimes and analyzing the patterns of crimes. It appears that the official crime data are most widely used by researchers and policy-makers, and the use of the data seems to be increasing. The critic of the police crime data should note that the police statistics are improving in accuracy, although the improvement may not be sufficient. For a practical reason, it must be recognized that the FBI data are the only national crime statistics readily available without cost to researchers and policy-makers, and no reasonable alternative is presently in sight.

NOTES TO CHAPTER TWO

1. *The Challenge of Crime in a Free Society* (Washington, D.C.: U.S. Government Printing Office, 1967), p. 1.
2. In 1971, the offenses for these 19 categories of crimes totaled 1,844,208, which was a 14.2 percent decrease from the preceding year's 2,149,968 offenses.
3. Properties lost in crime can often be compensated through insurance, but the irony is that those who can least afford the loss of material possessions such as the poor in ghettos and marginal businesses in high crime areas usually do not carry adequate insurance for two major reasons: (1) the insurance rates are exceedingly expensive in such areas; and (2) residents and businesses in ghetto areas are either unable to afford to carry insurance or unaccustomed to the idea of insurance, or both. See *Report of the National Advisory Commission on Civil Disorders* (A Bantam Book, 1968), pp. 360–62.
4. For example, young children having lost a parent in criminal homicide, a young woman sexually assaulted, or an old person robbed and manhandled suffer the consequences for a long time, if not the rest of their life in terms of financial disaster, emotional anguishes, or terrorizing nightmares haunting such victims.

5. For the precise definition of SMSA, see U.S. Bureau of the Census, *U.S. Census of Population: 1960,* Vol. 1, *Characteristics of the Population,* part 1, *United States Summary* (Washington, D.C.: U.S. Government Printing Office, 1964), pp. XXXI–XXXII.

6. Some historical studies and their findings do not agree with the arguments that urban crime is highest today and that it is growing at an unprecedented rate. A study of the New York Police Department statistics from 1916 to 1936 concluded that the crime rate for offenses against persons was not only higher than the rate for the same offenses today, but also the crime rate for the same offenses steadily decreased during the period. A study of the arrest reports of the Boston Police Department from 1849 to 1951 concluded that "The overall crime rate for the seven major offenses has declined steadily to a level of about one-third that in 1875. See, for the New York City study, Harry Willback, "The Trend of Crime in New York City," *Journal of Criminal Law, Criminology, and Police Science,* 29 (May–June, 1938), pp. 62–75 and, for the Boston study, see Theodore N. Ferdinand, "The Criminal Patterns of Boston Since 1849," *American Journal of Sociology,* 73 (July 1967), pp. 84–99.

7. Marvin E. Wolfgang, "Uniform Crime Reports: A Critical Appraisal," *University of Pennsylvania Law Review,* Vol. III, No. 6 (April, 1963), pp. 708–738 as reprinted in Bruce J. Cohen (ed.), *Crime in America* (Itasca, Illinois: P.E. Peacock Publishers, Inc., 1970), pp. 38–46.

8. Harry M. Shulman, "The Measurement of Crime in the United States," *The Journal of Criminal Law, Criminology, and Police Science,* Vol. 57, No. 4 (December, 1966), pp. 483–92, as reprinted in Cohen (ed.), *ibid.,* pp. 29–37. The quotation is from Cohen, p. 36.

9. Cohen, *ibid.,* p. 40.

10. *Loc. cit.*

11. Elinor Ostrom, "Institutional Arrangements and the Measurement of Policy Consequences: Applications to Evaluating Police Performance," *Urban Affairs Quarterly* Vol. VI, No. 4 (June, 1971), 447–475.

12. Shulman, *op. cit.*

13. See Wolfgang, *op. cit.*

14. See James Q. Wilson, *Varieties of Police Behavior* (Cambridge: Harvard University Press, 1968); James Q. Wilson, "The Police and the Delinquent in Two Cities," in James Q. Wilson, *City Politics and Public Policy* (New York: John Wiley & Sons, Inc., 1968), pp. 173–195; and John A. Gardiner, "Police Enforcement of Traffic Laws: A Comparative Analysis," in James Q. Wilson, *ibid.,* pp. 151–172.

15. Wolfgang, "Uniform Crime Reports: A Critical Appraisal," in Bruce J. Cohen (ed.), *Crime in America,* p. 43.

16. The President's Commission on Law Enforcement and Administration of Justice, *The Challenge of Crime in a Free Society* (Washington, D.C.: U.S. Government Printing Office, 1967), p. 21.

Chapter Three

The Politics of Crime and Crime Policy

Crime seems to be unusually durable in dominating public concern and political controversy. Since the mid-1960s when crime was suddenly catapulted into prominence as a top domestic problem, crime has become increasingly more significant as a social problem and as a political issue. It was a 1966 survey conducted by the National Opinion Research Center (NORC) that first uncovered the intense public concern about crime in recent years. Until then, various national polls failed to detect the importance of the crime problem in the minds of American public. The NORC survey asked the respondents to choose the most important domestic problem from a list of 6, which included poverty, inflation, education, race relations, and unemployment in addition to crime. Crime was the second most important problem, next to race relations.[1]

Crime became a key component of the so-called "law and order" issue in the 1968 Presidential elections, which infused a generous dose of fear, anger, and avenge into politics. The law and order issue continued to dominate the 1969 municipal elections in many of the major cities and other subsequent elections.

In 1973, crime was still the leading domestic problem. A 1973 Gallup poll, for example, found that crime was the worst problem facing the community. To no one's surprise, crime was found much worse in large cities than elsewhere.[2]

A social problem does not necessarily become a matter of public importance simply because it exists. A social problem must be discovered and brought to public attention in order to provoke controversy and demand political responses. For a social problem to become a political issue and to generate political responses, it is also necessary that the political climate at the time must be receptive to the challenge of the problem.[3]

Political responses shape the character of public policy for the solution of a problem, and ultimately, such character determines the effectiveness of the political system in meeting the pressure of a social problem. For any public policy to be effective, the substance of the policy must be relevant to the nature of the problem and the level of the policy must be adequate for the magnitude of the problem.

In the final count, no crime policy may be considered effective unless it is capable of reducing crime through prevention of crime and rehabilitation of criminals, and according to this test of effectiveness, public action in recent years has, by and large, failed. Crime has been a top social problem—if not the top—as well as a leading campaign issue in presidential, mayoral, and other elections for several years. Policy responses to crime problems have been rather vigorous in terms of the variety of programs initiated and the increase in public resources allocated for crime control and law enforcement. Yet, the crime rate has been growing higher.[4] More importantly, the fear of crime by the citizens has been growing worse.

The politics of crime has never brought the crime problem within proper policy perspectives. The confluence of fear and anger that dominate political debate on crime has generated more agitating rhetorics than sensible policy alternatives toward crime control. Thus, while crime has been a burning campaign issue in recent elections, political rhetorics have hardly shed an illuminating light on the nature of the crime problem. Consequently, the principal policy measures recently devised to counter the crime wave have tended to be more repressive and control oriented than preventive or rehabilitative.[5]

The central objective of this book is to describe and measure various public policies and programs that are considered relevant for control or prevention of crime while analyzing systematically the impact of such policy measures on the tendency of crime incidence. As a step toward breaking ground for this purpose, here we draw a spotty sketch of recent political experience in dealing with crime problems. The sketch includes public attitude toward crime, crime as an election issue, and thrust of recent crime policy.

PUBLIC ATTITUDE TOWARD CRIME AND CRIME POLICY

Unraveling the attitude of the American public toward crime and crime policy is no less than piecing together a puzzle, using the results of various public opinion polls. Various pollsters and survey teams utilize different samples, structure their questions differently while seeking the same or similar answers, and do not include in their questionnaires some of the questions for which responses are needed by data consumers. However, while the existing data drawn from diverse sources may unduly reduce consistency of a particular attitudinal matter, they seem adequate for assessing the input of public attitude in the political and policy-making processes.

Public attitude toward crime as a social problem shows a high degree of consistency among the different survey results: crime is one of the few most worried about problems; crime is getting worse; the fear of crime is increasing; and society is to blame for the crime problem more than are individual persons. Attitudes toward crime policy, however, reveal less consistency. The public tends to support a "tough" crime policy, although they do not believe it will accomplish the desired end.

Fear and Concern

The people are worried about crime, violence, and drug abuse, all of which are closely interrelated. As noted earlier, a 1973 Gallup poll showed that crime was the top domestic problem. However, a 1972 study by Potomac Associates in Washington (the data for this study was actually gathered by the Gallup Organization) showed that crime was not *the* most worried about problem, but *one of the few* most worried about problems. According to the scoring scale devised by the Potomac Associates' researchers, violence and inflation received the highest worry score with 90 each, while crime and drug addicts received the second highest score of 89. The third most worried about problems included water pollution (84), medical care (83), and air pollution (83). Of the 19 problems included in the questionnaire, mass transportation scored the lowest point, only 56.[6] Even before the current wave of crime controversy began, juvenile delinquency was one of the problems most concerned about among domestic affairs.[7]

Those who are afraid of street crimes and change their habits because of fear not only account for a substantial proportion of the population but a proportion that is increasing, according to both Gallup poll and Harris survey findings. In a number of opinion surveys, the Gallup poll asked the question: "Is there any area around here—that is, within a mile—where you would be afraid to walk alone at night?" In 1968, 31 percent of the respondents answered "Yes" and 69 percent "No." In 1972, the "Yes" percentage was increased substantially to 41 percent in March and 42 percent in December. The Harris survey in September 1970 asked: "Compared to a year ago, do you personally feel more afraid and uneasy on the streets today, less uneasy, or not much different from the way you felt a few years ago?" In response, 73 percent of the women and 59 percent of the men questioned answered more afraid and uneasy. Only 3 percent of female and 5 percent of the male respondents answered less afraid and uneasy.[8]

McIntyre, after reviewing a number of recent survey studies of public attitude toward crime, concluded that "the crimes which they fear were crimes which might endanger their personal safety, especially attack by a stranger."[9] Because of the fear of violent crime, the majority of the respondents to the Bureau of Social Science Research (BSSR) survey in Washington and those to a survey by Albert J. Reiss, Jr. said they had changed their habits to protect themselves from crime.[10]

McIntyre made an interesting point that "the fears are not consistent with the objective risks." She maintained that " . . . violence and the threat of violence do not present as great a hazard as do other risks in an industrial society. The number of accidental injuries calling for medical attention or restricted activity of one day or more is far greater than the 1.8 offenses per 1,000 Americans involving violence or threat of violence."[11]

More recently, a 10-city study by the Urban Observatory project of the National League of Cities showed that the majority of the respondents in 8 of the 10 cities felt "very safe" or "pretty safe" in their neighborhood at night. In Albuquerque and San Diego, 76 percent of the respondents said "very safe" or "pretty safe." In only 2 cities, Baltimore and Boston, more than half of the respondents said they felt "very unsafe" or "pretty unsafe" in their neighborhoods at night.[12] The same report also pointed out that drug sales, burglary, and robbery are three priority crimes feared most by the citizens. This finding that drugs are feared more than violent crimes is a significant shift from the earlier findings of field surveys conducted for the President's Commission on Law Enforcement and Administration of Justice in 1966.

In earlier days, the drug problem was largely confined within Negro ghettoes. However, in recent years drug abuse has invaded white, middle-class communities and has tipped the balance of terror. In a highly perceptive and critical article on black crime, Fred P. Graham writes:

> In the early 1950s there were always more narcotics arrests of Negroes each year than whites. This changed. Middle-class whites started smoking marijuana, and the police started arresting them for it. The narcotics arrest rate of Negroes is still high, but for the past few years more whites than Negroes have been arrested on narcotics charges . . . [13]

Crime Getting Worse

Not only do FBI statistics show that the crime rate has been increasing everywhere in the United States but also the majority of the respondents of the Gallup polls and Harris surveys report that crime is increasing in their neighborhoods. The Harris survey in October 1970 asked: "In the past year, do you feel the crime rate in your area has been increasing, decreasing, or has it remained the same as it was?" Sixty-two percent answered "increasing"; only 3 percent, "decreasing"; and 30 percent, "remained the same." Two Gallup polls in 1972 asked a similar question—that is, "Is there more crime in this area than there was a year ago, or less?" The two polls showed a marked difference in their results, but both of them showed a less pessimistic feeling than the results of the 1970 Harris survey. In March 1972, 35 percent answered "more"; 11 percent, "less"; and 42 percent, "the same." In December of the same year, 51 percent said "more"; 10 percent, "less"; and 27 percent, "the same." Although the trend is not clear-cut, we may conclude from this evidence that there are fewer people who think that crime is increasing lately than a few years ago.

Crime Worse Elsewhere

The surveys also found that the people felt their neighborhoods were safer than the rest of the city. The 1966 NORC study showed that "60 percent of those questioned compared their own neighborhood favorably to other parts of the community in which they lived, with regard to the likelihood that their home would be broken into, while only 14 percent thought that their area presented a greater hazard."[14]

The 1971 Urban Observatory Study of 10 cities showed that more people felt safer in their neighborhood than elsewhere in their community in most of the 10 cities. The proportion of the respondents who felt there was less crime in their neighborhood ranged from 74 percent in Kansas City, Kansas, and 73 percent in Kansas City, Missouri, to 42 percent in Boston. In 7 of the 10 cities, more than 60 percent felt their neighborhood had less crime. The proportion of the respondents who felt that there was more crime in their neighborhood ranged from a high of 13 percent in Boston to a low of only 2 percent in San Diego.[15]

Sliding Crime Fight and Policy Preference

There are more people who believe that the country is losing the fight against crime than those who believe it is making progress. There are more people who believe that the nation's law enforcement system does not really discourage crime than those who believe it does. The 1972 Potomac Associates' Study asked the respondents if they believed the country in its fight against crime "made much progress," "some progress," "stood still," "lost some ground," or "lost much ground." Only 1 percent said the country made much progress in fighting crime, while 19 percent said the country lost much ground; 19 percent said some progress, while 32 percent said lost some ground.[16] Thus, there were more than twice as many people who believed that the country was losing ground than those who believed the country was making progress.

The Harris poll asked the respondents whether or not they felt the law enforcement system worked really to discourage people from committing crimes. There were more than three times as many people (68 percent) who believed it did not discourage crime as those who believed it really discouraged crime (18 percent), and 3 percent of the respondents volunteered to say that the system encouraged crime.[17]

The remedies for crime reduction believed to be effective by the public has shifted over time from a "repressive measure" emphasis to a "social amelioration" or "moral inculcation" emphasis.[18] In 1966, the BSSR survey in Washington, D.C. asked the respondents what they thought was the most important thing to do to reduce crime in the city. The response was:

Sixty percent recommended repressive measures such as more police, police dogs, stiff sentences, or "cracking down on teenagers." Forty percent believed that the solution lay in social amelioration or moral inculcation. These included such measures as more jobs, recreation and youth programs, better housing, improved police–community relations, better child-training, religious training and revival, community leadership, or simply inculcating discipline.[19]

However, the nationwide study of the Potomac Associates in 1972 found that *social service policies* were much more preferred than *control policies* as the best measure for crime reduction. The most preferred measure (chosen by 61 percent) was: "Cleaning up social and economic conditions in our slums and ghettoes that tend to breed drug addicts and criminals." The least preferred measure (chosen by 22 percent) was: "Putting more policemen on the job to prevent crimes and arrest more criminals." Thus, those who picked the latter were only slightly more than one-third of those who chose the former.[20] "Improving conditions in our jails and prisons so that more people convicted of crimes will be rehabilitated and not go back to a life of crime" was selected by 40 percent of the respondents, while "really cracking down on criminals by giving them longer prison terms to be served under the toughest possible conditions" was preferred by 35 percent.[21]

Inconsistencies and Contradictions

There are unmistakable inconsistencies and contradictions in the public attitude toward specific crime policies in terms of preference, satisfaction, or support. As shown by the Potomac Associates' study, putting more policemen on the job was not believed to be useful for crime control, nor was our law enforcement system believed to be capable of discouraging crime. Yet, a preponderant majority of the people (83 percent) think that "the police and other law enforcement agencies should be tougher than they are now in dealing with crime and lawlessness." While only a small minority (14 percent) thought they should not be tougher.[22]

In spite of the prevailing feeling of the inefficacy of the police and law enforcement in crime control, local police departments or local police protection services are rated favorably by a great majority in a number of recent studies. The Urban Observatory study reported that some 70 percent of the respondents rated their city police forces either "very good" or "good enough." However, the study found there was a sharp difference between whites and blacks in their assessment of police performance. For example, some 60 percent of the whites in Boston said that police came right away when called, while less than 25 percent of the blacks questioned said the same. However, the white–black gap was much smaller for some other cities such as Kansas City, Missouri, where the percentage was slightly less than 80 percent for the whites and slightly over 60 percent for the blacks.[23]

The citizens' evaluation of the police performance in 3 selected neighborhoods in the city of Indianapolis and 3 suburban communities of matching characteristics in a recent study also indicates that a predominant majority of the citizens rate their local police rather favorably.[24] The police response to calls for assistance was considered prompt (less than 5 minutes) by the majority in all of the 6 study units and the quality of assistance was rated satisfactory by more than 70 percent of the respondents in all of the 6 study units. However, the police follow-up performance in criminal victimization cases was rated high by only one-third or less than one-half of the respondents in all except 1 of the 6 study units, where 55 percent rated the particular service high.

The Ostrom–Whitaker findings are highly revealing in that the local police performance generally pleases the citizens in non-criminal service functions, but the local citizens are not satisfied with the police service in criminal matters. The citizens' experience-based evaluation of the local police performance in criminal matters in the Indianapolis area helps to explain why the public views the law enforcement system as generally ineffective in crime control.

A recent study of 5 metropolitan areas in Florida (4 central cities, 4 metropolitan counties, and 1 city–county consolidated police department) also showed that citizens' evaluation of the local police is favorable to the police.[25] Sixty-eight percent of the respondents said that their city police or county sheriff was either "good" or "very good," while only 7 percent said "poor," and 21 percent said "fair."

Harsh punitive treatment of criminals was not necessarily considered the best measure of controlling crime in the findings of the Potomac Associates' study, but a series of the Gallup polls found that the proportion of the respondents thinking that the courts in the area were not harsh enough in dealing with criminals had grown from 48 percent in 1965 to 63 percent in 1968 and 75 percent in 1969. Only 2 percent thought the courts were too harsh in all 3 surveys.

Support for Spending Increase

There is an undisputable concensus in support of governmental spending for the police and other criminal justice agencies. A Gallup poll in November 1970 found that 91 percent of the respondents said that Congress should vote more money to help police and other law enforcement agencies to deal with crime. The Potomac Associates' study also uncovered that 77 percent of the questioned favored increased spending for combating crime, whereas only one percent favored reduction in spending for the purpose.[26] In a list of 19 domestic problems, crime ranked first in the level of public support for increased governmental spending for the problem.[27]

The Urban Observatory study of 10 selected cities included a question on whether governmental spending should be "increased," "remain the same," or "reduced" for 16 specific governmental functions, including police patrolling at night. The percentage of the respondents supporting increased spending exceeded 50 percent in 7 of the 10 cities; the support is particularly strong in those cities where the respondents felt the crime problem was serious—that is, in Boston (70 percent) and Baltimore (70 percent). In contrast, the support for increased spending for night patrol by the police was weak in those cities where crime problem was not considered very serious—that is, in San Diego (33 percent) and Milwaukee (41 percent).[28]

CRIME AS AN ELECTION ISSUE: "LAW AND ORDER"

The "law and order" issue, which is a collective condemnation of crime, violence, and civil disorders, became the number one campaign issue in the 1968 presidential elections. The law and order campaign was aimed at a mixture of social problems. However, crime was a key component, if not the most important one, of the entire issue.

Why Suddenly?

The first question to be considered here is why crime became a dominant election issue in 1968, even though crime had been increasing rapidly since the early part of the 1960s. As a matter of fact, Senator Barry Goldwater attempted to make a campaign issue out of the crime problem in the 1964 presidential election, but it did not catch the electoral fire at that time. In his address to the 1964 Republican Convention in San Francisco, Goldwater said:

> The growing menace in our country tonight, to personal safety, to life, to limb and property, in homes, in churches, on the playgrounds and places of business, particularly in our great cities, is the mounting concern of every thoughtful citizen in the United States. Security from domestic violence, no less than from foreign aggression, is the most elementary and fundamental purpose of any government, and a government that cannot fulfill this purpose is one that cannot long command the loyalty of its citizens.[29]

There are, however, a number of reasons why crime suddenly loomed large as a social problem in the second half of the 1960s and became the top campaign issue in the 1968 presidential election as well as subsequent elections. The more important reasons include: (1) the racial implications of the so-called new "crime wave"; (2) the riots and violence in the Negro ghettoes; and (3) other events—such as protest marches and civil disobediences—that contributed to the decline of social order.

It was not merely the increasing crime rate that frightened the American electorate, but also the increased threat to the security and safety of the white middle class by the new crime wave. As noted previously, drug abuse invaded the white middle class and tipped the balance of terror to include those who formerly felt less involved in the problem. Violent crimes such as murder, rape, robbery, and assault had traditionally been more often committed by Negroes and their victims had nearly always been the same race as the offenders.[30] Nonetheless, many times more Negroes are still arrested for violent crimes than whites, relative to the total population of the respective races.

However, the police used to ignore the violent crimes among Negroes in the ghetto subcommunity. David Hardy, a staff of *The New York Daily News,* testified to the National Advisory Commission on Civil Disorders as follows:

> To put it simply, for decades little if any law enforcement prevailed among Negroes in America, particularly those in the ghettoes. If a black man kills another black man, the law is generally enforced at its minimum. Violence of every type runs rampant in a ghetto.[31]

Further, the Negro crime situation had not been publicized in the annual release of the FBI statistics or the press commentaries and reports.[32] Graham points out that the appalling picture of Negro crime began to become a public knowledge when Ramsey Clark, then Attorney General, testified before the National Commission on the Causes and Prevention of Violence in 1968 and subsequently when the FBI compiled detailed statistics on Negro crime in compliance with the commission request.

In his testimony, Clark stated:

> Negroes, 12 percent of the total population, were involved in 59 percent of the arrests for murder: 54 percent of the victims were Negro. Nearly one-half of all persons arrested for aggravated assault were Negro and the Negro was the primary victim of assault. Forty-seven percent of those arrested for rape were Negro and again studies show the Negro is the primary victim. Sixty-one percent of all arrested for robbery were Negro. Less than one-third of the persons arrested for property crime are Negroes.[33]

Further, the FBI study, covering the 1964 to 1967 period, provided devastating testimony that urban crime and violence were a Negro phenomenon much more than people had realized. Because of the Negro leaders' fear of projecting a lawless image of blacks, they have never made an issue of the bleak crime situation in the ghettoes or of the inadequate police protection there.[34]

More importantly, however, evidence started to grow that Negro crime was no longer confined among the Negroes in the ghetto but had begun spilling over the traditional boundaries to victimize more white persons than before. For example, Edward Banfield found that the cases of assault with deadly weapons by blacks against whites in Oakland, California, increased drastically from 1962 to 1968. Banfield said:

In 1962, 6 percent of arrests for assault with deadly weapons involved a black suspect and a white complainant and 3 percent involved a white suspect and a black complainant. In 1968 the corresponding figures were 27 percent and 3 percent. The findings are based on a random sample in which every fifth assault was selected. The numbers in the sample were 65 in 1962 and 120 in 1968. The data were supplied to the writer by the chief of the Oakland Police Department.[35]

Some of the increased crimes in which black suspects and white victims are involved may be considered as a natural consequence of the sharp increase in inter-racial contacts and interactions following the rapid progress in the civil rights movement in the early part of the 1960s. A sense of black revenge for white injustice may also account for a part of the increase.[36]

The black ghetto riots frightened and infuriated the "Electoral Americans," on whom the election of president, governor, and mayor are traditionally and essentially dependent. In the mid-1960s the Electoral Americans were "unyoung, unpoor, and unblack," as they are characterized by Richard Scammon and Ben Wattenberg. On their TV screens, these Electoral Americans saw all of the riots, beginning with the Harlem riot of 1964, then Watts in 1965, Hough in 1966, and all over the country in nearly every city in 1967 and 1968. They saw the burnings, destructions, and lootings and wanted order.

In fact, any of the numerous 1960s protest movements, whether civil rights or against the war in Vietnam, infuriated the Electoral Americans when violence or breach of law was involved, as was often the case. Even the anti-war rally at the 1968 Democratic Convention in Chicago ended up in violence, as further emphasis of the prevailing social disorder.

These are some of the reasons why crime and violence suddenly became the dominant campaign issue in the second half of the 1960s. To recapitulate, the increasing crime rate, particularly the increasing black crime rate and the increasing white victimization by black offenders, frightened and infuriated the Electoral Americans. The black ghetto riots frightened and infuriated the Electoral Americans. Other violence in the streets, such as the war protests, infuriated the Electoral Americans. In pursuit of electoral victory, the candidates and their electioneers often took advantage of this state of fear by appealing to the righteous indignation of the irate Electoral Americans.

"Law and Order" in the
Presidential Campaign

It was Governor George Wallace who set the tone of the law-and-order campaign for the 1968 presidential election. Governor Wallace's segregationist credentials are well known; he is the one who proclaimed "Segregation now, segregation forever!" Wallace's slogan of law and order, however, carried a hidden message: the condemnation of black crime, black lawlessness, black riots, as well as other violent behavior by political and social radicals and nonconformists. Thus, the law and order slogan was more than a denouncement of rampant crime and violence. It also became a code name for racism, so to speak. Graham made a highly perceptive comment on this point as follows:

> Every nation has its equivalent of the mythical emperor who wore no clothes. In the fable, nobody could bring himself to believe what he saw until a child blurted out the truth, and then everyone had a laugh at the emperor's expense. In the United States the naked emperor was for years the high Negro crime rate; the boy who broke the spell was George Wallace, and nobody laughed.
>
> In his campaign for President, Governor George Wallace did not shout that the emperor had no clothes; a politician with his segregationist credentials could make his point without calling a spade a spade. Instead, he preached incessantly about rising crime. Everyone knew that it was Negro crime that was being deplored.
>
> Wallace's early strength forced his rivals to talk tough about crime, too. Soon, so many politicians had vowed that they weren't necessarily criticizing Negroes when they demanded "law and order" that everybody understood that the term really was a racial slur of sorts.[37]

Both candidates of the major parties, Vice President Hubert Humphrey and Mr. Richard Nixon had crime and violence as one of their major campaign issues. Early in May, Mr. Nixon issued a position paper entitled "Toward Freedom from Fear." Three months later in August, Mr. Humphrey released a position paper called "Order and Justice: The Right to Life." Humphrey's order and justice position was summed up in his National Press Club speech:

> Yes, crime and violence have to be stopped. But I disagree with those who sneer at the Constitutional guarantees, and propose shortcuts to justice across the quicksand of contempt for due process of law.[38]

Mr. Nixon in his acceptance speech in Miami made his pledge:

> Time is running out for the merchants of crime and corruption in American society. The wave of crime is not going to be the wave of the future in the United States of America. We shall reestablish freedom from fear in America . . . [39]

Throughout the campaign, Mr. Nixon repeatedly attacked the Supreme Court for such decisions as *Miranda* and *Escobedo* among others and emphasized the needs for appointing to the court men "who are thoroughly experienced and versed in the criminal laws of the land."[40] Reiss pointed out that Nixon made no suggestion that they be versed in civil liberties and civil rights as well.[41]

In *Time* magazine's October 4, 1968, issue, just one month before the election, Samuel Lubell's conclusion on the nation's mood toward the election was quoted as follows: "To most voters, crime and lawlessness and the Negro are part of the same issue. The vehemence and profanity with which white voters voice their racial views have risen over the last two months." The same issue of the magazine also reported that "the Aldine Printing Company in Los Angeles, the world's largest manufacturer of bumper stickers, reports that its bestseller is SUPPORT YOUR LOCAL POLICE, the old Birch slogan."

Some Results of Law-and-Order Campaigning

In 1966, the voters' fear of crime and support for police became a political headline when New York City's newly established Civilian Review Board was abolished by a near 2-to-1 margin in a referendum.[42] The Civilian Review Board, established by an executive order of Mayor Lindsay, had consisted of 4 civilians appointed by the Mayor and 3 policemen named by the police commissioner. The board had been "empowered to accept, investigate, and review any citizen complaints of police misconduct involving unnecessary or excessive force, abuse of authority, discourteous or insulting language, or ethnic derogation."[43]

The opposition campaign to the board was led by the Policemen's Benevolent Association, which argued that the board would impair police efficiency and would lower the police morale. The board plan was supported by liberal political leaders, including two U.S. Senators from New York—Jacob Javits and Robert Kennedy. The proponents of the board maintained that the board would help restore public confidence in the police.[44] The voting results on the referendum showed that the German, Irish, and Italian vote heavily supported abolishing the board, while Jewish voters split. These results reflect more a fear of crime and disillusionment with civil rights than racial bigotry.[45]

In the 1969 mayoral elections, crime, violence, and racial tension played a dominant role in a number of major cities. It was unfortunate that toughness on crime was equated with racial prejudice and that American political leaders, particularly the candidates, failed to clarify that a law-and-order message did not have to be a code word for racism. Many of the liberal candidates disavowed law-and-orderism in order to keep themselves pure on racial and civil rights stance. Thus, law-and-orderism became a political lash for the conservative candidates to whip the liberal candidates to their defeat.[46]

The mayoral elections of Minneapolis, Detroit, and New York attracted the national attention for the prominence of the law-and-order issue in the campaigns and for the election results. The Minneapolis election—won by Charles S. Stenvig, an obscure police detective running on law and order—was most surprising since Minneapolis had always been known as a city of political liberalism under the firm control of the Democratic–Farmer–Labor organization for decades. The city had a low crime rate, a small black population, and little racial tension; yet, Charles Stenvig defeated two opponents, Gerard Hegstrom, the Democratic–Farmer–Labor candidate, and Dan Cohen, a liberal Republican, City Council President, and a lawyer with a Harvard education. Cohen called the Stenvig brand of law and order "nothing more than the George Wallace in Minneapolis clothes."[47]

Detroit's mayoral election was not as clear-cut a case of law-and-order victory as that of Minneapolis. In Detroit, the contest between Richard Austin, a black and Wayne county auditor, and Roman S. Gribbs, a white and Wayne county sheriff, was overshadowed by the influence of race; whites voting for a white and blacks voting for a black. Both candidates were centrists and moderate. However, it is believed that Gribbs might owe some degree of his victory in that riot-torn and violence-prone city to his image of professional lawman.

In New York City, the incumbent mayor John Lindsay lost the Republican primary to the state senator John Marchi, an ex-policeman and political conservative. The Democratic primary nominated Mario Procaccino, also a conservative known as a simplifier of complex issues. As a Liberal party candidate, Lindsay won the general election, with less than a majority of the vote, by dividing the conservative and law-and-order votes between his two opponents.

In other cities such as Los Angeles and Seattle, the politics of fear and crime had decisive influence in the mayoral elections, and additional law-and-order mayors were elected in subsequent elections, including that of Frank Rizzo, the Police Commissioner of Philadelphia who won the mayoralty race in 1971 by successfully waging a law-and-order campaign.

It is evident that the 1970 Congressional elections were also strongly affected by crime problems. Crime and the drug problem apparently occupied an extremely important place in the thinking of the voters in that election. A Gallup poll in November 1970 asked: "When people around here go to vote on November 3rd for a candidate for Congress, how important will crime and drug addiction be in their thinking?" Eighty-four percent answered "extremely important"; 11 percent, "fairly important"; and only 3 percent, "not so important."

PUBLIC POLICY RESPONSES

The fear of crime and violence and anger against criminals have dominated public sentiment ever since the mid-1960s. By feeding on such public sentiment, the law-and-order issue overshadowed all domestic issues in the 1968 Presidential elections, the 1969 mayoral elections of many major cities throughout the country, and to a lesser degree subsequent elections at all levels of government.

The crime policy measures generated by the politics of fear and avenge have tended to be more repressive and punitive than preventative of crime and rehabilitative of criminal offenders. We shall discuss a broad range of public policies relevant to crime prevention and crime control and their effectiveness in creating the desired impact in great details in subsequent chapters. Here we will only highlight some of the law-and-order responses to crime and violence.

The major thrust of public policy to control crime and violence was directed toward: (1) spending more money for police and other criminal justice agencies and programs in order to increase the system capability of criminal justice operations by expanding the staff, improving their pay, and equipping them (the police in specific) with more powerful hardwares; (2) making judicial and correctional policies more punitive and avengeful in such a case as the restoration of capital punishment in many states; and (3) giving controversial discretionary powers to the law enforcement officers at the possible expense of the civil liberty of criminal suspects.

Empirical studies of crime correlates have consistently evidenced that social and economic deprivations (such as poor education, unemployment, lower income, and crowded or dilapidated housing, for example) are the more influential forces underlying a high crime incidence and violence in the cities. However, public policies for the rehabilitation of social and economic environment of the deprived and disadvantaged in the cities have never been envigorated by law-and-order politics. For example, all of the landmark federal legislation establishing innovative programs for the urban poor or city development occurred before 1966 and include, to name a few, the Manpower Development and Training Act of 1962; the Economic Opportunity Act of 1964; the Elementary and Secondary Education Act of 1965; and the Demonstration Cities and Metropolitan Development Act of 1966. Many of the programs established under such legislation have been weakened or dismantled by the Nixon Administration.

The fact remains that crime has not been reduced with the emergence of law-and-order policies; the crime rate has kept increasing. While the ghetto riots and mass violence, which began in 1964 in Harlem and climaxed in the summers of 1967 and 1968, have become a thing of the past,[48] how much have repressive control policies contributed to the ending of that era of mass violence? Probably a great deal. However, it must be recognized that there is a distinct difference between such mass violence as ghetto riots and so-called crime in the street, such as robbery and rape. A show of force by the National Guards may be effective in controlling mass violence but futile in reducing crime in the streets, which is individualized behavior.

Financing Policies
Criminal justice financing has come to command the budget priority at all levels of government, particularly at the municipal or county level. The federal government created a new grant program for law enforcement and a new office (Law Enforcement Assistance Administration in the Department of Justice) by the enactment of the Omnibus Crime Control and Safe Street Act of

1968. The legislation also put a new machinery of state law enforcement planning agency into motion in everyone of the 50 states for the administration of the law enforcement assistance grants.[49]

In the first year of the operation of the Law Enforcement Assistance Administration in 1969, $30 million were appropriated and some $300 million were appropriated for 1970.[50] In 1971, the LEEA grants approached $340 million.[51] The National Urban Coalition after studying the allocation pattern of the grants in 12 states in the initial year indicated that the predominant share (74 percent) of the grants was spent for the police, mostly for equipment. "The emphasis changed somewhat for 1970, as the percentage spent on corrections—probably the most poorly funded part of the criminal justice process—doubled to 26 percent of the total, and the amount for police dropped from 74 to 49."[52]

Many of the municipal governments throughout the country have taken extraordinary measures to expand their police forces and to meet the financial requirements for the expansion. The District of Columbia Metropolitan Police Department, for example, nearly doubled its personnel during a 5-year period—that is, from 3,301 full-time equivalent employees in the 1966–67 fiscal year to 6,073 in the 1970–71 fiscal year. The expenditures of the police department increased slightly less than two and a half times, from $35 million to $85 million during the same period.[53]

What Akron, Ohio, did for its police in 1968 and 1969 would not be quite unfamiliar in many other cities for the corresponding period. The Akron voters approved a charter amendment in the November 1968 election that was to add 120 policemen to the city's police force (30.5 percent increase from 393) and to provide an automatic pay increase for policemen and firemen reflecting the increase in the cost of living.

To raise funds to pay for the additional policemen and the expected pay increase, a proposal to increase the municipal income tax rate from 1 percent to 1.5 percent over the next 3 years was placed on the September 1969 primary election ballot. "The Committee for a Safer Akron" was formed to lead the campaign for the passage of the income tax issue. The name of the committee is suggestive enough; it was a law-and-order campaign with no disguise. The issue passed by a margin of 834 votes. When Robert Blakemore, then the chairman of the Summit County Central Committee of the Democratic Party, was asked by a reporter to comment on the tax election, he said:

> I think it is a reflection of the general law-and-order theme that is going throughout the country. It's obvious the campaign was presented that way. It was the only way the income tax could be sold.[54]

Capital Punishment

Between 1846 and 1965, 23 states abolished capital punishment, totally or in part; and between 1878 and 1961, 8 of the 23 states restored the death penalty. Thus, by 1965 there were 15 states that had abolished capital punishment.[55] During the 1960s executions declined rapidly from 56 in 1960 in 20 states to only 1 in 1966, although death sentences were issued rather steadily at a rate of around 100 a year.[56] During the 30-year period from 1936 to 1966, public opinion polls showed that public approval of the death penalty declined sharply from 62 percent to 38 percent, while support for abolition increased from 33 percent to 47 percent.[57] What the Bedau's study is showing us here is that capital punishment was pretty much on the way out in terms of non-executions, public disapproval, and abolition in a respectable number of states.

Finally, in June 1972, the U.S. Supreme Court ruled that the death penalty, as currently imposed in most states, was unconstitutional.[58] The ruling, however, left the door open for reinstating the death penalty, provided that it be imposed uniformly. By May 1973, capital punishment was restored in 13 states, and in 2 states the measures passed by the legislatures were waiting for the governor's signature. In 8 states, the measures for the restoration of the penalty were defeated; one bill, passed by legislature, was vetoed by the governor.[59]

In California, for example, the death penalty was reinstated by a referendum with a support of 67.5 percent of those who voted on the issue. Governor Reagan and his attorney general led the campaign for reinstatement. Richard A. McGee, the former California Director of Corrections who had presided over the executions of 170 men and women, opposed the reinstatement of death penalty on the following grounds:

> . . . as a practical man I have been convinced on purely rational grounds that the death penalty is futile and inappropriate in a modern society . . . . It is my conviction, from the vantage point of my experience, that vengeance and retribution carried to the point of taking human life in this deliberate fashion is beneath the dignity of a modern democratic government.[60]

Criminal Procedures

Some of the recent legislation has changed criminal procedures and increased the power of the law enforcement officers while endangering the civil liberties of the suspect. The District of Columbia Court Reform and Criminal Procedure Act of 1970, which provoked a heated controversy during Congressional deliberation, allows nighttime search warrants as well as "no knock" search and arrest warrants. The law also allows pretrial detention in certain cases.[61]

The title 3 of the Omnibus Crime Control and Safe Street Act of 1968 as well as the District of Columbia Court Reform and Criminal Procedure Act of 1970 permit wiretapping and electronic surveillance under specific circumstances for certain serious crimes. New York State adopted legislation "which allows preventive detention, uncorroborated testimony of accomplices, and arrests without a warrant on the basis of suspicion rather than on that of first-hand knowledge."[62]

Firearms Control

Firearms are the major homicide weapons used to kill some 20,000 people each year in addition to causing injury to some 100,000 others. Not only has the sale of firearms been growing rapidly, but the percentage of homicides caused by guns has also increased in recent years. Hand gun sales quadrupled from 1962 to 1968, and the percentage of homicides committed by firearms increased from 53 percent in 1961 to 65 percent in 1968.

The controversy over firearms control legislation at federal, state, and local levels of government has a long history, but none of the efforts to adopt a strong gun control measure have been successful. Ordinarily, firearms control has been most vigorously and persistently opposed by the conservatives and those who claim to detest violence and crime. The Omnibus Crime Control Act (Title IV) offers some federal role in the regulation of interstate and foreign commerce of firearms by restricting the acquisition of firearms through mail-orders. This restriction, however, is not likely to cut down the sale of handguns or the private possession of the dangerous weapons.

A meaningful gun control program can only be provided by federal and state action. Isolated local actions will have too many loopholes for enforcement and lack uniformity.

NOTES TO CHAPTER THREE

1. Philip H. Ennis, "Attitude Toward Crime," Interim Report to the President's Commission on Law Enforcement and Administration of Justice, 1966 (Mimeo), as cited in President's Commission on Law Enforcement and Administration of Justice, *Task Force Report: Crime and Its Impact—An Assessment* (Washington, D.C.: U.S. Government Printing Office, 1967), p. 86.
2. Thirteen percent of the nationwide sample picked "crime" as the worst problem in the community in response to the question: "What do you regard as your community's (city's) worst problem?" In large cities, the respondents picking crime as the worst problem accounted for 21 percent.
3. For example, it may be said that the contemporary poverty problem was discovered by liberal intellectuals in the late 1950s and early 1960s. The problem of poverty was politicized and generated political responses for the rising aspiration of the "new frontierism" during the two Kennedy and Johnson administrations, was receptive to the challenge of poverty problem for political action.
4. However, for the first time in many years, the 1972 preliminary report of the FBI crime statistics showed a slight decline in the overall crime rate from the 1971 level.
5. C. Ray Jeffery similarly maintained that the crisis of crime has generated suppressive crime policy when he said: "The high rate of crime and

violence have brought more popular support for the police and suppressive measures . . . " See his *Crime Prevention Through Environmental Design* (Beverly Hills: Sage Publications, 1971), p. 246.

6. William Watts and Lloyd A. Free (eds.), *State of the Nation,* A Potomac
    Associates Book (New York: Universe Books, 1973), p. 313.

7. Except for local taxes, juvenile delinquency was most often selected from a
    list of 39 problems in a 1963 Gallup poll as the top problem facing
    the community.

8. *The Harris Survey Yearbook of Public Opinion,* 1970, p. 63.

9. Jennie McIntyre, "Public Attitude Toward Crime and Law Enforcement,"
    The Annals of The American Academy of Political and Social Science,
    Vol. 374 (November 1967), pp. 34–46.

10. McIntyre, *ibid.,* p. 39.

11. McIntyre, *ibid.,* p. 40.

12. "City Taxes and Services: Citizens Speak Out," An Urban Observatory
    Report, *Nation's Cities* (August, 1971), pp. 21–22. This source will
    be referred to as the Urban Observatory Report in the subsequent
    notes.

13. Fred P. Graham, "Black Crime: The Lawless Image," *Harper's Magazine*
    (September, 1970), pp. 64–71. The quote is from p. 70.

14. Jennie McIntyre, *op. cit.,* p. 38.

15. The Urban Observatory Report, *op. cit.,* p. 22.

16. William Watts and Lloyd A. Free (eds.), *State of the Nation,* p. 116.

17. *The Harris Survey Yearbook of Public Opinion,* 1970, p. 65.

18. These terms were used by Jennie McIntyre. Her repressive measure corres-
    ponds to what I call control policy and her social amelioration
    measure corresponds to what I call social service policy.

19. McIntyre, *op. cit.,* pp. 41–42.

20. Watts and Free (eds.), *op. cit.,* pp. 118–119.

21. Watts and Free (eds.), *ibid.*

22. Gallup poll, August 1972.

23. The Urban Observatory Report, *op. cit.,* p. 23.

24. Elinor Ostrom and Gordon Whitaker, "Does Local Community Control of
    Police Make a Difference? Some Preliminary Findings," *American
    Journal of Political Science,* Vol. XVII, No. 1 (February 1973),
    pp. 48–76.

25. Richard Chackerian and Richard F. Barrett, "Police Professionalism and
    Citizen Evaluation," *Urban Affairs Quarterly,* Vol. 8, No. 3 (March
    1973), pp. 345–349.

26. Watts and Free (eds.), *op. cit.,* p. 117.

27. Watts and Free (eds.), *ibid.,* pp. 320–322 (Table A–7).

28. The Urban Observatory report, *op. cit.,* pp. 14–15.

29. As quoted in Richard M. Scammon and Ben J. Wattenberg, *The Real
    Majority* (New York: Coward-McCann, Inc., 1970), p. 37.

30. This generalization is strictly based on arrested suspects. Those offenders
    who are not arrested and whose identity is unknown to the police
    are disregarded in making this generalization.

31. *Report of the National Advisory Commission on Civil Disorders* (New York: A Bantam Book, 1968), p. 308.
32. Fred P. Graham, "Black Crime: The Lawless Image," *op. cit.,* pp. 64–65.
33. Graham, *ibid.,* p. 64.
34. For example, Graham points out that Mrs. Patricia Harris, a Negro member of the National Commission on the Causes and Prevention of Violence, insisted that the FBI study not be made public. Mrs. Harris believed the publicity of the study would give ammunition to segregationists. See Graham, *ibid.,* p. 68.
35. Edward C. Banfield, *The Unheavenly City* (Boston: Little, Brown and Company, 1968), p. 298. (Footnote 22 in chapter 8).
36. For example, Eldridge Cleaver in his book *Soul on Ice* talks about the numerous rapes that he committed against white women and he explains his behavior with attraction–repulsion syndrome toward white women which was created in him by racial injustice. Eldridge Cleaver, *Soul on Ice* (New York: Delta, 1968), pp. 13–14.
37. Graham, "Black Crime . . . " *op. cit.,* p. 64.
38. Albert J. Reiss, "Crime, Law & Order as Election Issues," *Trans-action* (October, 1968), pp. 2–4. Quote from p. 3.
39. Richard M. Scammon and Ben J. Wattenberg, *The Real Majority* (New York: Coward-McCann, Inc., 1970), p. 41.
40. Reiss, *op. cit.,* p. 3.
41. Reiss, *ibid.*
42. Murray S. Stedman, Jr., *Urban Politics* (Cambridge, Mass.: Winthrop Publishers, Inc., 1972), pp. 274–277.
43. Conrad G. Paulsen and Richard Bonnie, "Securing Police Compliance with Constitutional Limitations: The Exclusionary Rule and Other Devices," in James S. Campbell, Joseph R. Sahid, and David P. Stang (eds.), *Law and Order Reconsidered* (New York: Praeger Publishers, 1970), pp. 390–436. The quote is from page 411.
44. Stedman, *op. cit.,* pp. 275–276.
45. Lucy S. Dawidowicz, *The 1966 Elections: A Political Patchwork* (New York: The American Jewish Committee, April, 1967); and David W. Abbott, Louis H. Gold, and Edward T. Rogowsky, *Police, Politics and Race* (New York: The American Jewish Committee, 1969).
46. An exception to this is the case of Mayor Henry Maier in Milwaukee. Mayor Maier ran against David Walther, a liberal white and won the election by a landslide in the wake of a riot in the city in April 1968. Mayor Maier was a known liberal and added toughness on crime in his electoral arsenal. Even in those riot precincts, Maier polled 35 percent to 40 percent of the vote. See Richard M. Scammon and Ben J. Wattenberg, *The Real Majority* (New York: Coward-McCann, Inc., 1970), p. 238–239.
47. Bernard Casserly, "One Issue: L & O," *Commonwealth* (July 20, 1969).
48. The Lemberg Center for the Study of Violence at Brandeis University, which was organized in 1966, announced its plan to close down in August 1973.

49. As the first-run experiment of the block grant system, the state government was given the administrative responsibility for the disbursement of the grants within a set of federal guidelines. See, for example, B. Douglas Harman, "The Politics of Law Enforcement Assistance," *The Municipal Year Book, 1970* (Washington, D.C.: The International City Management Association, 1970), pp. 470–479.

50. Harman, *ibid.*

51. The National Urban Coalition, *Counterbudget* (New York: Praeger Publishers, 1971), p. 218.

52. The National Urban Coalition, *ibid.*, p. 218.

53. The figures for employment and expenditures were derived from U.S. Bureau of the Census, *Criminal Justice Expenditures and Employment for Selected Governmental Units, 1966–67,* GSS–No. 51 (Washington, D.C.: U.S. Government Printing Office, 1969) for 1966–67 and from Law Enforcement Assistance Administration and Bureau for the Census, *Expenditure and Employment Data for the Criminal Justice System, 1970–71,* GSS–No. 64 (Washington, D.C.: U.S. Government Printing Office, 1973) for 1970–71.

54. *Akron Beacon Journal,* September 11, 1969, p. A 1.

55. Hugo Adam Bedau, "The Issue of Capital Punishment," *Current History* (August, 1967), pp. 82–87 and 116. See Table IV on page 85 for the above information.

56. Bedau, *ibid.*, p. 83.

57. Bedau, *ibid.*, p. 84.

58. *Furman* v. *Georgia,* 408, U.S. 238, (1972).

59. "Death Penalty Has Been Restored by 13 States," *The New York Times,* May 10, 1973.

60. As quoted in *The Nation* (December 4, 1972), p. 548.

61. P.L. 91–358.

62. C. Ray Jeffery, *Crime Prevention Through Environmental Design,* p. 246.

Chapter Four

The Criminal Justice System in the United States

The criminal justice system represents the entire array of governmental institutions that function as the instrument of a society to enforce its standards of conduct necessary for the protection of the safety and freedom of individual citizens and for the maintenance of the order of the society. The criminal justice system performs this task by means of detecting, apprehending, prosecuting, adjudicating, and sanctioning those members of the society who violate the established rules of behavior as prescribed by the constitutional and statutory laws of the society.

America's criminal justice system is highly complex and diverse both in its organizational structure and operational procedures. Its principal components include the police, the prosecutorial offices, the courts, and the correctional institutions and programs. Defense counsel is also an essential part of the criminal process since the American system of justice guarantees adversary process in its criminal proceedings. Jury trial, too, is an inherent part of America's criminal justice process whereby the peers of the defendant in the community are brought into the adjudicating process of the courts.

In this chapter, we shall highlight the major characteristics of the criminal justice system in the United States. In specific, we shall outline the overall characteristics of the American criminal justice system in terms of the nature of its role orientation, organizational structure, and operational procedures.

THE ROLE OF THE CRIMINAL JUSTICE SYSTEM

The main thrust of America's criminal justice system is directed toward the control of crime and criminal offenders after the crime is committed rather than the prevention of crime before the crime has occurred. The central role of the criminal justice system in the United States may be called "palliative" in the sense that the system is preoccupied with the crime already committed; the crime is a symptom rather than a cause of violent and other deviating behavior as a social problem. America's criminal justice system is, in fact, not meant to be preventive or curative of crime, for it is not designed to eliminate the causes of crime so that crime can be prevented from occurrence.

Some of the police work, particularly police patrols, are expected to contribute to the deterrence of crime by reducing the opportunities for crime. While police patrols may, in fact, head off some criminal acts temporarily, they do not modify the crime-inducive influences within the community. The President's Crime Commission recognizes this reality when it states:

> . . . the fact remains that the mission of the police is not to remove the causes of crime, but to deter crime, and to deal with specific criminals whoever they are, and with specific crimes whenever, wherever, and however they occur.[1]

The prosecuting attorneys and the courts deal only with the criminal offenders detected and arrested by the police. The charges brought against criminal offenders by the prosecutors and the disposition of criminal cases, whether conviction or dismissal, by the courts do not touch upon the causes of crime, although it is hoped that the prosecutor's charges and the court actions create a deterrent effect.

The correctional system at least in theory comes closest to a curative response of the criminal justice system to crime. A part of the correctional function is to treat the causes of criminal behavior of the convicted offenders so that their future commission of crime can be prevented. An ACIR report notes that:

> Action taken against lawbreakers is designed to serve three purposes beyond the immediately punitive one: remove dangerous people from the community; deter others from criminal behavior; and *give society an opportunity to attempt to transform lawbreakers into law-abiding citizens.*[2]

In practice, however, the prisons and other correctional programs hardly rehabilitate the criminal offenders. Rather, they remain largely custodial and punitive, contrary to the manifest goal of corrections service, as Freed argues:

> . . . the typical prison experience is degrading, conviction records create a lasting stigma, decent job opportunities upon release are rare, voting rights are abridged, military service options are curtailed, family life disruptions are likely to be serious, and the outlook of most ex-convicts is bleak.[3]

Some correctional institutions have recently adopted innovative programs and have reportedly achieved respectable success in rehabilitating their inmates, but the fact is that the correctional institutions alone are far too limited to change the social environment into which the rehabilitated offenders are to be released.

The correctional processes in particular and the criminal justice system in general are neither curative of criminal offenders nor preventive of crime. A high rate of crime and a high rate of recidivism, ranging from one-third to two-thirds, in spite of the increasing efforts to strengthen the criminal justice programs, are, in a way, an indication of such reality.

ORGANIZATIONAL STRUCTURE

When public policy and policy performance are the focus of analysis, the organizational structure of governmental agencies may not be considered important. Particularly in the behavioral tradition of policy analysis, policy measurement and policy determinants occupy the central concern of the analysis, not the governmental organization. Although governmental organization is considered as one of the many variables influencing policy outcomes in the models for empirical analysis of public policies, it is still important to understand the organizational structure, for it is the vehicle through which public policies are formulated and implemented. Likewise, the organizational structure of the criminal justice system outlined below will provide for the institutional context of criminal justice policies.

The Federal System

The organizational structure of America's criminal justice system is as complex, fragmented, and diverse as the federal system of American government. All levels of government, federal, state, and local, are involved in law enforcement and administration of criminal justice by providing police protection, adjudication, and corrections. The institutional arrangements and assignment of criminal justice functions among federal, state, and local governments were not created all at once by a systematic design, but evolved through time in a piecemeal fashion. Each level of government assumed a new function or adjusted its institutional arrangements as the need arose without necessarily coordinating the new aspects with older ones or those of other governmental units. The piecemeal development of criminal justice institutions through time and the autonomy of federal, state, and local governments in determining functional and institutional adjustments are the major reasons why the organizational structure in particular and the criminal justice system in general in the United States are so complex and diverse.

As with most other domestic service functions of American government, state and local governments are primarily responsible for criminal justice. Among the individual states, however, there is a remarkable variation in the state–local system of criminal justice. The assignment of criminal justice functions between state and local governments and the resulting institutional arrangements vary from state to state and often from locality to locality within the same state. In general, however, it is local government, particularly large cities and counties, that carry the principal burden of police protection, the most costly of all the criminal justice functions. But the state–local sharing pattern of other criminal justice functions, such as judicial and correctional services, is not as much under local control as police protection.

THE POLICE SYSTEM

The police system in the United States is a perfect replica of the federal system of American government with an extreme degree of decentralization and fragmentation. Federal government maintains several police forces separately organized and having specialized functions. All state governments, except for Hawaii, have a state police or state highway patrol department with limited jurisdiction.[4] Some 40,000 local governments—cities, counties, towns, and special districts—have independent local police departments. It is the local police, as noted previously, that have the broadest responsibility for enforcing laws and controlling crime in American society.

Federal Police Forces.   There is not a centrally controlled police system in the federal government. Rather, there are 22 units of federal agencies with the police functions of providing protection as well as criminal investigation services. These agencies include the Federal Bureau of Investigation and Bureau of Narcotics and Dangerous Drugs of the Department of Justice; U.S. Park Police and Park Rangers of the Department of the Interior; Alcohol, Tobacco, and Firearms Division, Intelligence Division, and Internal Security Division of Internal Revenue Service and U.S. Secret Service of the Department of Treasury; U.S. Border Patrol of U.S. Immigration and Naturalization Service; Postal Inspection Service of U.S. Postal Service; and Federal Protective Service Division of General Service Administration among others. Sky Marshall is a new addition created to deal with the recent problem of airplane hijacking.

The functional jurisdiction of each of these federal agencies, which have police power, is narrow and specific. The only exception to this generalization is the Federal Bureau of Investigation, which has the enforcement jurisdiction over the violation of all federal laws other than those specifically assigned to other agencies. In 1971, the FBI employed more than 19,000 full-time employees. The 22 federal law enforcement units together employ over 56,000 persons full-time equivalent.[5]

State Police.   Forty-nine of the 50 states have state police forces which vary greatly in size and scope of responsibility. In 1971, the size of the state police force ranged from a 141-man unit in North Dakota to a 9,570-man force in California. All of the state police departments combined employed

69,375 full-time equivalent employees. The total state police forces represents 14.6 percent of the state and local combined police employees. However, the state percent of the state–local police force showed a marked variation among the states, ranging from less than 10 percent in Massachusetts, Nevada, New York, and Wisconsin to more than 40 percent in Alaska, Delaware, and Vermont.[6]

Most of the state police departments perform a limited number of police functions. Highway patrol is the single most important and common function for all the state police departments. Only a small number of states provide a full range of police services. According to an ACIR report, for example, in Alabama, Oklahoma, and North Carolina, the state police spent more than 90 percent of their time on highway patrol, while those in New York and Delaware spent more than 40 percent of their time on state-wide criminal investigation activities. As many as 23 states do not have state-wide crime control responsibilities, and in 11 states even the patrol activities were restricted to unincorporated areas only. The ACIR report summarizes the diverse character of the state police organizations as follows:

> Certain states have not chosen to vest their police agencies with a full range of police responsibilities. Some separate their police and investigative agencies and have both report to a common public safety director (e.g. Idaho, Illinois, Oklahoma, and Utah). Others vest criminal identification, criminalistics, and investigation responsibilities in 'special' police agencies, apart from the State police (e.g. Colorado, South Carolina, South Dakota, and Wyoming).[7]

Local Police. Local autonomy in law enforcement is a uniquely American tradition. There is no national or state police force that exercises central control over law enforcement and crime control as we find in other modern nations. Police protection for the day-to-day safety and security of ordinary citizens from the so-called "crime in the streets" is mainly provided by nearly 40,000 local police agencies, which include municipal police departments, county sheriff's departments, and town or township police units. The size of local police departments and their law enforcement capacity vary tremendously depending on the size of the community and range from a 40,311-man department in New York City, a 15,825-man unit in Chicago, and a 10,053-man force in Los Angeles to 1-man departments in many small towns and villages. In 1971, all of the local police departments together employed 402,691 persons full-time equivalents, of which 333,844 persons were employed by municipal police departments and the remaining 68,847 persons were employed by county police departments.[8]

Since local police departments are a part of general local government, fragmentation of police forces is a more serious problem for effective law enforcement in metropolitan areas where local government fragmentation is more extensive than elsewhere. The 1967 census of governments reports 227 SMSA's that include 404 counties, 4,977 municipalities, and 3,255 towns or townships.

Nearly all of these counties and municipalities, as well as some of the towns and townships, have their own independent police departments. One consequence of the autonomy and fragmentation of local police agencies in metropolitan areas is a perennial problem of ineffective cooperation among police departments. The President's Commission on Law Enforcement and Administration of Justice cautions:

> The boundaries that define and limit police operations do not hinder the movements of criminals, of course. They can and do take advantage of ancient political and geographical boundaries, which often give them sanctuary from effective police activity.[9]

A report of the Advisory Commission on Intergovernmental Relations is more specific in pointing out that inadequate cooperation and poor coordination resulting from fragmentation create obstacles "to improve service, increase efficiency, and reduce costs," particularly in the special technical fields such as "communications, identification, criminal statistics, and laboratories."[10]

Many local governments, however, do cooperate in their police work in various ways, although such cooperation does not necessarily overcome the problem created by fragmentation. Such cooperation takes the form of service contracts, formal agreements, and informal agreements. Service contract is a means "whereby one (government) provides all or selected aspects of the police function for the other government or governments."[11] The ACIR report indicates the extent of service contract as of 1967:

> . . . 43 localities of more than 10,000 population contracted with another local government for the provision of "total" police services. . . . Most of these localities were either in Los Angeles County, California, or Nassau and Suffolk Counties, New York. In the bulk of these interlocal contracts a locality contracted with an established county force for the provision of police services within the locality.[12]

The formal agreements are a means enabling 2 or more governments to "undertake jointly any functions and responsibilities which each of the agreeing governments could undertake singly," while informal agreements are a cooperative measure with less binding powers than formal agreements most often used "in such areas as police communications, criminal investigations, jail and traffic services."[13] A 1972 survey of local police chiefs in 3 metropolitan areas in Northeastern Ohio suggests that not only are intergovernmental agreements widely used for police cooperation, but also the method is considered an effective means for the improvement of law enforcement and crime control by the police chiefs. Of the 70 respondents answering the question "Does your department have a formal agreement with other departments for cooperation?," 81.4 percent answered "yes." Of the same respondents, 90 percent said "effective" answering to the question: "How effective do you think such a cooperative agreement is for the improvement of law enforcement and crime control?"[14]

Development of an Organized Police Force in America

The origin of the American experience of developing an organized police force can be traced to the British tradition. England had developed a system of justices and constables, along with paid night-watchmen, and such system was adopted by the growing towns and cities in the 18th and 19th centuries. Recognizing the need for better law enforcement, civic associations of London formed offices consisting of 3 justices authorized to employ 6 constables to police the streets and highways of London. By the beginning of the 19th century, London had 9 of these offices, and in 1829 the establishment of the British Metropolitan Police Department marked a new era by creating a London-area force of 1,000 uniformed men under 2 administrative Commissioners.[15]

Early American efforts at law enforcement were primarily expended in urban areas, and the police forces consisted of constables, voluntary citizen patrols, and paid night-watchmen. New York City was the first American city to follow London's example by organizing a unified police department in 1844.[16] Following the example of New York City, other major cities that began to organize unified police departments included Chicago in 1851, New Orleans and Cincinnati in 1852, and Boston and Philadelphia in 1854. Organized police forces became universal for all major cities by the turn of the twentieth century.[17]

Police Function and the Role of Policemen

Unified municipal police forces were organized in the 19th century to control crime and mass violence in the rapidly growing and industrializing cities. Police were then and are today synonymous with "crime fighters" as far as public expectations or public image is concerned. However, the nature of the functions that the police actually performed in the past and that they are performing today is debated among the scholars. Westley, an ex-police officer, claims that the function of the American police was "to support and enforce the interests of the dominant social, political and economic interests of the town and only incidentally to enforce the law."[18] Richardson concurs with Westley's contention in his study of New York City police of the 19th century when he says that:

> The respected elements of society drew a sharp line between themselves and the undeserving poor; the police were to treat the former with respect and the latter with whatever methods kept them in line. It was not what the police did that mattered, but to whom they did it.[19]

Large city police departments today are more bureaucratic and professional forces than ever before. Two primary functions are usually ascribed to the police. For example, James Q. Wilson views order maintenance and law enforcement as the central functions of the police. In performing the order maintenance function, the police act to prevent situations that may result in criminal actions. The law enforcement function is the process of applying legal sanctions to persons deemed in violation of the law by apprehending them and processing them through the criminal justice processes.[20] Goldstein similarly believes that the police have 2 specific functions: the control of crime through such activities as patrol and apprehension of criminal suspects; and service functions such as resolving family disputes that otherwise may result in criminal acts.[21]

However, these two police functions are considered to be in conflict under the bureaucratic and professional police system. The conflict between law enforcement and order maintenance is that promotion and recognition of professional achievements are primarily based on measureable productions, such as the number of arrests and traffic tickets issued, rather than the social services rendered, which are generally less conducive to measurement. This tendency is believed to discourage the performance of social service functions of the police.[22]

Germann, an ex-police chief, who is highly critical of the current developments in police role argues that police functions tend to become paramilitary and coercive political activities more than being crime prevention and social services. He writes:

> Common observation indicates that not only are we not stressing crime prevention and social services, but we seem to be moving in the direction of paramilitary and political police, expanding the repressive and coercive role of police.
>
> From coast to coast, police and sheriff departments have initiated radical changes in programs and equipment as they prepare themselves for riots or guerrilla warfare. This has been done with very little questioning of the property of American police to assume duties and functions which traditionally have been the responsibility of the National Guard or Regular Military Forces of the nation . . . the American policeman welcomes the role of 'soldier' and some police leaders have used that exact word in describing current police role.[23]

It seems evident that American police today perform diverse functions, which include order maintenance, law enforcement, and political control of social behavior. The degree of emphasis placed on these functions appears to vary from city to city and under different circumstances within the same city.

THE JUDICIAL SYSTEM AND CRIMINAL JUSTICE

The independent judiciary is the citadel for the preservation of the rule of law in a democratic society and to sustain order with justice in the society. It is the courts that determine guilt or innocence of the accused and prescribe appropriate penalties for the convicted offenders in criminal cases. It is the courts that ultimately settle disputes among individuals and groups in civil cases. The society expects the judicial process to be a reservoir of wisdom, integrity, and impartiality and to deliver equitable and just solutions to criminal proceedings and civil contentions. The collective authority of the state (the civil government) to determine the rights and wrongs and fairness or inequities is vested in the judicial system.

The courts are seldom organized separately for criminal and civil purposes. Criminal and civil matters are usually transacted in the same courts, although many courts, particularly the courts of general jurisdiction, maintain a separate criminal division. However, it is not practicable to isolate that part of the court system that is exclusively concerned with criminal matters for the discussion of court structure.

The judicial system involves more than the courts and judges. Several other institutions are inseparably woven into the judicial processes. Prosecution, jury system, defense counsel, and bail system are the major institutions that partake in the judicial process in addition to the court itself.

As in the case of police and law enforcement, the court system's organizational base is the federal structure of American government. Federal and state—local governments have developed their own court system to enforce the criminal codes and other legal and constitutional disputes of the respective levels of government. In both federal and state—local levels of government, the courts have a number of tiers in the hierarchical structure. They include the court of last resort, usually called the supreme court; intermediate courts whose primary function is to review the cases already ruled on in the courts of original incidence; the courts of general jurisdiction that have original jurisdiction over most legal cases; and finally the courts of limited jurisdiction or special jurisdiction. The hierarchical structure of the court organization for the federal and state—local governments is illustrated in Figure 4—1.

Federal Courts

The federal court system consists of the U.S. Supreme Court, 11 Circuit Courts of Appeals, 93 District Courts, and a number of special courts. The U.S. Supreme Court is the highest court in the nation and the last resort of appeals. The Supreme Court's rulings have a great impact, both in setting guidelines and providing the framework for interpretation of the U.S. Constitution

Figure 4–1.   The Court Structure in the United States

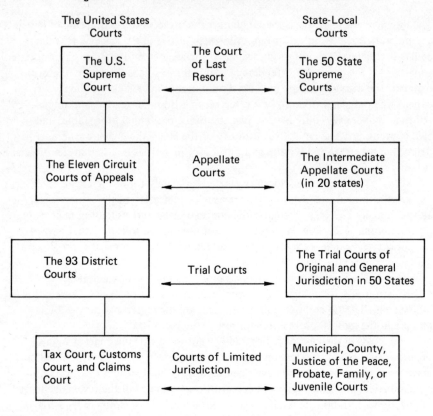

Source: Adopted and Modified from Advisory Commission on Intergovernmental Relations, *State–Local Relations in the Criminal Justice System* (Washington, D.C.: U.S. Government Printing Office, 1971), p. 88.

and federal laws not only for the other federal courts but also for the state courts in their judicial deliberations.

The 11 Circuit Courts of Appeals are the Appellate Courts to review decisions of the district courts within their circuit and some of the actions taken by the independent regulatory agencies when appealed. The district courts are trial courts of original jurisdiction, and they are the "workhorses of the federal judiciary." There is at least one district court in each state; New York state has 4 U.S. District Courts, 2 of which are in New York City. Each district court is composed of at least 1 judge or as many as 24 judges, depending on the size of the population served by the district.

The district courts are the only federal courts employing grand and petit juries regularly. District judges are assisted by a pool of staff, such as clerks, bailiffs, stenographers, and court reporters. The district courts are primarily concerned with federal laws, but they also apply appropriate state laws when necessary in cases, for instance, that involve citizens of different states.

There are a number of special courts created by U.S. Congress: the Courts of Claims, Tax Courts, the Customs Court, and the Court of Customs and Patent Appeals. These special courts have limited jurisdiction in the functional areas for which the courts are established.

Other staff agencies of the federal judiciary include the U.S. Marshalls Service, the Administrative Office of the United States Courts, and the Federal Judicial Center. U.S. Marshalls no longer function as a federal police force but as staff officers for federal courts to maintain order in the courtroom and to carry out other court orders—serving summonses for witnesses, for example. The Administrative Office of the United States Courts was created in 1939 to supervise and coordinate administrative staff services for all of the U.S. courts other than the Supreme Court.[24]

The federal judicial system employed 7,421 persons full-time equivalent in 1971. Federal judges are all appointed by the president with the consent of the Senate. There are 9 justices for the Supreme Court, 84 judgeships for the Courts of Appeals, and over 330 district judgeships.

State—Local Courts

The state—local court system shows a structure parallel to the United States court organization in that each of the 50 states has a court of last resort, as many as 20 states have an intermediate appellate court, all states have various trial courts and a variety of minor courts of limited jurisdictions. In all but New Hampshire, the state supreme courts are established by the state constitutions.[25] In many states, the appellate courts and trial courts are also created by the state constitutions. Minor courts of limited jurisdictions are usually established by legislative enactments.

The minor courts of limited jurisdictions are most complex and least consistent among the states and among different areas within the same state. Often counties, municipalities, and towns or townships have their courts of limited jurisdictions to handle minor civil and misdemeanous criminal cases. The complexity of minor or local courts may be illustrated by the state of Ohio. In Ohio, the Court of Common Pleas is the state trial court with original and general jurisdiction, but the court is financed by county revenues. Each county has a court of common pleas and the number of judges and court staff vary depending on the population size of the county. The court of common pleas has such specialized divisions as criminal, probate, domestic relations, and juvenile. However, in some counties juvenile division is a part of the probate division, in some others it is a part of the domestic relations division; and in still others—such as in Cuyahoga County—the juvenile court is a separate unit independent of the court of common pleas.

Municipal court is a major statutory court of limited jurisdiction at the subcounty level in Ohio. A municipal court usually serves more than one municipality, and the territorial jurisdiction of the court often does not coincide with the boundaries of any one local government. The number of judges and the size of staff are determined by the population size of the court jurisdiction. The Cleveland Municipal Court, the largest in the state, has a chief justice and 12 judges, while those municipal courts with less than 100,000 population in the jurisdiction are served by a single judge.

Many villages and cities in Ohio also maintain mayor's courts, which have limited jurisdiction over cases involving municipal ordinances and moving traffic violations. For example, as many as 29 municipalities in Cuyahoga County had mayor's courts in June, 1971. The mayor of the municipality serves in a dual capacity as mayor and judge of the court.

County courts and police courts are still a part of the local court system in Ohio statutes, but they are virtually extinct today. In the 3 metropolitan areas (the Cleveland, Akron, and Elyria–Lorain SMSA's) studied, there was only 1 county court and no police court in function.

Justice of the peace courts are the most traditional local court handed down from the colonial period. The justice of the peace is usually not required to be an attorney-at-law, and he is not paid by salary but financed by fines and fees. Since the 19th century, this court has been a target of court reform designed either to abolish the court or to supplant it with other courts such as county or municipal courts. Justice of the peace courts have been totally abolished in 17 states and "have been replaced in selected cities in 4 more." In those states and areas where justice of the peace courts still exist, "they continue to exercise petty criminal jurisdiction and petty civil jurisdiction."[26]

Significance of Lower Criminal Courts

The trial courts and local minor courts of limited jurisdictions are the most crucial part of the judicial system in determining the quality of criminal justice. As the Advisory Commission on Intergovernmental Relations indicates:

> These are the courts before which arrested persons are first brought, either for trial of misdemeanors or petty offenses, or for preliminary hearing on felony charges. Ninety percent of the Nation's criminal cases are heard in these courts, although public attention may focus on sensational felony cases and on the trials conducted in the prestigious felony courts. Also, to the extent that the citizen becomes involved with the criminal courts, the lower court is usually the court of last resort.[27]

Contrary to the ramifications of the workings of the lower criminal courts in determining the quality of criminal justice produced by the American judicial system, these courts are most often poorly staffed and poorly supported and, thus, least capable. The President's Commission on Law Enforcement and Administration of Justice expressed this concern succinctly as follows:

> ... the significance of these courts to the administration of criminal justice lies not only in the sheer numbers of defendants who pass through them but also in their jurisdiction over many of the offenses that are most visible to the public. Most convicted felons have prior misdemeanor convictions, and although the likelihood of diverting an offender from a career of crime is greatest at the time of his first brush with the law, the lower courts do not deal effectively with those who have come before them ... [28]

QUALITY OF JUSTICE

The differences in the judicial system, its capability, and criminal codes among other reasons contribute to the variation of the outcomes of court decisions on criminal cases. Understaffed courts with overcrowded dockets necessarily delay the hearings of the pending cases and their trials. The variance of state–local criminal codes contributes to the variance in the outcomes of criminal proceedings. An extreme example is the case of capital punishment. As of March of 1972, 39 states retained the death penalty for selected crimes, while 11 states did not. In most of the states retaining the death penalty, this punishment is applicable to first degree murder, while in 5 of the states, its imposition is limited to such offenses as murder of a police officer or prison guard. In one state, Alabama, as many as 17 offenses were punishable by death.[29] In recent years, capital punishment has been in a state of suspended animation in those states that do retain the penalty. However, if this penalty is enforced, the resulting inequity among the states will surely be appalling. It is generally true that criminal codes among the states lack uniformity. For example, nearly all forms of gambling do not constitute crime in Nevada, but nearly all forms of gambling are considered crimes in most other states.

Further, the perspective of individual judges in applying criminal codes produces different results in the rulings of similar criminal cases. In fact, a case study of the sentencing practices of individual judges on felony cases in the Los Angeles City Branch of the Superior Court of Los Angeles County (the trial court of original and general jurisdiction in California) reveals a shocking variation among the individual judges as shown in Table 4–1.

The conviction rate not only varies from one category of crime to another for the same judge but also varies from judge to judge for the same category of crime. The findings of the Los Angeles study indicate that criminal cases of the same category can produce different sentencing results. These differences depend on the judge who presides over the case or on a judge who might render different sentences, depending on the particular types of criminal cases that he handles.

Table 4-1.   Sentencing Patterns of Individual Judges: Felony Sentence Rate, by Superior Court Judges, Los Angeles County, 1970 *(percent)*

Judges (City of L.A.)	Possession Dangerous Drugs	Burglary	Posession Marijuana	Robbery	Forgery	Sale of Narcotics
1	45	53	30	79	66	87
2	23	35	21	83	40	92
3	25	38	18	76	63	61
4	19	9	3	70	38	77
5	13	26	16	82	38	67
6	8	22	6	84	25	50
7	48	46	47	86	65	87
8	45	39	26	47	49	65
9	18	32	4	58	62	64
10	14	17	5	48	15	33
11	54	44	58	85	49	63
12	19	36	10	58	18	81
13	15	17	6	51	48	48
14	25	41	56	44	48	67
County Total 35	28	42	20	75	43	72

Note: Only judges who have sentenced 300 or more defendants are included in this table.

Source: Sorrel Wildhorn and Robert Greenwood, *Prosecution of Adult Felony Defendants* as quoted in *Psychology Today* August, 1973, p. 14.

PROSECUTION

The prosecutor occupies the interface position between the police arrest of criminal suspects and the court proceedings of the criminal cases. The powers and functions of the prosecutor in handling criminal cases are wide ranging and significant:

> He has authority to determine whether an alleged offender should be charged and what the charge should be, and to obtain convictions through guilty plea negotiations. He influences and often determines the disposition of all cases brought to him by the police and often works closely with them on important investigations. His decisions significantly affect the arrest practices of the police, the volume of cases in the courts, and the number of offenders referred to the correctional system. The prosecutor, therefore, is potentially a key figure in coordinating the various enforcement and correctional agencies in the criminal justice system.[30]

The prosecutor partly supersedes the role of the judges and grand jury in the matter of obtaining preliminary evidence against a defendant, as pointed out by the President's Crime Commission:

> Theoretically the examination of the evidence against a defendant by a judge at a preliminary hearing, and its reexamination by a grand jury, are important parts of the process. Practically they seldom are because a prosecutor seldom has any difficulty in making a prima facie case against a defendant. In fact most defendants waive their rights to preliminary hearings and much more often than not grand juries indict precisely as prosecutors ask them to. The prosecutor wields almost undisputed sway over the pretrial progress in most cases.[31]

"Plea bargaining" is widely used as a method of expediting criminal cases in overloaded courts, particularly in large cities. In return of a plea of guilty, the prosecutor reduces his original charges and recommends lenient sentences for the defendants. The necessity of plea bargaining has often been recognized in view of the excessive delays and overcrowded dockets of criminal cases in many urban courts, while a sort of "justice at discount rate" impression projected by plea bargaining has been intensely criticized. The views of the President's Crime Commission also reflect this delemma:

> Plea bargaining may be a useful procedure, especially in congested urban jurisdictions, but neither the dignity of the law, nor the quality of justice, nor the protection of society from dangerous criminals is enhanced by its being conducted covertly.[32]

Federal Prosecutors

United States Attorneys act as the prosecutors for the federal courts. There is one U.S. Attorney in each District Court. The 93 District Attorneys' offices employed 5,800 full-time equivalent employees in 1969.[33]

State–Local Prosecutors

Within the states, the prosecutor is a local official, except for those in 3 states. The prosecutorial system, however, varies widely among the states in the methods of selection, powers and functions, and organizational structure. The local prosecutors are generally independent of the state attorney general. In most states, the attorney general only participates in appellate cases.

The prosecutor is elected in 45 states and appointed in 5 states. He is elected by county in 29 states, by judicial district in 12 states, and from both county and judicial district in 4 states. In most states, the prosecutor has both criminal and civil responsibilities, but in 12 states he has only criminal duties. The Advisory Commission on Intergovernmental Relations classifies the prosecutor systems of the states into 9 categories as follows:

1. State prosecutor systems: Alaska, Delaware, and Rhode Island;
2. State-appointed local prosecutors: Connecticut and New Jersey;
3. Local (judicial district) prosecutors with criminal and appeals responsibilities: Georgia and Massachusetts;
4. Local (judicial district) prosecutors with solely criminal responsibilities: Arkansas, Colorado, Indiana, New Mexico, North Carolina, and Tennessee;
5. Local (judicial district) prosecutors with civil and criminal justice responsibilities, but no appeals duties: Alabama, Louisiana, Oklahoma, and South Carolina;
6. Local (county) prosecutor with criminal and appellate responsibilities: Hawaii, Illinois, Kansas, Michigan, Minnesota, New York, North Dakota, Ohio, Oregon, Pennsylvania, Vermont, and Washington;
7. Local (county) prosecutors with solely criminal responsibilities: Missouri and Texas;
8. Local (county) prosecutors with criminal and civil, but not appellate responsibilities: Arizona, California, Idaho, Iowa, Maine, Maryland, Montana, Nevada, Nebraska, New Hampshire, South Dakota, Virginia, West Virginia, Wisconsin, and Wyoming; and
9. Overlapping county–judicial district prosecutors: Florida, Kentucky, Mississippi, and Utah.[34]

In addition to state, county, or judicial district prosecutors, many large cities maintain city prosecutors. These municipal prosecutors are called police prosecutors in Ohio cities.

The 1971 statistics show that employment for legal services and prosecution in the 50 states totalled 34,087, of which 8,133 were employed by the states, 16,102 were employed by counties, and 9,852 were employed by municipalities.[35]

COUNSEL FOR THE INDIGENT DEFENDANT

The adversary system is an essential requirement for fair trial in the American procedures of criminal justice. The defendants enjoy the constitutional rights of representation by attorney in their defense against any criminal charge. However, this constitutional protection has not often been fully extended to the indigent defendants who do not have the means to hire legal counsel, which thus impairs the quality of justice. As a way of resolving this problem, a number of rulings by the United States Supreme Court in recent years have made it the obligation of the government to provide legal counsels for the indigent defendants.[36] More recently, the Supreme Court ruled it unconstitutional to impose prison sentence upon a misdemeanant indigent not represented by a lawyer.

To provide counsel for indigent defendants is primarily the state and local government's responsibility. Two methods have been employed for the purpose: the assigned counsel system and the public defender system. The assigned counsel system provides a counsel for the indigent defendant by the court's appointment of a lawyer in private practice to represent the defendant. The counsel so assigned is paid by public funds from state or local sources. The assigned counsel system has been criticized for frequently providing less experienced and less dedicated lawyers who perform the assignment in a perfunctory manner.

The public defender system provides salaried lawyers who devote all or a substantial part of their time to defending indigents. The public defender system is exclusively financed by government funds, and it is considered a better means of providing legal counsel for indigents than the assigned counsel system.

There are 2 other systems for providing indigent defense: the private defender system and the public-private defender system. The former is sponsored by non-governmental organizations such as the legal aid society and the latter is operated by independent organizations with public and private contributions.[37]

As of 1969, "11 states have statewide defender offices and 23 other states have defender offices in major urban areas. Public defender organization increased from 136 to 330 between 1964 and 1969."[38] In 1971, state, county, and municipal governments throughout the nation employed 3,458 full-time equivalent employees for the indigent defense. This is a considerable improvement from 1969 when employment for the indigent defense was 2,099.[39]

JURY SYSTEM

The jury system is an inherent part of the American judicial processes and is rooted in the common law tradition. There are two types of juries: grand and trial. The grand jury consists of 12 to 24 property owners, and its two major functions are: (1) to decide whether persons brought before it by the prosecutor should, according to the evidence, be held for trial and (2) to conduct investigations into the existence of a crime, or of crime generally, and to hold for trial, through a 'presentment,' persons it believes may be guilty of crimes, even if the prosecutor has not acted."[40] The trial jury consists of 12 persons and unanimity is required for a verdict. Traditionally, the jury is to decide the questions of fact, while the judge is to decide the questions of law.

Today, jury trial is under severe criticism. Jurors are considered unrepresentative, emotional, or incompetent to deal with complex criminal issues. Most of all, jury trial is blamed for judicial delays and expenses for questionable results. Earlier criticisms, as summarized by Professor Willoughby, seem to remain valid:

> . . . A jury is in the nature of a fifth wheel; that real responsibility for the bringing of criminal charges is in fact exercised by the prosecuting attorney, the grand jury doing little or nothing more than

follow his suggestions; that it entails delay . . . ; that it renders prosecution more difficult through important witnesses getting beyond the jurisdiction . . . or through memory of facts becoming weakened by lapse of time; that it entails unnecessary expense to the government; and that it imposes a great burden on the citizen called upon to render jury service.[41]

However, the value of trial by jury is not entirely lost. The jurors can reflect the changing values of society in criminal procedures. The jury can bring an indictment for a case when there exists a compelling evidence of crime and particularly when the prosecutor does not take action on the case for the reasons of political corruption or personal bias. Opinion surveys found the public favors the retention of jury system. Annually some 2 million persons are called to serve as possible jurors in some 150,000 federal, state, and local trials.[42]

A number of changes are recommended by various groups to reform the trial jury. Such changes include the reduction of the jury to a 6-man panel, majority rule rather than unanimous decision for a verdict, more effective management in the use of jurors to reduce cost, delay, and the number of jurors called.[43]

MONEY BAIL SYSTEM

A defendant waiting for trial is either imprisoned or released. The pretrial release is contingent upon money bail or personal recognizance. Bail is used as a method of insuring the defendant's appearance for trial. From the perspective of insuring justice, however, money bail has been criticized as unfair to the poor. The poor are usually those who cannot afford to post bail bonds and suffer pretrial incarceration. When the poor can manage to post the bail bond, their financial hardship is likely to be greater because the amount of bail is determined by the type of crime for which the defendant is accused, not by the economic means of the defendant.

Therefore, which defendant will be subject to pretrial incarceration and which defendant will be staying out of jail while waiting for the trial is largely determined by the economic ability of the defendant. This reality is not only unfair to those who suffer pretrial incarceration but also results in the incarceration of a large number of defendants not yet proven guilty, which creates a financial burden to the community and a situation of crowded jails. Further, the indiscriminate use of money bail can result in either the release of "dangerous" defendants or the incarceration of "safe" defendants.

A number of changes are recommended for the money bail system. The abolishment of money bail altogether is one of them. To replace the money bail, a careful screening method may be instituted to determine whether a defendant should be released on personal recognizance or held in prison. The Vera Institute of Justice experiment in New York in obtaining pretrial release of a defendant on personal recognizance based on relevant information concerning the defendant and careful analysis of the information has demonstrated a measure of success and potential usefulness.[44]

CORRECTIONS

There are two major components in the corrections system: the institution-based corrections and the community-based corrections. The institution-based corrections are characterized by the incarceration of convicted offenders in various correctional institutions, such as prisons, jails, workhouses, juvenile detention homes, juvenile training schools, and so forth. In this case, the convicted offenders are kept isolated from the community for punishment, rehabilitation, and training in an effort to prepare them for reintegration into the community. In contrast, community-based corrections keep the convicted offenders in the community under the supervision and guidance of corrections officers. Probation and parole constitute the major traditional community-based correctional services. In recent years a number of special innovative programs have been developed for community-based corrections. These programs may be grouped into 5 categories as follows: "guided group interaction programs; foster homes and group homes; prerelease guidance centers; intensive treatment programs; and reception center parole."[45]

Punishment of criminals has always been and still is a significant part of correctional practice despite a series of evolutions in correctional theory. In earlier days, criminal punishment was no more than revenge against criminals by the state. In the mid-18th century, the concept of deterrence was developed in criminal punishment and imprisonment began to be used as a means of punishment for deterrence. At the same time, the concept of reformation was added to the purpose of imprisonment, "for the prison was intended to serve as a place for reflection in solitude leading to repentence and redemption."[46]

The subsequent development of correctional theory has led to the present emphasis on treatment of the criminal offender. In the treatment-oriented correctional concept, the offender is viewed "as a person with social, intellectual, or emotional deficiencies that should be corrected to a point that would permit him to resume his place in the community."[47] Today correctional services include a wide-ranging variety such as education, vocational training, religious guidance, and psychotherapy, both in the institution-based and the community-based correctional programs. Yet, punishment and retribution persist in the popular concept of corrections, as well as in the actual correctional practices. Ubiquitous prison riots in recent years can at least in part be attributed to the persistence of punishment-oriented correctional practices.

In spite of the fact that rehabilitation has long been accepted as the primary goal of American correction in theory, such services for rehabilitation as education, vocational training, and psychological or psychiatric therapy are limited or unavailable in most correctional institutions or community-based correctional programs. Staff resources for correctional institutions are mostly committed to services and custodial functions of guard duty and maintenance services; only a minor fraction of the staff resources is made available for rehabilitative functions such as educational and counseling services. Community-based correctional programs, such as probation and parole, are also so woefully understaffed and underfinanced that supervision and counseling for the probationees and parolees are generally inadequate.

In 1965, all the correctional institutions in the United States employed a total of 102,748 persons, of which less than 10 percent were employed for rehabilitative services; 62 percent were employed for custodial functions; and 29 percent were employed for service functions.[48] It has also been recognized that community-based corrections is a more promising approach to rehabilitative and reintegrative goals of modern corrections. In fact, the tendency to place offenders in community-based correctional programs has been increasing and by the mid-1960s some two-thirds of the correctional population were under the jurisdiction of community-based correctional programs. However, resources committed to community-based corrections are far less than that for correctional institutions. Of a total of 121,163 employed for the entire corrections systems in the United States in 1965, only 18,415 (15.1 percent) served community-based programs. Of a total of $1,005,746,500 in operating costs for the entire corrections systems, only $195,548,200 were used for community-based programs in 1965.[49]

In short, the American corrections systems are either unequipped or poorly equipped to provide necessary services for the offenders entrusted to the correctional institutions and agencies. In the following, we shall outline the correctional institutions, agencies, and programs and their organizational structure.

Federal Corrections
Federal correctional services include prisons, probation, and parole. There are some 40 correctional institutions of various types under the control of the Bureau of Prisons. The bureau employed over 5,400 full-time equivalent employees in 1971;[50] inmates in federal institutions exceeded 19,000 at the end of 1967.[51]

The other major federal correctional agencies are the probation service attached to the United States District Courts and the Board of Parole of the Justice Department, which provide probation and parole services for federal offenders, respectively.

State—Local Corrections
As in other components of the America's criminal justice system, the state—local corrections systems carry the major burden of correctional services.

For example, when prison inmates alone are considered, there were 175,300 inmates in various state prisons on December 31, 1967, and 160,900 inmates in local jails on March 15, 1970, compared with 19,500 inmates in federal prisons on December 31, 1967.[52] State–local corrections institutions and programs together served a correctional population of 1.1 million during the 1967–68 fiscal year. Twenty-five percent were inmates of the institutions, while 75 percent were served by community-based programs. Adult males accounted for 60 percent of the correctional population; juvenile males, 26 percent; adult females, 6 percent; and juvenile females, 8 percent.[53]

The variance of state–local corrections systems among the states is enormous in regard to the correctional institutions and programs, their organizational and administrative structure, and their correctional theories and practices. The organization of corrections system in individual states is based on the types of services and facilities and offender groups, the most significant of which are juveniles and adults. Juvenile corrections programs include juvenile detention, juvenile probation, juvenile training schools, and juvenile aftercare, while adult corrections programs include misdemeanant probation, adult probation, correctional institutions for adults, and adult parole. The age definition for correctional purposes is not uniform among the states nor, sometimes, among particular cases of offenses.

Juvenile Detention. Juvenile detention refers to temporary custody of youthful offenders pending court disposition. This function is mainly a local one. Only 8 states provided direct juvenile detention service in 1965, although many states assisted their local governments by setting standards, providing subsidies, or consultation.[54]

The National Council on Crime and Delinquency survey in 1965 found that a daily average of some 13,000 delinquent juveniles were held in detention facilities, with an annual total of 409,000 juveniles having been admitted to detention homes, jails, or other institutions. The survey also discovered that some 93 percent of juvenile court jurisdictions lacked juvenile detention facilities; 11 states had no detention facilities for juveniles; whereas 1 state had 39 detention homes.[55]

Juvenile Probation. Probation services for delinquent juveniles are a device used to rehabilitate juvenile offenders while keeping them in the community under the supervision of probation officers. Juvenile probation services are a special function performed by juvenile courts; therefore, in most states the services are administered locally. However, the organization of probation services for the juveniles showed 3 types in 1965. They are "a centralized statewide system (11 states); a centralized county or city system supported by state supervision, consultation, standard setting, recruitment, in-service training and staff

development assistance, and by a partial State subsidy of local agencies
(28 states); or a combination of these, with the larger and wealthier local jurisdictions operating their departments and the State providing services in other
areas (11 states).[56]

The administrative agency for juvenile probation is the courts in
most states. The courts assume administrative responsibility for juvenile probation in 32 states, state correctional agencies in 5 states, state department of
public welfare in 7 states, other state agencies in 4, and other agencies or combination of agencies in 3 others.[57]

Juvenile Institutions. Juvenile institutions are diverse in the type of
facilities as well as services provided. Juvenile institutions include reformatories,
schools of industry, camps, and reception centers. The kind of services provided
by such institutions most often includes medical, recreational, dental, educational, casework, social work, psychological, and psychiatrical services.[58]

In recent years, many states have diversified their juvenile facilities
for specialized services. In most states, juvenile institutions are centrally administered by the state government. However, 16 states had locally-administered
juvenile facilities in 1965.[59]

The 1965 survey by the National Council on Crime and Delinquency
identified 220 juvenile institutions in the 50 states, Puerto Rico, and Washington,
D.C. The breakdown of the 220 institutions was as follows: 82 boys institutions;
56 girls institutions, 13 co-ed institutions, 49 camps, 14 reception centers, 4
residential centers, 1 vocational center, and 1 day treatment center.[60]

As far as the cost is concerned, the juvenile institutions are considered the most expensive of all correctional programs. The National Council on
Crime and Delinquency estimate of per inmate cost by the 220 state-administered
institutions was $3,411 in 1965.[61]

Juvenile Aftercare. Juvenile aftercare is a parole program for
juvenile offenders. The National Council on Crime and Delinquency survey shows
that 40 states had centrally-administered state juvenile aftercare programs, while
the remaining 10 states lacked centralized programs in 1965. "The types of aftercare supervision provided ranged from merely filing a monthly report to such
activities as foster home placement, group counseling, family services, and employment programs."[62]

The juvenile aftercare programs are most often administered by such
state agencies as departments of public welfare, state youth correctional agencies,
and departments of corrections. Contrary to the generally centralized administrative organization of the juvenile aftercare programs, the authority to grant
parole for the juvenile inmates from institutions is largely decentralized. Often
the authority responsible for making the parole decision does not have adequate
access to necessary information on inmates.[63]

Adult Probation. There are two types of adult probation, one for misdemeanants and the other for felons. In 1965, probation services were not available for misdemeanants in 11 states and in 3 of the 11, misdemeanants were ineligible for probation. Twenty-one states had a statewide system of misdemeanant probation, administered by corrections agencies, courts, or departments of public welfare. In 6 states, that function was shared by state and local governments, while decentralized local systems (county or city) were used by 13 other states.[64]

Adult defendants convicted for felonious crimes are placed on probation by the courts. However, various statutory restrictions were imposed on granting probation for felony convicts in 35 states. Those convicted of capital crimes—murder and rape—were most often ineligible for probation. In the beginning of 1966, more than 230,000 individuals were on probation.

Of the 51 jurisdictions that include the 50 states and the District of Columbia, adult probation was a county function in 14 states and primarily a state function in 37 other states. The administrative organization for probation was combined with that for parole in most states.

Correctional Institutions for Adults. In a predominant majority of the states, both state and local governments maintain correctional institutions for adults. The National Council on Crime and Delinquency's 1965 survey identified 358 state correctional institutions for adults, including penitentiaries, reformatories, industrial institutions, prison farms, conservation camps, forestry camps, and so forth. These institutions held a daily average of 201,220 inmates. The administrative organization of state institutions showed three distinct patterns: multi-functional correctional agencies (34 states); unifunctional state boards (13 states); separate administration of individual institutions (3 states).[65]

Local correctional institutions are more than ten times as numerous as state institutions. The 1970 National Jail Census identified 4,037 local jails for adults, which accommodated more than 160,000 inmates. The most complete data on local jails to date made available by this jail census are complex, but some of the more illustrious findings include: (1) some 70 percent of the jails received juveniles; (2) nearly 90 percent of the jails did not have recreational or educational facilities, although about 50 percent of them provided medical facilities; (3) only 5 percent of the jails were overcrowded, but they were mostly large city jails; and (4) only 69,096 inmates out of 160,863 were serving sentences—the remaining 91,767 inmates were those arraigned and awaiting trial, being held for other authorities or not yet arraigned, or awaiting further legal action following the initial conviction.[66]

Adult Parole. Parole is a method of releasing adult felons from correctional institutions under the supervision of parole officers after serving a part of the sentence. The objective of parole is primarily to accord rehabilitative opportunities within the community environment rather than the institution to those felony offenders who are believed ready for such opportunities.

The 1965 survey by the National Council on Crime and Delinquency found that more than 62,000 prisoners were paroled in a recent year and that number was twice as many as those who obtained unconditional discharge following the expiration of their sentences. Parole practices are subject to state statutory regulations and vary widely among the states. As the survey also discovered, there is "a wide spread inconsistency in the application of parole principles . . . the paucity of efforts to subject correctional practice to rational analyses . . . ."[67]

A state parole board, usually appointed by the Governor, is in charge of parole decision-making in most states. Forty-seven states have a centralized state parole board, 43 of which have full and exclusive power to grant and revoke parole. In the other states, the parole board has an advisory role or limited authority. The state parole boards often have additional responsibilities such as holding clemency hearings, commuting sentences, or administering parole services.

The administration of parole services is organized into two types of structure: (1) in 31 states, the parole executive is responsible to the parole board; and (2) in the 20 other states, he is responsible to the department that has general administrative responsibility for the correctional program.[68]

NONSYSTEM OF THE CRIMINAL JUSTICE SYSTEM

The ultimate and priority goal of a society in crime control lies in preventing crime and reducing crime. The criminal justice system, as presently constituted and empowered, has limited capacity to contribute toward this end. Even at its best, the criminal justice system is primarily designed to deal with crimes already committed and criminals already identified and apprehended rather than with the causes and prevention of crime.

Even the capacity to deal with the crime after the fact is severely impaired by the extreme degree of organizational decentralization, jurisdictional fragmentation, and lack of cooperation among the key components of the criminal justice system. The diverse criminal justice agencies with specific functions lack deliberate and purposeful cooperation and coordination to achieve the essential goals of criminal justice. Rather, hostility, jealousy, or competition is a common experience among the criminal justice agencies. As Daniel J. Freed contends, the criminal justice system in America is not working as a *system.* Freed argues:

> . . . police view courts as the enemy. Judges often find law enforcement officers themselves violating the law. Both see correctional programs as largely a failure.
> Mechanisms for introducing some sense of harmony into the sys-

tem are seldom utilized. Judges, police administrators, and prison officials hardly ever confer on common problems.

. . . every agency in the criminal process in a sense competes with each other in the quest of tax dollars. Isolation or antagonism rather than mutual support tends to characterize their intertwined operations.[69]

The inadequacy of the criminal justice operations as a system is perhaps best manifested in the faulty process of information exchange among the agencies, which thus inhibits the effective functioning of the criminal justice process at its crucial points of decision-making. The President's Commission on Law Enforcement and Administration of Justice's emphasis on this matter merits attention. The commission states:

Probably the single greatest technical limitation on the system's ability to make its decisions wisely and fairly is that the people in the system often are required to decide issues without enough information. A policeman who has just set out in pursuit of a speeding and suspicious looking car should be able to get immediate information as to whether or not the car is wanted; a judge about to sentence a criminal should know everything about him that the police know; and the correctional authorities to whom that criminal is delivered should know everything about him that the judge knows.[70]

Even when the criminal justice system, as narrowly defined here, is assumed to function as a coordinated system, it still cannot be fully effective in reducing crime and preventing crime if it continues to function in isolation from the other governmental and non-governmental agencies and programs that have an impact of vital importance on the well-being of individuals. Thousands of governmental and private agencies operate such social and economic programs as education, public welfare, social work, medical care, and jobs and employment, which together determine the opportunity structure and the distribution of wealth in the society. Since criminal behavior is, as other social behavior, anchored in the value system of a society, the concept of the criminal justice system must be broadened in such a way that police, judges, and correctional officers and their activities can be mutually complementary and reinforcive with educational, welfare, and other social service activities in the society so as to reduce the social forces inducive of criminal behavior. Unfortunate as it may be, this is not the case.

NOTES TO CHAPTER FOUR

1. The President's Commission on Law Enforcement and Administration of Justice, *The Challenge of Crime in a Free Society* (Washington, D.C.: U.S. Government Printing Office, 1967), p. 93.

2. Advisory Commission on Intergovernmental Relations, *State–Local Relations in the Criminal Justice System* (Washington, D.C.: U.S. Government Printing Office, 1971), p. 66. The italics were added by the author for emphasis.

3. Campbell, James S., Joseph R. Sahid, and David P. Stang (eds.), *Law and Order Reconsidered,* Report of the Task Force on Law and Law Enforcement to the National Commission on the Causes and Prevention of Violence (New York: Praeger Publishers, 1970), p. 270.

4. Advisory Commission on Intergovernmental Relations, *State–Local Relations in the Criminal Justice System,* p. 83.

5. U.S. Department of Justice, Law Enforcement Assistance Administration and the Bureau of the Census, *Expenditures and Employment Data for the Criminal Justice System, 1970–1971* (Wasnington, D.C.: U.S. Government Printing Office, 1973), p. 14.

6. See *ibid.,* pp. 36–40.

7. Advisory Commission on Intergovernmental Relations, *State–Local Relations in the Criminal Justice System,* pp. 83–86 (Quotation is from page 83). For a greater detail of specific functions performed by individual state police departments, see Table 12 on pages 84, 85, and 86.

8. U.S. Department of Justice, Law Enforcement Assistance Administration and U.S. Department of Commerce, Bureau of the Census, *op. cit.,* pp. 88–99.

9. The President's Commission on Law Enforcement and Administration of Justice, *The Challenge of Crime in a Free Society,* p. 119.

10. Advisory Commission on Intergovernmental Relations, *Performance of Urban Functions: Local and Areawide* (Washington: U.S. Government Printing Office, 1963), p. 120.

11. Advisory Commission on Intergovernmental Relations, *State–Local Relations in the Criminal Justice System,* p. 79.

12. *Loc. cit.*

13. *Loc. cit.*

14. Norman Pellegrini, "Priorities and Innovations in Police Administration," an Urban Studies Seminar Paper (Department of Urban Studies, The University of Akron, 1973), Appendix Tables 19 and 20.

15. The President's Commission on Law Enforcement and the Administration of Justice, *Task Force Report: The Police* (Washington, D.C.: U.S. Government Printing Office, 1967), pp. 3–6.

16. *Ibid.,* p. 5.

17. Advisory Commission on Intergovernmental Relations, *State–Local Relations in the Criminal Justice System,* p. 72.

18. William A. Westley, "The Police: A Sociological Study of Law, Custom, and Morality" (unpublished Ph.D. dissertation, University of Chicago, 1951), p. 30 as cited in Arthur Niederhoffer, *Behind the Shield: The Police in Urban Society* (New York: Doubleday & Company, 1967), pp. 12–13.

19. James F. Richardson, *The New York Police: Colonial Times to 1901* (New York: Oxford University Press, 1970), p. 285.

20. James Q. Wilson, "Dilemmas of Police Administration," *Public Administration Review* (Sept.–Oct., 1968), 28: pp. 407–417.

21. Herman Goldstein, "Police Response to Urban Crisis," *Public Administration Review* (Sept.–Oct., 1968), 28: pp. 417–423.

22. The President's Commission on Law Enforcement and Administration of Justice, *Task Force Report: The Police,* pp. 141–143 and Albert J. Reiss, Jr. and Daniel J. Bordua, "Environment and Organization: A Perspective on the Police," in Daniel J. Bordua (ed.), *The Police: Six Sociological Essays* (New York: Wiley and Sons, 1967), p. 34.

23. A.C. Germann, "The Police: A Mission and Role," *The Police Chief* (January, 1970), pp. 16–19.

24. For a discussion of the organizational structure of the United States judiciary, see James MacGregor Burns and Jack Walter Peltason, *Government by the People,* fifth edition (Englewood Cliffs: Prentice-Hall, Inc., 1963), pp. 484–490; the President's Commission on Law Enforcement and Administration of Justice, *The Challenge of Crime in a Free Society* (Washington, D.C.: U.S. Government Printing Office, 1967), pp. 125–130; and Committee for Economic Development, *Reducing Crime and Assuring Justice* (New York: CED, 1972), pp. 18–22.

25. Advisory Commission on Intergovernmental Relations, *State–Local Relations in the Criminal Justice System,* p. 88.

26. *Ibid.,* p. 89.

27. *Ibid.,* p. 90.

28. The President's Commission on Law Enforcement and Administration of Justice, *Task Force Report: The Courts,* (Washington, D.C.: U.S. Government Printing Office, 1967), p. 29.

29. Congressional Digest, *Controversy Over Capital Punishment: Pro & Con,* January, 1973, p. 3.

30. Advisory Commission on Intergovernmental Relations, *State–Local Relations in the Criminal Justice System,* p. 112.

31. The President's Commission on Law Enforcement and Administration of Justice, *The Challenge of Crime in a Free Society,* pp. 10–11.

32. *Ibid.,* p. 11.

33. CED. *Reducing Crime and Assuring Justice,* p. 82.

34. ACIR, *op. cit.,* p. 113.

35. U.S. Department of Justice, Law Enforcement Assistance Administration and U.S. Department of Commerce, Bureau of the Census, *Expenditures and Employment Data for the Criminal Justice System, 1970–71* (Washington, D.C.: U.S. Government Printing Office, 1973), p. 37.

36. Gideon v. Wainwright, 372 U.S. 335 (1963); Miranda v. Arizona, 384 U.S. 436 (1966); U.S. v. Wade, 388 U.S. 218 and Gilbert v. California, 388 U.S. 263 (1967) among others.

37. The methods for the indigent defense discussed here are primarily based on Advisory Commission on Intergovernmental Relations, *State–Local Relations in the Criminal Justice System,* pp. 118–119.

38. *Loc. cit.*
39. U.S. Department of Justice, Law Enforcement Assistance Administration and U.S. Department of Commerce, Bureau of the Census, *Expenditures and Employment Data for the Criminal Justice System,* the volumes for 1968–69 and 1970–71.
40. Charles R. Adrian, *State and Local Governments* (New York: McGraw-Hill, 1960), p. 362.
41. W.F. Willoughby, *Principles of Judicial Administration* (Brookings Institution, 1929), p. 186 as cited in James M. Burns and Jack W. Peltason, *Government by the People* (Englewood Cliffs: Prentice-Hall, 1963), p. 202.
42. Murray Teigh Bloom, "On Trial: Trial by Jury," *National Civic Review* (July, 1973), pp. 358–361.
43. *Ibid.*
44. The President's Commission on Law Enforcement and Administration of Justice, *The Challenge of Crime in a Free Society,* p. 131.
45. The President's Commission on Law Enforcement and Administration of Justice, *Task Force Report: Corrections* (Washington, D.C.: U.S. Government Printing Office, 1967), p. 38.
46. *Ibid.,* p. 3.
47. *Ibid.,* p. 4.
48. *Ibid.,* p. 51, Table 2.
49. *Ibid.,* p. 1, Table 1.
50. U.S. Department of Justice, Law Enforcement Assistance Administration and U.S. Department of Commerce, Bureau of the Census, *Expenditure and Employment Data for the Criminal Justice System,* 1970–1971, p. 15.
51. CED, *Reducing Crime and Assuring Justice,* p. 83.
52. Committee for Economic Development, *Reducing Crime and Assuring Justice,* p. 83.
53. Joint Commission on Correctional Manpower and Training, *A Time to Act: Final Report* (Washington, D.C.: The Joint Commission, October, 1969) as cited in Advisory Commission on Intergovernmental Relations, *State–Local Relations in the Criminal Justice System,* p. 120.
54. The President's Commission on Law Enforcement and Administration of Justice, *Task Force Report: Corrections,* p. 199.
55. *Ibid.,* pp. 121–122.
56. Advisory Commission on Intergovernmental Relations, *State–Local Relations in the Criminal Justice System,* p. 126.
57. The President's Commission on Law Enforcement and Administration of Justice, *Task Force Report: Corrections,* p. 133. Puerto Rico is counted as a state here.
58. ACIR, *op. cit.,* pp. 127–128.
59. *Loc. cit.*
60. The President's Commission on Law Enforcement and Administration of Justice, *Task Force Report: Corrections,* p. 144.
61. *Ibid.*

62. ACIR, *op. cit.,* p. 129.
63. ACIR, *loc. cit.*
64. ACIR, *ibid.,* pp. 129–130. Puerto Rico was counted as a state here.
65. The President's Commission on Law Enforcement and Administration of Justice, *Task Force Report: Corrections,* pp. 178–180.
66. U.S. Department of Justice, Law Enforcement Assistance Administration, *1970 National Jail Census* (Washington, D.C.: U.S. Government Printing Office, 1971).
67. The President's Commission on Law Enforcement and Administration of Justice, *Task Force Report: Corrections,* p. 185.
68. *Ibid.,* p. 189.
69. Daniel J. Freed, "The Nonsystem of Criminal Justice," in James S. Campbell, Joseph R. Sahid, and David P. Stang (eds.), *Law and Order Reconsidered: Report of the Task Force on Law and Law Enforcement to the National Commission on the Causes and Prevention of Violence* (New York: Praeger Publishers, 1970), p. 267.
70. The President's Commission on Law Enforcement and Administration of Justice, *The Challenge of Crime in a Free Society,* p. 13.

Chapter Five

The Rising Cost for Criminal Justice Services: An Overview

FISCAL CRISIS

The unreceding crisis of crime in our cities has intensified the public clamor for safe streets and "freedom from fear." The law-and-order theme has dominated campaign issues in many of the important national and local elections. The resulting political responses have generally envigorated law enforcement and criminal justice policies: old programs have been expanded; new programs and services have been added; and not infrequently operational procedures have been reorganized. However, the expansive responses of public policy are subject to constraints, the most important of which is the limitation of resources.

Public policy decisions, to be most ideal from the standpoint of problem solution and need satisfaction, should be made in such a way that governmental services rendered or governmental regulations imposed are fully sufficient to satisfy the public needs. Then, to meet the resource requirements for the support of such policies and programs, whatever resources necessary should be raised for the purpose. However, the reality of governmental policy-making process is usually the other way around: namely, policies and programs are tailored to match the resources available.

Local governments, especially those in metropolitan areas, are most hard-pressed for expansive responses of law enforcement and criminal justice policies. The reasons are many. As a consequence of historical evolution, a preponderant share of governmental responsibility for law enforcement and criminal justice in America is assigned to local governments. Thus, the local government must raise the funds necessary for most of the law enforcement and criminal justice services, and the central cities of metropolitan areas are most pressed for immediate and massive response to crime control because crime problem is most serious there.

The resource constraints to finance criminal justice services in metropolitan areas are further compounded by the rapid increase in overall financial needs to meet the challenge of the so-called urban crisis. The crisis of urban crime is only a part of the urban crisis. Although there is no single definition acceptable to all, the urban crisis may be viewed as a conglomerate of problems that threatens to break down the role of the cities as the center of opportunity, convenience, diversity, interaction, and creativity.[1] The problems that constitute the urban crisis may include the deterioration of education, housing, race relations, job opportunity, transportation, and manpower development, to name a few. All of these problems and more are in competition with crime and law enforcement problems for a thicker slice of the limited public resource pie.

Any actions for the strengthening of the capability of criminal justice agencies require additional financial commitments. In recent years, the political climate has been generally in favor of more generous financial support for criminal justice functions, especially for the police. Measurable improvements have been made in such areas as personnel, equipment and facilities, and utilization of new technology for information and communication, and so forth. Nevertheless, financing for criminal justice functions, as for other governmental functions and programs, has been caught in the local fiscal crisis. The fiscal crisis epitomizes the urban crisis from the standpoint of public policy-making.

The financial difficulties experienced by local governments in the Northeastern Ohio area are illustrative of the local fiscal crisis, for they are not dissimilar to the general experience of local governments throughout the country. The recent financial plight of Cleveland has been repeatedly headlined in the nation's mass media. To head off the forthcoming financial shortage, the then Mayor Carl B. Stokes's Administration proposed an increase in the city's income tax. The tax proposal, however, was voted down twice, in the November 1970 general elections and in the February 1971 special election. The last minute scramble to patch-up the financial "swiss cheese" by the Stokes Administration in the latter part of 1971 led to a layoff of some 1,750 city employees, including some 200 police officers.

Not surprisingly, tax and city finance was one of the most controversial issues in the city's mayoral election of November 1971. Mayor Ralph Perk, succeeding Mayor Stokes, immediately faced an estimated deficit ranging from $11 million to $21.5 million. The Perk Administration again laid off some 500 city employees and proposed a 10 percent pay-cut for the remaining city employees. While the mayor's pay-cut proposal was soundly repudiated by the city employee unions, an agreement was reached to defer payment of the 10 percent of employees' salaries until August 31 of 1972 instead of cutting it. This financial crisis, after all, was not solved, but merely postponed.

The Summit County government has had recurrent experience of budget shortage during the last few years. As early as in 1969, a shortage in the county's general fund budget resulted in a 10 percent pay-cut for all sheriff's deputies. This pay-cut decision prompted a "sick call" walkout. Only 5 percent of the pay reduction was subsequently restored.

The city of Akron has been relatively free from financial problems. A 1 percent city income tax was adopted in 1962, and a plan for a rate, increase in the tax to 1.5 percent over a 3-year period was adopted in 1969. However, in 1972, the city began to feel a fiscal squeeze, mainly due to a wage and salary clause built into the city charter in 1968, which allows policemen and firemen automatic salary raises that reflect increases in living costs. The revenue projection for the 1972 to 1973 fiscal year precluded the possibility of complying with this charter provision. The city council voted for a ceiling in salary increase at $418. The employee unions and the administration failed to reach an agreement. The unions sued the city for the breach of the charter provision, and the case lasted until the summer of 1973.[2]

Why Fiscal Crisis?

Why are our local governments trapped in such a fiscal crisis? The reasons for local fiscal crisis are complex and not always obvious. Nevertheless, some of the more important reasons are identifiable.

First, we live in an era of "rising expectation." The public expectation for more and better municipal services is certainly no exception. Thus, increasing demands are pressed for both traditional and new municipal services. The traditional services include criminal justice functions, streets and highways, and parks and recreation, while included in the new services are community development, development of human resources, and protection of environment, for examples.

Second, the rapid rise in tax burdens required to finance these expanding services has prompted a "taxpayers' rebellion." It is a fact that the tax burden in the United States is the lowest among the Western industrialized nations.[3] In American political culture, however, private use of resources is more highly valued than governmental (public) use of resources.[4] This political culture largely dictates local tax policy in that local tax rates are mainly determined by popular referendum. Voters, however, tend to repudiate more-tax propositions more often than ever.

Three, local taxes are generally regressive and unproductive. Property taxes are the predominant source of local tax revenues. However, the burden of property taxes is relatively heavier on those who have less income than on those who have more income. In addition, property taxes are perhaps the least responsive to income growth of all taxes, meaning that the revenue productivity of property taxes does not correspond to the income growth or economic growth. In Ohio, unlike most other states, the municipal income taxes are as important a source of local tax revenues as property taxes for cities and villages. However, the municipal income taxes are imposed at a flat rate. Usually the tax rate ranges from 0.5 percent to 1.5 percent among the Ohio municipalities. And the taxable income includes only wages and salaries—this being the reason why this tax is often called a "payroll tax." Due to the flat rate of the tax structure and exclusion of unearned income, the municipal income taxes are also regressive.[5]

Four, local government structure is believed to play a significant role in the current fiscal crisis. In general, the local government system is highly fragmented, particularly in metropolitan areas. As a result, most of the local government units are rather small in population size and land area. For this reason, most local government units, whether they be municipalities or school districts, lack economies of scale for the performance of urban services in such a way as to maintain quality and economy with the available public resources.

Five, as a related part of the problem described above, there exists a problem of mismatch between resources available and the extent of governmental service problems.[6] In specific, this mismatch phenomenon looms large when the metropolitan central cities are compared with their suburbs. Invariably, the metropolitan central cities are concentrated with a disproportionate share of social problems relative to resources available to combat these problems, while often the suburbs enjoy excess resources and lack such serious social problems as the central cities face. As a rule, the low-income minority population, which has little to contribute to municipal taxes but is in the greatest need of public services, is increasing rapidly in central cities. At the same time, the tax bases in the central cities are declining in absolute terms or in relative terms compared with suburban areas. The suburban tax bases are growing and the newly gained population there is most likely middle- or upper-middle-income whites. When a metropolitan area is viewed as a whole, the tax base appears to be growing, but it is actually weakening in the central city.

In summary, the local fiscal crisis in urban America does not seem to be caused by *economic bankruptcy*. Economy is strong and growing in metropolitan areas as a whole, and local tax bases are also strong and growing in metropolitan areas as a whole. But growing fiscal problems of our urban governments are undoubtedly attributable to *political bankruptcy*. Voters are generally reluctant, to put it mildly, to support local taxes, and the fragmented local government structure in metropolitan communities is an inadequate and outdated governmental mechanism, unable to tap the resources where they are available and use them where they are needed throughout the metropolitan areas.

NATIONAL SUMMARY OF FEDERAL, STATE, AND LOCAL EXPENDITURES FOR CRIMINAL JUSTICE

How much does it cost to finance all governmental programs and services for criminal justice by all governments in the United States? Comprehensive expenditure data for criminal justice spending have just become available since the 1968–69 fiscal year as a joint undertaking between the Bureau of the Census of the Department of Commerce and Law Enforcement Assistance Administration of the Department of Justice.[7] Fiscal data relating to criminal justice operations prior to that date are fragmentary and incomplete.

In the following, the national aggregate of criminal justice spending of federal, state, and local governments for the 3 fiscal years from 1968–69 to 1970–71 will be presented in three ways: (1) the level of spending and its trends; (2) the relations between criminal justice spending and total spending for all functions; and (3) distribution patterns of criminal justice spending among the levels of government and among the different functions of criminal justice.

The Level and Trends of Criminal Justice Spending

Table 5–1 presents total expenditures for criminal justice by level of government and by function for 3 consecutive fiscal years from the 1968–69 fiscal year to the 1970–71 fiscal year. During the 1970–71 fiscal year, federal, state, and local governments together expended $10,513 million for all criminal justice functions, which was an average of $50.97 per person. Of this total, local government spending was $6,621 million ($32.10 per capita), state spending $2,681 million ($13.00 per capita), and federal spending $1,211 million ($5.87 per capita). Among the individual functions, the cost of police protection was most expensive, with $6,165 million ($29.89 per capita), followed by corrections with $2,291 million ($11.11 per capita) and judicial functions with $1,358 million ($6.58). The total expenditures for all criminal justice operations by all governments were $8,571 million ($42.18 per capita) in the 1969–70 fiscal year and $7,340 million ($36.36 per capita) in the 1968–69 fiscal year.

The growth rate of criminal justice spending is shown in Table 5–2. Per capita total expenditures for all criminal justice functions by all governments increased by 40.2 percent during the 3-year period from the 1968–69 fiscal year to the 1970–71 fiscal year. Of the 3 major functions (police, judicial, and corrections), expenditures for corrections increased most with a 53.5 percent growth, while judicial expenditures increased least with a 32.7 percent rise. Of the 3 levels of government, federal expenditures have grown most with a 48.2 percent increase, while local government expenditures had the smallest percentage increase of 38.1.

In spite of the rapid increase in total spending for criminal justice as a whole, the growth rate of expenditures for individual functions and that for each level of government have maintained a remarkable degree of stability. Except federal spending for prosecution (a 4.4 percent decrease), every function at every level of government has experienced a considerable increase in expenditures ranging from a low of 25.0 percent increase in federal judicial spending, a 29.9 percent increase in state judicial spending to a high of a 75.8 percent

Table 5–1.   Total Direct Expenditures for Criminal Justice by Function and Level of Government, 1968 to 1971
(Current Dollars)

	All Governments		Federal		State		Local	
	In Millions	Per Capita	In Millions	Per Capita	In Millions	Per Capita	In Millions	Per Capita
1970–71								
Total	10,513	50.97	1,211	5.87	2,681	13.00	6,621	32.10
Police	6,165	29.89	804	3.90	873	4.23	4,488	21.76
Judicial	1,358	6.58	134	.65	314	1.52	911	4.42
Corrections	2,291	11.11	111	.54	1,323	6.41	857	4.15
Prosecution	491	2.38	89	.43	108	.52	295	1.43
Indigent Defense	128	.62	61	.30	16	.08	51	.25
Miscellaneous	79	.38	13	.06	47	.23	20	.10
1969–70								
Total	8,571	42.18	978	4.81	2,139	10.53	5,454	26.84
Police	5,080	25.00	589	2.90	689	3.39	3,803	18.71
Judicial	1,190	5.86	129	.63	282	1.39	779	3.83
Corrections	1,706	8.40	83	.41	1,051	5.17	572	2.81
Prosecution	442	2.18	102	.50	83	.41	257	1.26
Indigent Defense	102	.50	56	.28	9	.04	37	.18
Miscellaneous	50	.25	21	.10	24	.12	6	.03

1968–69

Total	7,340	36.36	800	3.96	1,849	9.16	4,691	23.24
Police	4,430	21.94	492	2.44	621	3.08	3,317	16.43
Judicial	1,002	4.96	106	.52	236	1.17	660	3.27
Corrections	1,462	7.24	71	.35	914	4.53	477	2.36
Prosecution	369	1.73	92	.45	71	.35	207	1.02
Indigent Defense	78	.39	40	.20	7	.04	31	.15
Miscellaneous	—	—	—	—	—	—	—	—

Sources: Bureau of the Census and LEAA, *Expenditure and Employment Data for the Criminal Justice System*, (Washington D.C.: U.S. Government Printing Office). The issues for the 1968–69, 1969–70, and 1970–71 fiscal years.

Table 5–2.   Change in Direct Expenditures for Criminal Justice, by Function and Level of Government, 1968 to 1971
(Percent Change in Per Capita)

	All Governments	Federal Government	State Governments	Local Governments
Total	40.2	48.2	41.9	38.1
Police	36.2	59.8	37.3	32.4
Judicial	32.7	25.0	29.9	35.2
Corrections	53.5	54.3	41.5	75.8
Prosecution	30.1	-4.4	48.6	40.2
Indigent Defense	59.0	50.0	100.0	66.7
Others	–	–	–	–

Source: Bureau of the Census and LEAA, *Expenditure and Employment Data for the Criminal Justice System* (Washington D.C.: U.S. Government Printing Office). The issues for the 1968–69, 1969–70, and 1970–71 fiscal years.

increase in local corrections spending and a 100.0 percent increase in state spending for indigent defense.[8]

The trends of criminal justice expenditures, as shown in Table 5–2, indicate that some changes are emerging in the emphasis of criminal justice policy. For example, the increase in correctional expenditures in excess of 50 percent seems to indicate that the pattern of policy responses toward corrections is changing, perhaps, from custodial to rehabilitative services and from punitive to humane treatment. Although the total amount of money involved is modest, the rapid increase in expenditures for indigent defense is also significant. The growing public support for the defense of indigent defendants may help improve the change for equal justice between the rich and poor. A number of recent rulings of the U.S. Supreme Court have imposed increasing responsibility upon government to provide legal counsel for the indigent defendants.[9] It is only during the past few years that such court decisions began to show their impact on governmental expenditures for criminal justice.

Fiscal System Context of Criminal Justice Spending

Since governmental budget-making is a competitive process of allocating limited resources among various competing purposes, a specific share of the total budget pie allocated to a particular function may be viewed as an indicator of that function's budget priority. To approximate the relative priority of criminal justice spending within the total context of fiscal resource allocation, total criminal justice expenditures are computed as a percent of total direct general expenditures for all governmental purposes.[10] The percentage so computed will tell us whether the budget priority of criminal justice spending has been increasing, decreasing, or remaining unchanged relative to the rest of gov-

Table 5–3. Total Direct General Expenditures and Share of Criminal Justice Spending, by Level of Government, 1968 to 1971

	Total Direct General Expenditures (Millions of Dollars)	Share of Criminal Justice Spending (Percent)
1970–71		
All Governments	301,096	3.49
Federal	150,422	.96
State	56,478	5.17
Local	94,196	7.07
1969–70		
All Governments	275,017	3.12
Federal	143,685	.68
State	48,749	4.39
Local	82,582	6.60
1968–69		
All Governments	255,924	2.87
Federal	139,197	.57
State	43,244	4.28
Local	73,483	6.38

Source: Bureau of the Census and LEAA, *Expenditure and Employment Data for the Criminal Justice System* (Washington, D.C.: U.S. Government Printing Office). The issues for the 1968–69, 1969–70, and 1970–71 fiscal years.

ernmental functions. Table 5–3 shows total direct general expenditures for all governmental functions and the percent of the total for criminal justice of the 3 fiscal years.

Table 5–3 demonstrates that expenditures for criminal justice have taken an increasingly greater share of total budget of federal, state, and local governments. All governments combined, total criminal justice spending accounted for 2.87 percent of total direct general expenditures in the 1968–69 fiscal year and that figure was increased to 3.49 percent in the 1970–71 fiscal year. The share of the budget allocated to criminal justice purposes was the greatest at the local level, and it has grown from 6.38 percent in the 1968–69 fiscal year to 7.07 percent in the 1970–71 fiscal year. Federal government spends the smallest share of its budget for criminal justice, but the share of criminal justice budget has increased fastest at this level. Thus, not only the level of criminal justice spending has increased at every level of government and in every function, but also the criminal justice share of the total budget has been increasing consistently at a rapid rate.

Distribution Patterns

As shown in Table 5–4, local governments carry the heaviest financial burden for criminal justice of the 3 levels of government. Local government expenditures account for nearly two-thirds of total spending for criminal justice by all governments, state spending about one-quarter of the total, and federal spending slightly over one-tenth. Local spending is predominant in 3 functional areas—police protection, judicial function, and legal services and prosecution. State spending is dominant in corrections, while federal spending is dominant in indigent defense.

Table 5–4. Distribution of Total Direct Expenditures for Criminal Justice Among the Levels of Government, 1968 to 1971
(Percent)

	All Governments	Federal Government	State Governments	Local Governments
1970–71				
Total	100.0	11.5	25.5	63.0
Police	100.0	13.0	14.2	72.8
Judicial	100.0	9.9	23.1	67.0
Corrections	100.0	4.8	57.8	37.4
Legal Services and Prosecution	100.0	18.1	21.9	60.0
Indigent Defense	100.0	47.6	12.8	39.6
Others	100.0	16.2	59.1	24.7
1969–70				
Total	100.0	11.4	25.0	63.6
Police	100.0	11.6	13.6	74.9
Judicial	100.0	10.8	23.7	65.5
Corrections	100.0	4.8	61.6	33.5
Legal Services and Prosecution	100.0	23.1	18.8	58.1
Indigent Defense	100.0	54.6	9.2	36.2
Others	100.0	41.0	47.5	11.5
1968–69				
Total	100.0	10.9	25.2	63.9
Police	100.0	11.1	14.0	74.9
Judicial	100.0	10.5	23.6	65.9
Corrections	100.0	4.9	62.5	32.6
Legal Services and Prosecution	100.0	24.9	19.2	56.1
Indigent Defense	100.0	51.2	9.4	39.4
Others	100.0	100.0	–	–

Sources: Bureau of the Census and LEAA, *Expenditure and Employment Data for the Criminal Justice System* (Washington, D.C.: U.S. Government Printing Office). The issues for the 1968–69, 1969–70, and 1970–71 fiscal years.

Functional distribution pattern of criminal justice spending is also ascertained and shown in Table 5–5. Both local and federal governments spend more than 60 percent of the total criminal justice budget for police protection, while state governments allocate nearly one-half of the total crime budget for corrections. No drastic changes in the distribution pattern have occurred during the period examined here.

Summary

Criminal justice services cost more than $50 per capita to federal, state, and local governments in the 1970–71 fiscal year. The total crime budget has increased more than 40 percent from the 1968–69 to the 1970–71 fiscal year. The criminal justice cost as a percent of total direct general expenditure has

Table 5–5. Functional Distribution of Criminal Justice Expenditures by Levels of Government, 1968 to 1971 *(Percent)*

	All Governments	*Federal Government*	*State Governments*	*Local Governments*
1970–71				
Total	100.0	100.0	100.0	100.0
Police	58.6	66.4	32.6	67.8
Judicial	12.9	11.1	11.7	13.8
Corrections	21.8	9.2	49.3	12.9
Prosecution	4.7	7.3	4.0	4.5
Indigent Defense	1.2	5.0	.6	.8
Others	.8	1.1	1.8	.3
1969–70				
Total	100.0	100.0	100.0	100.0
Police	59.3	60.1	32.2	69.7
Judicial	13.9	13.1	13.2	14.3
Corrections	19.9	8.5	49.2	10.5
Prosecution	5.2	10.4	3.9	4.7
Indigent Defense	1.2	5.7	.4	.7
Others	.6	2.1	1.1	.1
1968–69				
Total	100.0	100.0	100.0	100.0
Police	60.3	61.5	33.6	70.7
Judicial	13.6	13.2	12.8	14.1
Corrections	19.9	8.9	49.4	10.2
Prosecution	5.0	11.4	3.8	4.4
Indigent Defense	1.1	5.0	.4	.7
Others	–	–	–	–

Sources: Bureau of the Census and LEAA, *Expenditure and Employment Data for the Criminal Justice System* (Washington, D.C.: U.S. Government Printing Office). The issues for the 1968–69, 1969–70, and 1970–71 fiscal years.

also been increasing. The intergovernmental distribution of criminal justice spending is local-dominant, while the interfunctional distribution is police-dominant.

NOTES TO CHAPTER FIVE

1. For an incisive discussion of urban crisis, see Alan K. Campbell (ed.), *The States and the Urban Crisis* (Englewood Cliffs: Prentice-Hall, 1970), chapter 1.
2. The financial experiences of Cleveland, Summit County, and Akron are adopted from Yong Hyo Cho, *Local Financing for Criminal Justice in Northeast Ohio: Patterns, Trends, and Projections* (Akron: Center for Urban Studies, University of Akron, 1972), pp. 32–34.
3. *Time* magazine reported that total tax collections in the U.S. as a percent of GNP was 30.6 compared with 33.6 in West Germany, 37.0 in Canada, 40.7 in Sweden, and 43.0 in Britain. March 13, 1972, p. 72.
4. See for a detailed discussion on this matter, John K. Galbraith, *The Affluent Society* (Boston: Houghton Mifflin, 1958).
5. See Ohio Tax Study Commission, *The State and Local Tax Structure of Ohio* (Columbus, 1967), pp. 34–35.
6. Many of the recent studies treated this particular aspect of metropolitan fiscal problem. See, for example, Advisory Commission on Inter-governmental Relations, *Fiscal Balance in the American Federal System, Vol. 2, Metropolitan Fiscal Disparities* (Washington, D.C.; U.S. Government Printing Office, 1967); Alan K. Campbell and Seymour Sacks, *Metropolitan America: Fiscal Patterns and Governmental Systems* (New York; The Free Press, 1967); and Committee for Economic Development, *Fiscal Issues in the Future of Federalism* (New York: CED, 1968).
7. Law Enforcement Assistance Administration, U.S. Department of Justice and Bureau of the Census, U.S. Department of Commerce, *Expenditure and Employment Data for the Criminal Justice System* (Washington, D.C.: U.S. Government Printing Office). An annual publication beginning the 1968–69 fiscal year.
8. Since the sum of money involved in indigent defense is negligible, the high rate of growth does not significantly affect the growth rate of total spending.
9. The court cases affecting governmental responsibility for providing legal counsel for indigent defendants include: *Gideon v. Wainwright* (372 U.S. 335 (1963)); *Miranda v. Arizona* (398 U.S. 436 (1966)); *Gilbert v. California* (388 U.S. 263 (1967)); *Mempa v. Rhay* (389 U.S. 128 (1967)); *Hamilton v. Alabama* (368 U.S. 62 (1962)); and *Douglas v. California* (372 U.S. 353 (1963)).
10. General expenditure is used here instead of total expenditure because general expenditure excludes utility expenditure, liquor stores expenditure, and insurance-trust expenditure, all of which are not subject to the general process of budgetary allocation annually for expenditure decisions. Direct expenditure avoids the possibility of

double counts of the same fund more than once by different governments. Direct expenditure excludes intergovernmental expenditure from expenditure total of the government that transfers the fund to another government, but includes it in the expenditure total of the government that actually spends the fund, for example, for police training.

Chapter Six

The Pattern of State–Local Expenditures for Criminal Justice

As shown clearly in Chapter 4, complexity and diversity characterize the state–local system of criminal justice in the United States. However, the criminal justice system is not the only one that is characterized by the massive interstate variation; the entire system of state and local governments varies greatly from state to state. One of the ways devised for a systematic measurement of the state-by-state differences in the state–local governmental systems is what is called the "fiscal assignment system." The fiscal assignment system is a concept developed for the description of the allocation pattern of expenditure or revenue responsibility between a state government and all of the local governments within the state.[1]

Professors Campbell and Sacks, in their pioneering study of state–local assignment of fiscal responsibility described the fiscal assignment systems as follows:

> There are 50 state–local governmental systems and the District of Columbia system in the United States, each with its own unique characteristics; and within each state–local system there are distinct local subsystems, usually more than one within each state . . .
>
> Although there are various ways in which these systems can be described and classified, one of the most useful is to base the classification on fiscal characteristics. The relevant fiscal characteristics for describing state–local systems are: allocation between state and local governments of general expenditure and revenue responsibility . . . [2]

The subsequent studies have also uncovered that the variation of the fiscal assignment system is one of the key determinants of the variance in the level of local or state fiscal policy outcomes among the states.[3] The state–local criminal justice systems can also be described and classified by the pattern of assigning expenditure responsibility for criminal justice between the state government and all local governments within the state. Undoubtedly, the pattern of the variation of local or state expenditures for criminal justice among the states is believed to be, in a significant way, a function of the variance in the expenditure assignment for criminal justice.

Here, we present the comparative summary of state–local spending systems and spending behavior for criminal justice of the 50 states. Our comparison is focused on the following: (1) the expenditure assignment of criminal justice; (2) the level of expenditures for criminal justice; and (3) the criminal justice share of total general expenditures.

THE EXPENDITURE ASSIGNMENT OF CRIMINAL JUSTICE SYSTEM

The local percent of state and local expenditures for criminal justice represents the expenditure assignment of criminal justice. Table 6–1 reports the summary of the distribution pattern of the 4 measures of the assignment among the 50 states. The 4 measures of assignment include total expenditures, police expenditures, judicial expenditures, and corrections expenditures. Their distribution patterns are measured by mean, standard deviation, coefficient of variation, and the lowest and the highest states.[4]

The assignment of total expenditures for criminal justice averaged 61.5 percent among the 50 states, and it ranged from a low of 17.2 percent in Alaska to a high of 79.1 percent in New York. For the 3 major functions, the assignment of police expenditures averaged 76.5 percent;[5] that of judicial expenditures, 62.6 percent; and that of corrections expenditures, only 25.6 percent. In general, police function is most local (over three-fourths); while corrections responsibility is least local (one-fourth). However, each of the 3 functional assignments is highly various among the 50 states. As the coefficient of variation indicates, the assignment of corrections expenditures varies most,

Table 6–1.   Summary of Local Expenditures for Criminal Justice as a Percentage of State–Local Expenditures for the 50 States, 1970–71

	Mean	Standard Deviation	Coefficient of Variations	Lowest	Highest
Total	61.5	13.9	22.4	17.2	79.1
Police	76.5	11.5	15.0	31.4	99.0
Judicial Function	62.6	26.5	42.4	0.0	89.9
Corrections	25.6	15.2	59.4	0.0	73.5

Sources: U.S. Department of Justice, Law Enforcement Assistance Administration and U.S. Department of Commerce, Bureau of the Census, *Expenditure and Employment Data for The Criminal Justice System,* 1970–71 (Washington, D.C.: U.S. Government Printing Office, 1973).

while the expenditure assignment for police protection shows the lowest variance. The police system was least decentralized in Alaska (31.4 percent of the state and local expenditures for police was local), whereas it was most decentralized in Hawaii (99.0 percent of its state–local expenditures for police was local). The judicial assignment ranged from 0 percent local in Hawaii to 89.9 percent local in Ohio. The corrections assignment ranged from 0 percent local in Delaware and Rhode Island and only 0.1 percent local in Connecticut and Vermont to as high as 73.5 percent local in Pennsylvania.

THE EXPENDITURE LEVEL

The spending level of criminal justice is measured by per capita. Per capita expenditures for criminal justice are computed for all criminal justice functions combined and for selected functions individually, on the one hand. On the other hand, the per capita figures are computed for the combined expenditures of state and local governments, state expenditures only, and local government expenditures only. The 50 states' summary of the state–local spending level is presented first, then followed by the spending level of state government and that of local governments.

The Level of State–Local Spending

Table 6–2 shows the interstate variation pattern in per capita state–local expenditures for criminal justice, total and selected functions. The level of state and local expenditures for criminal justice varies greatly from state to state, as shown by the coefficient of variation as well as the range of variation (the difference between the highest and lowest). The spending level for indigent

Table 6–2. Summary of Per Capita State–Local Expenditures for the Criminal Justice System, by Function, for the 50 States, 1970–71

	Mean ($)	Standard Deviation ($)	Coefficient of Variation (%)	Lowest ($)	Highest ($)
Total	39.53	17.52	44.3	18.53	110.11
Police	22.37	8.92	39.9	10.89	49.47
Judicial	5.60	3.70	66.1	2.18	27.71
Legal Services & Prosecution	1.92	1.45	75.5	0.55	9.73
Indigent Defense	.28	.32	114.3	0.00	1.86
Corrections	9.08	5.10	56.2	3.38	29.27
Other Criminal Justice	0.34	0.28	82.4	0.01	1.49

Sources: U.S. Department of Justice, Law Enforcement Assistance Administration and U.S. Department of Commerce, Bureau of the Census, *Expenditure and Employment Data for The Criminal Justice System,* 1970–71 (Washington, D.C.: U.S. Government Printing Office, 1973).

defense varied most with a coefficient of variation of 114.3 percent, whereas the spending level for police protection varied least with a coefficient of variation of only 39.9 percent.

The mean of state and local expenditures for all criminal justice functions was $39.53 per capita, but the total spending level ranged from a low of less than $20.00 at the one extreme ($18.53 in West Virginia and $19.48 in Arkansas) to a high of over $80.00 at the other extreme ($110.11 in Alaska, $85.44 in New York, and $80.59 in Nevada). The level of police expenditures averaged $22.37 per capita. In several states, however, the spending level for police was below $15.00 (such as $10.89 in West Virginia, $12.82 in Arkansas, and $14.03 in Alabama for example), while in a few other states, the spending level exceeded $40.00 ($49.47 in New York and $44.32 in Alaska). The 50 states' mean for judicial expenditures was $5.60. Again, Alaska was the highest spending state for this function ($27.71), while the lowest spending state was Arkansas ($2.18). The spending level for corrections averaged $9.08 per capita. For this function, several southern or rural states spent less than $4.00 (Mississippi, North Dakota, Arkansas, and West Virginia), while Alaska and New York spent more than $20.00 per capita.

The Level of State Spending

Table 6–3 summarizes the pattern of per capita state expenditures for criminal justice. The interstate variation in state expenditures is greater than that in state and local combined expenditures for each of the corresponding functions. As we observed earlier, one of the key reasons for such variation lies in the difference of the expenditure assignment systems among the states.

Total state expenditures for criminal justice averaged $16.91 per capita and they ranged from a low of $7.95 in Arkansas to a high of $91.48 in Alaska. The state police expenditure averaged $5.35 per capita, but its variation was even greater, ranging from less than $1 per capita in Hawaii (35 cents) to

Table 6–3. Summary of Per Capita State Expenditures for Criminal Justice System, by Function, for the 50 States, 1970–71

	Mean ($)	Standard Deviation ($)	Coefficient of Variation (%)	Lowest ($)	Highest ($)
Total	16.91	12.93	76.5	7.95	91.48
Police	5.35	4.21	78.7	0.35	30.49
Judicial Function	2.48	3.50	141.1	0.44	22.86
Correction	6.92	4.20	60.6	2.75	27.23

Sources: U.S. Department of Justice, Law Enforcement Assistance Administration and U.S. Department of Commerce, Bureau of the Census, *Expenditure and Employment Data for The Criminal Justice System,* 1970–71 (Washington, D.C.: U.S. Government Printing Office, 1973).

$30.49 in Alaska. State judicial expenditures averaged $2.48 per capita among the 50 states, but the interstate variation in the spending level of this function was greater than all others with a coefficient of variation of 141.1 percent. Several states spent less than $1 (including Arizona, Arkansas, California, and Georgia among others), while the state government of Alaska spent as much as $22.86 per capita for judicial function. State expenditures for corrections averaged $6.92 per capita and the interstate variation was relatively moderate compared with the other functions.

The Level of Local Spending

The interstate variation of per capita local expenditures for criminal justice is not as great as that of per capita state expenditures as the comparison of Tables 6—3 and 6—4 makes apparent. As the coefficient of variation indicates, per capita local expenditures for corrections varied most and those for police varied least.

Per capita total local expenditures for criminal justice averaged $23.85. At the one extreme, local governments in Vermont spent $8.62 per capita for all criminal justice functions, whereas local governments in New York spent as much as $67.59 per capita for all criminal justice operations, at the other extreme. The 50 states' mean of local police expenditures was $17.31 per capita. In several states, local police expenditures did not even reach $10.00 per capita (such as $6.97 in West Virginia, $8.36 in Vermont, $9.76 in South Carolina, $9.79 in South Dakota, and $9.83 in Arkansas), whereas in 2 states, local spending for police exceeded $40.00 per capita ($45.43 in New York and $41.14 in Nevada). The interstate variance in the level of local expenditures for judicial function and corrections is much more drastic than that for police primarily because of the greater variation of the expenditure assignment for courts and corrections than that for police.

Table 6—4. Summary of Per Capita Local Expenditures for the Criminal Justice System by Function for the 50 States, 1970—71

	Mean ($)	Standard Deviation ($)	Coefficient of Variation %	Lowest ($)	Highest ($)
Total	23.85	12.52	52.5	8.62	67.59
Police	17.31	8.24	47.6	6.97	45.43
Judicial Function	3.04	1.84	60.5	0.0	7.59
Corrections	2.38	2.40	100.8	0.0	11.56

Sources: U.S. Department of Justice, Law Enforcement Assistance Administration and U.S. Department of Commerce, Bureau of the Census, *Expenditure and Employment Data for The Criminal Justice System,* 1970—71 (Washington, D.C.: U.S. Government Printing Office, 1973).

THE TOTAL BUDGET CONTEXT OF CRIMINAL
JUSTICE SPENDING

Table 6–5 presents the summary of interstate variation in the criminal justice percent of total general expenditures, computed for the state and local government expenditures combined, state expenditures only, and local expenditures only. As discussed elsewhere, this measure of criminal justice spending can be considered as an indicator of the budget priority of the criminal justice services or the fiscal burden of the criminal justice operations.

The interstate variance in the criminal justice percent of total general expenditures is generally moderate compared with the level variance. However, the range of variation is still considerable for this measure as well. The criminal justice percent of the combined expenditures of state and local governments ranged from a low of less than 5.0 percent in several states (such as 3.9 percent in West Virginia, 4.4 percent in North Dakota, 4.8 percent in Hawaii, and 4.9 percent in Tennessee) to a high of more than 11.0 percent in a few states (such as 11.4 percent in Florida, 11.3 percent in Nevada, and 11.0 percent in Illinois) with an average of 7.1 percent. Thus, the budget burden of criminal justice in Florida is nearly three times as great as that in West Virginia.

The criminal justice percent of total state general expenditures ranged from a low of less than 2.0 percent in such states as North Dakota (1.6 percent) and West Virginia (1.8 percent) to a high of 6.0 percent in Delaware and 6.3 percent in Maryland, with a mean of 3.3 percent. The criminal justice share of total local general expenditures varied from over 20 percent (20.6 percent in Pennsylvania and 20.3 percent in Illinois) to less than 5.0 percent (3.2 percent in Alaska and 4.7 percent in North Carolina), with an average of 11.8 percent.

SUMMARY

One characteristic is consistent and stands out in this summary of the 50 states' comparison of state and local expenditure systems and spending behavior for criminal justice—that is, the variance that is prevalent among the states. First of all, the system of assigning the expenditure responsibility for criminal justice between state and local governments varies greatly among the states. In some states, local governments assume only a fraction of total expenditure responsibility for criminal justice in the states (17.2 percent in Alaska, for example), while in some others local governments assume a predominant share of the responsibility (79.1 percent in New York).

The level of expenditures for criminal justice as measured by per capita demonstrates a vast variance among the states although the degree of variance differs depending on the type of functions and the level of governments. In general, however, police expenditures vary less than other functional expendi-

Table 6–5. Summary of Criminal Justice Spending, Percentage of Total Direct Expenditures, for the 50 States, 1970–71

	Mean (%)	Standard Deviation (%)	Coefficient of Variation (%)	Lowest (%)	Highest (%)
State—Local	7.1	1.9	27.2	3.9	11.4
State Only	3.3	1.0	30.8	1.6	6.3
Local Only	11.8	4.2	35.8	3.2	20.6

Sources: U.S. Department of Justice, Law Enforcement Assistance Administration and U.S. Department of Commerce, Bureau of the Census, *Expenditure and Employment Data for The Criminal Justice System,* 1970–71 (Washington, D.C.: U.S. Government Printing Office, 1973).

tures and local government expenditures vary less than state expenditures among the states.

Finally, criminal justice expenditure as a percent of total general expenditures indicates that the financial burden of criminal justice service is uneven among the states. The criminal justice burden on state and local budget ranges from less than 5 percent to more than 11 percent. The criminal justice burden is nearly three times as heavy on local budget as on state budget on the average. Further, the burden on local budget shows a greater variance among the states than that on state budget. The variance in the state and local expenditure policies for criminal justice demonstrates a unique quality that makes them suitable for a quasi-experimental research design for comparative policy analysis. Although the policy variance is not created by deliberate design, the variance seems sufficiently meaningful for the evaluation of the differential impact of policy difference on the achieving of the policy goals.

NOTES TO CHAPTER SIX

1. Originally, this concept of describing and classifying the state—local governmental systems was developed by Alan K. Campbell and Seymour Sacks. See their article, "Administering the Spread City," *Public Administration Review* (September, 1964), pp. 141–152.
2. Campbell and Sacks, *Ibid.,* p. 142.
3. Alan K. Campbell and Seymour Sacks, *Metropolitan America: Fiscal Patterns and Governmental Systems* (New York: The Free Press, 1967); and Yong Hyo Cho, "The Effect of Local Governmental Systems on Local Policy Outcomes in the United States," *Public Administration Review* (March, 1967), pp. 31–38.
4. This format will be used for all tabular presentation in this chapter.
5. The assignment of police expenditures has been consistently shifted toward the state governments throughout this century. In the beginning of this century, police function was almost entirely a local function.

Chapter Seven

Local Spending for Criminal Justice: The Case of the Northeast Ohio Urban Region

It was in the 1966–67 fiscal year that the Bureau of the Census began to compile comprehensive financial data for selected largest cities and counties.[1] Although this data is extremely valuable for comparative fiscal studies for criminal justice administration, the limited period of time covered by that data is simply insufficient for a meaningful analysis of fiscal trends.

To explore the trends of local expenditures for criminal justice, we employed a case study of the northeast Ohio urban region: namely, the jurisdiction of the Northeast Ohio Areawide Coordinating Agency (NOACA).[2]

THE NOACA REGION

NOACA was formed in 1968 as a regional political organization for areawide review and planning of federal grant applications.[3] NOACA contains three SMSA's that consist of 7 counties: the Cleveland SMSA comprises 4 counties (Cuyahoga, Geauga, Lake, and Medina counties); the Akron SMSA comprises 2 counties (Summit and Portage counties); and the Lorain-Elyria SMSA comprises of a single county of Lorain. NOACA has been troubled by two sets of recurrent conflicts among the constituent governments. The first set was the conflict between the city of Cleveland under Mayor Carl B. Stokes and the NOACA board. The apparent issue underlying the conflict was Cleveland's underrepresentation in the NOACA board membership, but different interests between Cleveland and the rest of the region were considered a fundamental reason for the conflict. This conflict resulted in the decertification of NOACA as the regional review agency by the Department of Housing and Urban Development in 1971. The NOACA's certification was reinstated in 1972 when a compromise was worked out between Cleveland and the NOACA board.[4]

The other conflict was a rivalry between the Akron area and the Cleveland area. The Akron area has always disliked to be bound together with the Cleveland area in the same regional organization and advocated its separation from NOACA and the Cleveland area whenever opportunity presented. Following a nearly year-long study of state administrative service districts and regional planning districts by the Ohio Department of Economic and Community Development and Ohio Local Government Service Commission, Governor Gilligan announced in the spring of 1973 the reorganization of regional planning agencies and state administrative service districts; the Akron area (Summit, Portage, and Medina counties) were taken out of NOACA and combined with Stark and Wayne counties to form a new regional planning and review agency. The Cleveland area appealed to the Department of Housing and Urban Development to disapprove the governor's reorganization scheme soon after the announcement.

In 1969, NOACA was also designated as the region's law enforcement planning district to coordinate planning and program development in law enforcement and criminal justice with the financial assistance of the law Enforcement Assistance Administration of U.S. Justice Department. The Omnibus Crime Control and Safe Street Act of 1968 that provided block grant to the states for law enforcement assistance required state agency of law enforcement planning as well as regional agency in metropolitan areas to plan and coordinate federally supported programs in law enforcement. Thus, NOACA has assumed dual responsibilities of regional review and coordination of federal grant applications in general and law enforcement planning and its coordination in particular in the region.

The NOACA region is a significant part of the Great Lakes industrial belt along with the Detroit area, the Chicago area, the Buffalo area, and the Milwaukee area, among others. The total population in the region slightly exceeded 3 million in 1970, as shown in Table 7–1. More than two-thirds of the population lived in the Cleveland metropolitan area. Population by county ranged from 1,721,300 in Cuyahoga county to only 62,977 in Geauga county. Non-white population was most heavily concentrated in Cuyahoga and Summit counties and particularly in the cities of Cleveland (39.0 percent) and Akron (17.8 percent).

Population density was also highest in Cuyahoga county with 3,775 persons per square mile and lowest in Geauga county with 155 persons per square mile. The degree of urbanization was exceeded 90 percent in two counties (Cuyahoga and Summit), nearly 90 percent in 2 counties (Lake and Lorain) in the neighborhood of 50 percent in 2 counties (Medina and Portage) and only 14.6 percent in Geauga.

LOCAL GOVERNMENT STRUCTURE
AND CRIMINAL JUSTICE SYSTEM

Criminal justice agencies are a part of four types of general local government in Ohio. They are county, city, village, and township governments. In 1972, the

Table 7–1. Population in the NOACA Region, 1970

	Total Population	Density	% Non-White	% Urban
Regional Total	*3,000,276*	*1,028*	*13.9*	*90.9*
The Cleveland SMSA	2,064,194	1,297	16.6	94.0
Cuyahoga County	1,721,300	3,775	19.6	99.6
Cleveland	750,903	9,880	39.0	100.0
Geauga County	62,977	155	1.6	14.6
Lake County	197,200	854	1.6	89.2
Medina County	82,717	195	1.0	49.5
The Lorain–Elyria SMSA	256,843	519	4.9	89.2
Lorain	78,185	4.115	10.2	100.0
Elria	53,427	3,816	11.1	100.0
The Akron SMSA	679,239	752	8.2	84.6
Summit County	553,371	1,350	9.6	90.4
Akron	275,425	5,196	17.8	100.0
Portage	125,868	254	2.4	53.7

Sources: Bureau of the Census, Census of Population: 1970, Vol. 1, *Characteristics of Population,* (Washington, D.C.: U.S. Government Printing Office, 1971), and Bureau of the Census, *Area Measurement Reports,* Series GE–20, No. 37, (Washington, D.C.: U.S. Government Printing Office, 1967).

U.S. Census of governments counted 233 units of the four types of general local governments within the NOACA jurisdiction. They include 7 county governments, 134 municipalities (which include city and village governments), and 93 units of townships.[5]

Police Departments

A 1969 survey counted 155 local police departments in the NOACA region as shown in Table 7–2. The 155 local police departments included seven county sheriff's departments, 61 city police departments, 70 village police departments, and 17 township police departments. The jurisdiction of local police departments is as highly fragmented as that of general local governments. A great majority of the police departments are small with less than 10 police officers.

The number of police departments in each county varied from 61 in Cuyahoga county and 26 in Summit county to 11 each in Medina and Portage counties. The county sheriff's department has the statutory police jurisdiction throughout the county, but in practice the sheriff's police function is mainly restricted to the unincorporated areas. Summit county had the largest department of a 217-man force, while Geauga county the smallest, a 14-man department. The city police departments are the most important local police agencies, for they serve the most populous urban communities where crime rate is high

Table 7–2. Number of Police Departments in the NOACA Region, by Types of Government and by County, 1969

	Total	County	City	Village	Township
Total	*155*	*7*	*61*	*70*	*17*
Cuyahoga	61	1	35	21	4
Geauga	12	1	0	5	6
Lake	19	1	6	11	1
Lorain	15	1	8	6	0
Medina	11	1	3	6	1
Portage	11	1	2	8	0
Summit	26	1	7	13	5

Source: Derived from the NOACA List of Local Law Enforcement Agencies Prepared for a Survey for the 1970 Comprehensive Law Enforcement Plan.

and various social problems requiring police attention are prevalent. The size of city police departments varied greatly from the largest, a 2,175-man department, in Cleveland, to the smallest, a five-man department, in Avon. The village and township police departments were particularly small. Of the 70 village police departments, only 5 had 10 or more sworn officers in 1969. Thirty-four departments had less than 5 full-time officers, while as many as 20 had a 1 or 2-man departments. All but one township police department had less than 10 officers. Ten of the 17 had a department of less than 5 officers.

Courts

There are three types of local courts in the NOACA region: the court of common pleas, municipal court, and mayor's court. Every county has a court of common pleas, and this is the major trial court of original and general jurisdiction. This court has several specialized divisions such as criminal division, domestic relations, probate, and juvenile, and so forth. In Cuyahoga county, however, the juvenile court is not a part of the court of common pleas, but a separate entity independently established in 1902.

Municipal court is a minor court of original jurisdiction. Its boundaries usually include more than one municipality. There were 24 municipal courts in the NOACA region in 1969. Thirteen of the 24 were in Cuyahoga county, 4 in Lorain, and 3 in Summit, 2 in Lake, and 1 each in the remaining 3 counties.[6] The number of judges for the municipal courts varies depending on the population size within the court jurisdiction. For example, the Cleveland Municipal Court, the largest in the region, has 13 judges, while those courts with less than 100,000 population within their jurisdiction are served by a single judge.

Mayor's Court. Many cities and villages maintain mayor's courts with a limited jurisdiction over cases involving municipal ordinances and moving traffic violations. As many as 29 municipalities in Cuyahoga county, for example,

Table 7–3. County Jails in Northeast Ohio, 1970

	Designed Capacity	*Inmates Population*	*Operating Expenditures (In Thousands of Dollars)*	*Number of Employees*	
				Full Time	*Part Time*
Total	*876*	*1,020*	*2,926*	*230*	*20*
Cuyahoga	350	609	1,939	156	1
Geauga	80	19	30	3	–
Lake	75	54	75	3	6
Lorain	58	62	100	9	8
Medina	45	28	68	9	–
Portage	56	46	54	5	5
Summit	212	202	665	45	–

Source: Derived from the unpublished data of the 1970 National Jail Census taken under a joint sponsorship of the Bureau of Census and the Law Enforcement Assistance Administration. This data was furnished by the LEAA to the author.

had mayor's court in June, 1971.[7] The mayor serves in a duel capacity as the mayor of the municipality and the judge of the court. The mayor's court is being gradually phased out in Ohio.

Correctional System

Correctional services in the NOACA region are primarily relying on institutional corrections; namely, jails. Parole is the function of the state government and the probation system is not well developed at the local level.

Each of the 7 counties has a county jail. Table 7–3 shows the capacity, inmates, operating expenditures, and employees of each of the 7 county jails. The Cuyahoga county jail, the largest urban county in the state, housed inmates more than 72 percent beyond its capacity unlike the jails of less urban counties where the jail capacity exceeded the inmates.[8] All of the county jails are operated by sheriff's deputies under the supervision of the county sheriff. However, beginning in the summer of 1973, Summit county started a new program of recruiting and training college graduate civilian correctional officers for the operation of the county jail. The civilian correctional officers are planned to replace the sheriff's deputies in a few years.

The National Jail Census of 1970 shows that 20 cities in the NOACA region have a municipal jail; 15 in Cuyahoga county, 2 in Lorain county, and 3 in Summit county. As shown in Table 7–4, municipal jails were not overcrowded, and except for a few of the larger city jails, most were operated by part-time staff.

Other criminal justice agencies include prosecutorial office, county coroner, jury, and public defender. Each of the counties has an elected county prosecutor and his appointed assistants. City solicitor or law director serves as prosecuter for the municipal courts.

Table 7–4.   Municipal Jails by County, 1970

| | Designed Capacity | Inmates Population | Operating Expenditures (Hundreds of Dollars) | Number of Employees | |
				Full Time	Part Time
Total	1,025	650	1,575	165	42
Cuyahoga County	839	564	1,333	151	32
Bedford	2	4	2	–	1
Berea	11	3	2	–	1
Brooklyn	4	1	1	–	1
Cleveland	700	497	1,199	151	5
East Cleveland	26	13	17	–	3
Euclid	12	8	12	–	2
Garfield Heights	11	3	3	–	1
Lakewood	19	5	62	–	6
Lyndhurst	3	2	2	–	–
Maple Heights	13	3	10	–	3
Mayfield Heights	5	5	3	–	1
North Royalton	7	3	2	–	1
Parma Heights	7	3	2	–	1
Strongville	14	9	7	–	4
University Heights	5	5	9	–	2
Lorain County	48	45	63	2	6
Elyria	20	20	28	1	3
Lorain	28	25	35	1	3
Summit County	138	41	179	15	4
Akron	120	37	172	15	1
Cuyahoga Falls	10	1	3	–	1
Twinsburg	8	3	4	–	2

Source: Derived from the unpublished data of the 1970 National Jail Census taken under a joint sponsorship of the Bureau of Census and the Law Enforcement Assistance Administration. This data was furnished by the LEAA to the author.

Each county has an elected coroner who is a licensed physician. The county coroner is responsible for determining the cause of death, particularly when the circumstances of the death are suspicious of the involvement of criminal acts. Each county has a jury commission that is responsible for the selection of jurors for grand and trial juries. Until the summer of 1973, when Summit county began its public defender system, Cuyahoga county was the only one with a public defender system in the region.

LOCAL SPENDING FOR CRIMINAL JUSTICE SYSTEMS IN THE NOACA REGION

We have collected local expenditure data for criminal justice functions for each of the counties, cities, villages, and townships in the region for 11 consecutive years, from 1960 to 1970. The annual financial reports of individual local governments were used as the primary source of our data. For the years from 1960 to 1966, we used the State Auditor's annual reports on local government finances, which were based on the individual government reports submitted to that office. For the subsequent years, the original reports of individual local governments as submitted to the State Auditor were used.

The specific items of criminal justice spending data collected are as follows: (1) for counties: expenditures for county sheriff's department; expenditures for corrections including jails, probation, and other miscellaneous correctional functions; expenditures for all courts under the county's financial responsibility; expenditures for prosecutions; and expenditures for coroner's office; (2) for cities: expenditures for city police department, city jail, and municipal court; and (3) for villages and townships: expenditures for their respective police departments.

However, to maintain clarity and simplicity in reporting our findings, we selected only 3 representative years, 1960, 1965, and 1970, for our presentation in this report. We believe that these 3 years will be adequate to establish trends in the spending pattern for criminal justice systems. First, the 3 years cover an 11-year period with an equal time interval among them. Second, the 11-year period covers two distinct eras in the latest history of criminal justice politics. During the first half of the 1960s, criminal justice was not a prominent political issue; however, it loomed large as one of the most controversial domestic policy issues in the second half of the decade. We believe that the 3 selected years will fully reflect the change in the issue context of criminal justice and law enforcement in domestic politics.

The 7-county area under the NOACA jurisdiction includes no less than 170 local government units that perform one or more criminal justice functions. Therefore, it is rather pointless to discuss the financial activities for criminal justice functions of each of these local government units in full detail. Rather, our emphasis here shall be on demonstrating the general pattern of local financing for criminal justice.[9]

Only the summary of our findings is reported here, and our summary presentation is organized as follows: (1) the level of expenditures for criminal justice; (2) the change pattern in the level of expenditures; and (3) criminal justice spending as a percent of total expenditures for all governmental functions. These modes of presentation attempt to ascertain the magnitude of expenditures for criminal justice, the rate of change in criminal justice spending, and the fiscal system context of criminal justice spending. Further, the data are organized in three ways: (1) total expenditures for all criminal justice functions by all local governments by county areas; (2) total expenditures by all local governments by criminal justice functions; and (3) expenditures for all criminal justice functions by type of local government.

The Level of Spending

Total criminal justice expenditures by all local governments in the NOACA region amounted to $101,644,124 ($33.88 per capita) in 1970, $55,603,908 ($19.40 per capita) in 1965, and $44,699,457 ($16.36 per capita) in 1960, as shown in Table 7–5. The inter-county difference in total criminal justice spending was tremendous, reflecting the population size and degree of urbanization of the counties. In each of the 3 selected years, the spending level was highest in Cuyahoga county and it was lowest in Geauga county. In 1970, for example, per capita total spending ranged from a high of $42.86 in Cuyahoga county and $27.92 in Summit county to a low of $11.78 in Geauga county and $13.57 in Portage county. A similar pattern of inter-county difference in spending levels prevailed in 1965 and 1960.

Table 7–6 reports the total criminal justice spending by all governments in the NOACA region by individual functions. A preponderant share of local criminal justice spending was devoted to police protection. The share of police spending exceeded 73 percent of the total spending in 1970 and 1965, though the 1960 percentage was slightly less than 70 (69.4 percent to be exact). In 1970, for example, of the total of $33.88 per capita, $24.99 was spent for police protection, $6.01 per capita for court, $2.11 for corrections, and less than $1 for prosecution and coroner. The interfunctional distribution of criminal justice spending showed a similar pattern in 1965 and 1960.

Total criminal justice spending by type of local government indicates that city and county governments carry most of the fiscal burden for criminal justice. As Table 7–7 displays, 62 cities together spent some $73 million while the 7 county governments spent nearly $25 million in 1970. Sixty-eight village governments spent $3.5 million and 34 township governments spent $657 thousands in the same year. Per capita expenditure was also the highest in cities with $29.73 compared with $21.04 for villages, $8.14 for counties, and only $3.78 for townships in 1970.[10] The 1970 spending pattern among the different types of local government prevailed in 1965 and 1960.

The Trends of Criminal Justice Spending

Table 7–8 presents the percent change of per capita expenditures for criminal justice by all local governments summarized for the region as a whole and for each county area. Per capita total local expenditures for criminal justice by all local governments in the region more than doubled during the 11-year period with an increase of 107.1 percent. However, this increase occurred mostly during the 1965 to 1970 period with a 73.7 percent increase compared to a 19.2 percent increase during the 1960 to 1965 period.

The trends of individual counties generally follow this regional trend although the variation among the counties is not inconsiderable. For the 11-year period, the intercounty variation in the percent change ranged from the lows of a 105.1 percent increase in Cuyahoga County and a 105.2 percent increase in

Table 7–5. Total Local Expenditures for Criminal Justice by all Governments in the NOACA Region, by County, 1970, 1965, and 1960

	1970		1965		1960	
	Total Dollars	*Per Capita*	*Total Dollars*	*Per Capita*	*Total Dollars*	*Per Capita*
Total	101,644,124	33.88	55,603,908	19.40	44,699,457	16.36
Cuyahoga	73,771,533	42.86	41,341,145	24.54	34,444,565	20.90
Geauga	741,775	11.78	339,179	6.49	265,289	5.58
Lake	3,634,417	18.43	2,244,626	12.98	1,335,471	8.98
Lorain	4,902,872	19.09	2,403,269	10.13	1,778,706	8.18
Medina	1,430,936	17.30	699,057	9.44	472,916	7.24
Portage	1,708,570	13.57	796,984	7.34	554,806	6.04
Summit	15,450,969	27.92	7,779,648	14.58	5,847,704	11.39

Table 7–6. Total Local Expenditures for Criminal Justice in the NOACA Region, by Function, 1970, 1965 and 1960

	1970		1965		1960	
	Total Dollars	*Per Capita*	*Total Dollars*	*Per Capita*	*Total Dollars*	*Per Capita*
Total	101,641,124	33.88	55,603,908	19.40	44,699,457	16.36
Police	74,979,248	24.99	40,880,097	14.26	31,038,084	11.36
Court	18,023,135	6.01	10,152,679	3.54	7,807,269	2.86
Correction	6,337,846	2.11	3,454,370	1.21	5,198,108	1.90
Prosecution	1,675,946	.56	989,877	.35	612,010	.22
Coroner	771,098	.26	84,580	.03	43,986	.02

Table 7-7. Total Local Expenditures for Criminal Justice in the NOACA Region, by Type of Government, 1970, 1965, and 1960

	1970			1965			1960		
	No. of Units	Total Dollars	Per Capita	No. of Units	Total Dollars	Per Capita	No. of Units	Total Dollars	Per Capita
Total	171	101,641,124	33.88	168	55,603,908	19.40	164	44,699,457	16.36
County	7	24,437,048	8.14	7	14,764,289	5.15	7	11,584,271	4.24
City	62	73,034,446	29.73	60	38,872,817	16.93	38	30,559,952	14.31
Village	68	3,512,600	21.04	74	2,068,090	14.39	91	2,445,488	8.92
Township	34	657,030	3.78	27	198,649	1.26	27	109,746	.83

Table 7—8.   Percent Change in Per Capita Total Local Expenditures for Criminal Justice in the NOACA Region, by County, 1960 to 1970 *(Percent)*

	1960–1970	*1960–1965*	*1965–1970*
Total	*107.1*	*19.2*	*73.7*
Cuyahoga	105.1	17.4	74.7
Geauga	111.1	16.3	81.5
Lake	105.2	44.5	42.0
Lorain	133.4	23.8	88.5
Medina	139.0	30.4	83.3
Portage	124.7	21.5	84.9
Summit	145.1	28.0	91.5

Lake County to the highs of a 145.1 percent increase in Summit County and a 139.0 percent increase in Medina County. During the 1960 to 1965 period, the increase rate ranged from 16.3 percent in Geauga County to 44.5 percent in Lake County. During the 1965 to 1970 period, the increase ranged from 91.4 percent in Summit County to 42.0 percent in Lake County. Except for Lake County, the percent increase for the second half is more than twice or thrice as great as that in the first half of the decade.

Table 7—9 summarizes the regional trends for each type of local government. As far as the rate of percent increase is concerned, township spending experienced the fastest increase with 355.4 percent, and followed by villages with 204 percent, cities with 107.8 percent, and counties with 92 percent. The increase rate is two to four times as high for the second half as for the first half of the decade.

The expenditure trends for different types of local government indicate that smaller communities such as villages and townships have increased their expenditures for police protection much faster than the cities and counties have increased their spending for criminal justice. This finding seems to imply that the fear of crime, if not the actual threat of crime, has rapidly spread to the suburban villages and towns, thus, prompting a speedy expansion of their police forces.

Table 7—10 presents the regional trends of criminal justice spending for selected functions. There is a marked difference in the growth rates of functional expenditures, the extremes ranging from a 154.5 percent increase for prosecution to a 11.1 percent increase for corrections for the 11-year period. Spending for police and courts increased by 120.0 percent and 110.1 percent, respectively.

During the 1960 to 1965 period, expenditures for correction decreased by 36.3 percent. We should note that this decrease does not mean an actual reduction in correctional spending during that period, but due to the incompleteness of spending data for correction in 1965 as reported in the official

Table 7-9. Percent Change in Per Capita Local Expenditures for Criminal Justice in the NOACA Region, by Type of Government 1960 to 1970 *(Percent)*

	1960–1970	*1960–1965*	*1965–1970*
Total	*107.1*	*19.2*	*73.7*
County	92.0	21.5	58.1
City	107.8	18.3	75.6
Village	204.0	61.3	115.7
Township*	355.4	51.8	200.0

*A part of township data, on which this computation is based, is an estimate.

Table 7-10. Percent Change in Per Capita Total Local Expenditures for Ciminal Justice in the NOACA Region, by Function, 1960 to 1970 *(Percent)*

	1960–1970	*1960–1965*	*1965–1970*
Total	*107.1*	*19.2*	*73.7*
Police	120.0	26.4	74.0
Court	110.1	23.8	69.8
Correction	11.1	−36.3	74.4
Prosecution	154.5	59.1	60.0
Coroner*	–	–	–

*Data for Coroner is incomplete.

financial reports of local governments in that year. Expenditures for prosecution increased by 59.1 percent from 1960 to 1965 and continued to increase at the same rate during the second half of the decade with a 60 percent increase.

"Too much emphasis on police at the expense of judicial and correctional improvements" has been one of the frequent targets of critics of law enforcement and criminal justice policy in recent years. The criminal justice spending trends during the 1960s bear out this criticism. However, during the second half of the decade, the rates of spending increase have largely evened out among the functions, though the interfunctional gaps in the spending level remain as wide as ever.

Criminal Justice Spending Relative to Total Expenditures

As a way of approximating the political priority of law enforcement and criminal justice functions over time, we measured per capita criminal justice spending as a proportion of per capita total local expenditures for the years, 1970, 1965 and 1960. Table 7-11 reports per capita total local criminal justice spending by all local governments as a percent of per capita total local expenditures for all functions for the region as a whole and for each county. The regional

Table 7—11.   Per Capita Local Criminal Justice Expenditures as a Percent of Per Capita Total Local Expenditures in the NOACA Region, by County, 1960 to 1970 *(Percent)*

	1970	*1965*	*1960*
Total	12.8	8.9	7.6
Cuyahoga	14.0	9.3	7.8
Geauga	9.7	8.3	8.3
Lake	10.2	7.9	5.1
Lorain	10.8	7.4	5.6
Medina	9.0	5.3	6.0
Portage	5.8	10.1	7.4
Summit	11.3	8.4	7.7

total clearly indicates that criminal justice has become increasingly more important in terms of its share in the local budget. The share of criminal justice spending in total local spending was 7.6 percent in 1960, increased to 8.9 percent in 1965, and to 12.8 percent in 1970.

The pattern of individual counties generally follows the regional pattern. Such counties as Cuyahoga, Lake, Lorain, and Summit show a consistent increase in the criminal justice percent of local total expenditures. Further, an increase in the proportion is generally greater from 1965 to 1970 than that from 1960 to 1965. However, the trends are not completely consistent in all counties. In Portage County, for example, there is a drastic downturn in the trend from 1965 to 1970. This is not because of decline in the level of criminal justice spending, but because of the unusually large total expenditures in 1970. In fact, criminal justice spending increased from $7.34 per capita in 1965 to $13.57 per capita in 1970, nearly doubling the level of spending. In comparison, total expenditures for all functions increased from $72.40 per capita in 1965 to $234.40 per capita in 1970 in Portage County, more than tripling the level of total spending.

Table 7—12 presents the proportion of criminal justice spending for each type of local governments. With the exception of county governments, the

Table 7—12.   Per Capita Local Criminal Justice Expenditures as a Percent of Per Capita Total Local Expenditures in the NOACA Region, by Type of Government, 1960 to 1970 *(Percent)*

	1970	*1965*	*1960*
Total	12.8	8.9	7.6
County	8.8	10.9	11.1
City	15.0	8.3	6.7
Village	17.3	11.6	8.7
Township	11.9	7.3	6.2

proportion has increased consistently throughout the period. The county proportion of criminal justice spending has consistently decreased from 11.1 percent in 1960, to 10.9 percent in 1965, and to 8.8 percent in 1970. This
downturn in the trend does not mean the decrease in the level of criminal justice
spending, but the more rapid increase in spending for other functions such as
public welfare, for example.

   In 1970, the proportion of criminal justice spending of counties
ranked at the bottom, while that of villages and cities ranked the first and second
with 17.3 percent and 15.0 percent, respectively. In 1965, the criminal justice
share of local budget was again highest in village governments and lowest in
townships. In 1960, however, the criminal justice share of local spending was
topped by counties and villages, while townships were the lowest. Nearly every
village government in Northeast Ohio has its own independent police department.
As discussed earlier, the village police departments are invariably small with a
few police officers. However, the fiscal burden of police protection is heaviest
for villages since the scale of village budget and population base of village government are also severely limited.[11]

SUMMARY

The cost for criminal justice has risen rapidly during the past decade in the
Northeast Ohio urban region. Total criminal justice expenditures by all local
governments in the region have grown from $16.36 per capita in 1960 to $33.88
in 1970. This growth represents a 107.1 percent increase during the 10 years,
thus averaging more than a 10 percent growth per year. The rise in the criminal
justice expenditures was nearly four times as fast in the 1965 to 1970 period as
the 1960 to 1965 period with 73.7 percent and 19.2 percent increases, respectively. The problems of crime and criminal justice in our cities became a controversial and sensitive public issue at all levels of politics in the second half of the
1960s. The rising crime rate and ubiquitous urban riots among others have produced a political climate favorable for generous fiscal responses to law enforcement and criminal justice activities, particularly the police. The relationship of
criminal justice spending to total local expenditures in the NOACA region clearly
demonstrates a drastic increase in criminal justice priority within the process of
local policy-making. Total criminal justice spending by all local governments
accounted for only 7.6 percent of total local expenditures for all functions in
1960 and it accounted for 12.8 percent of total local budget in 1970, thus,
criminal justice is taking an increasingly greater share of the total local budget
pie.

NOTES TO CHAPTER SEVEN

1. Bureau of the Census, *Criminal Justice: Expenditure and Employment for
   Selected Governmental Units, 1966–67* (Washington, D.C.: U.S.

Government Printing Office, 1969). This data series became a joint undertaking between the Census Bureau and Law Enforcement Assistance Administration beginning the issue for the 1968–69 fiscal year. In the issue of the 1969–70 fiscal year, the number of cities was increased to 153 and counties to 128. In the issue for the 1970–71 fiscal year, the number of governmental units included was further expanded to 384 city governments and 312 county governments.

2. This chapter is an excerpt from my research report, "Local Financing for Criminal Justice in Northeast Ohio: Patterns, Trends, and Projections," (Center for Urban Studies, the University of Akron, October, 1972). The research reported here was supported by the Northeast Ohio Areawide Coordinating Agency and the Ohio Department of Community and Economic Development from the criminal justice planning grants provided by the Law Enforcement Assistance Administration of U.S. Justice Department.

3. As a part of federal policy to develop metropolitanwide political organization for the coordination of planning and urban development, the Demonstration Cities and Metropolitan Development Act of 1967 (Section 204) required that certain federal grant applications originating in a metropolitan area should be reviewed by a metropolitan political organization with authority for areawide planning.

4. For a detailed discussion of the conflict between Cleveland and the NOACA board, see Frances Frisken, "The Metropolis and the Central City: Can One Government Unite Them?" *Urban Affairs Quarterly* (June, 1973), pp. 395–422 and Douglas Montgomery, "Federal versus Local Autonomy: Conflicts in Decertification and Recertification," a paper presented at the 1972 Annual Meeting of the American Political Science Association, held in Washington, D.C. September 5–9, 1972.

5. U.S. Bureau of the Census, Census of Governments: 1972, Vol. 1, *Governmental Organization* (Washington, D.C.: U.S. Government Printing Office, 1973), pp. 202–211.

6. Northeast Ohio Areawide Coordinating Agency, *District 4, 1970 Comprehensive Law Enforcement Plan* (Cleveland: NOACA, 1970), pp. 207–293.

7. The Governmental Research Institute, *Governmental Facts,* a monthly bulletin, (Cleveland, June, 1971).

8. Overcrowded jail has been the target of consistent criticism against the inadequacy of our correctional institutions. See Karl Menninger, *The Crime of Punishment* (New York: The Viking Press, 1968), pp. 38–40.

9. For a detail, see Yong Hyo Cho, *Local Financing for Criminal Justice in Northeast Ohio: Patterns, Trends, and Projections* (Center for Urban Studies, the University of Akron, 1972).

10. The per capita figures were computed by using the appropriate population base for each type of local government. For per capita spending of county governments, total population of the seven counties was used as the population base, while for that of cities, the total population of 62 cities was used for the computation, for example.

11. In Ohio, villages are incorporated municipalities with population of less than 5,000. When a village's population exceeds 5,000, the village becomes a city.

Chapter Eight

A Model for the Impact Analysis of Public Policy on Crime

This chapter and the ones that follow present a systematic inquiry into the measuring of the public policy impact on the crime rates of selected cities. Our inquiry attempts to seek answers to the following questions: What effect do the various measures of public policy have on the crime rates in our cities? Do any of the policy measures demonstrate measurable effect in reducing the crime rates? If they do, what are the specific policy measures and how significant are their crime-reducing effect?

In response to the rising crime rates in our cities, policy attention at all levels of government has been, and still is, focused on *control policies*. The control policies refer to those policies for law enforcement and criminal justice that directly affect governmental capacity to handle criminal acts and criminals. *Social service policies* are usually excluded from consideration for a development of comprehensive crime policy strategy. The social service policies refer to those policies that provide amenities and opportunities essential for the enhancement of the quality of urban life. They may contribute to the weakening of crime-inducive influences in the community and may be expected to be preventive of crime. Therefore, both control and service policy measures are included in the present study for the evaluation of their crime-deterring impact.

Public policies are conceived to be an intervention device in the process of criminal behavior at two separate points to suppress criminal tendency. To prevent crime, control policies are conceived to intervene primarily in the end process of criminal behavior—that is, to arrest, punish, or rehabilitate criminals. We want to test whether the differences in the level of control policies make a difference in the rates of crime occurrence. Service policies are conceived to intervene in the interaction process of the ecological forces of the environment. The service policy intervention is intended to weaken the crime-inducive influence in the ecological environment by improving the environmental quality for want gratification and life opportunity for self-fulfillment. We test here whether there is any evidence that the differences in the level of service policies make a difference in the rates of crime occurrence.

Obviously, this inquiry is complex and elusive as a problem for analysis. To accommodate the complexity and to capture the elusiveness in our analysis, we approach this inquiry from a number of methological and conceptual perspectives. First, we adopt a comparative and macro-analytic approach. Second, we adopt the approach of *problem-centered analysis* rather than that of *policy-centered analysis.* Third, we approach policy analysis from the conceptual perspective that public policy process—policy formulation, policy deliberation (conflict, negotiation, and persuasion), policy adoption (or rejection), and policy implementation—is an experimental process.

COMPARATIVE ANALYSIS OF POLICY IMPACT

Comparative policy analysis has been one of the most active areas of political science research in the past several years. Conceptual models have been advanced and refined. Public policy outcomes are measured (most often by the level of expenditures for various functions and by the level of revenues from various sources), variables influential in determining the policy outcomes are identified, and the policy variance among the different government jurisdictions is systematically explained.[1]

Only a few studies have attempted to examine whether the differences in the policy level produce different results in policy impact. Sharkansky related the expenditure policies to the service outcomes, such as relationship of expenditure level for highway function to highway safety, expenditure level for education to test scores, and expenditure level for natural resources to the frequency of recreational use of natural resources for hunting and fishing, etc.[2] State legislative apportionment as a policy outcome has been analyzed in several studies to measure its impact on the spending and taxing behavior of the states.[3]

Earlier studies have explored the relationships of some selected measures of crime control policy to crime rates. A number of sociologists have studied what legal sanction does to crime-deterrence.[4] Their findings tend to support the contention that punishment does in a way serve as a deterrent. They found that certainty of punishment is inversely correlated with various crime rates, while severity of punishment is inversely correlated with homicide rate only. Ira Sharkansky, a political scientist, examined the relationships between per capita expenditure for police protection and crime rates and found positive correlations. He interpreted this finding as an indication that money is spent where the problem is.[5]

Most comparative studies of crime have focused their attention on the analysis of criminal behavior; namely, ecological correlates of crime. Unfortunately, however, only a few empirical studies have been made to analyze the effect of public policy on crime,[6] and none of the studies attempted to evaluate a broad range of public policy variables.[7] The present study is an attempt to evaluate the effect of crime control policy measures, which can be identified and quantified, and that of social service policy variables, which are deemed relevant and quantifiable, on the crime rates of selected cities through a comparative analysis. The framework and the techniques of comparative analysis utilized by earlier studies vary. In designing the comparative framework for our analysis, we have had to deal with a number of conceptual or technical matters.

Unit of Analysis

Four types of units of analysis are most often used by comparative and empirical studies of criminal behavior: (1) individuals for inter-person comparison;[8] (2) sub-city areas for intra-city comparison;[9] (3) city as a whole for inter-city comparison;[10] and (4) states for inter-state comparison.[11] For our purpose here we use city as the unit of analysis. The reason is simply that cities are the basic unit of urban government that make or implement public policy decisions. Often the policy decisions made at a higher level of government, such as federal or state, are implemented by cities as the operating unit.

Although the decision to use the entire city as a unit of our analysis was inevitable, it was not a happy one. The reason is that an entire city is not an ideal geographical unit for the measurement of crime rates. As repeatedly demonstrated by earlier studies, there is a great deal of intra-city variation in crime rates and socio-economic conditions. The aggregate measure of crime rates and other ecological variables for the entire city fails to capture the complexity of their intra-city variance.

Sample

Two sets of cities are selected as sample: (1) a national sample of the 49 largest cities in the United States:[12] and (2) a state sample of the 40 largest cities in Ohio.[13] The cities selected for our analysis are not a sample in a strict sense of the term; their selection was not random, rather determined by availability of data or accessibility to the data. But we will consider the 2 sets of the cities as 2 sets of samples in their analytical treatment and the interpretation of the results of the analysis. There are some important differences between the 2 sets of samples, which include sizes of population and, more importantly, governmental systems of the cities.

Every city of the national sample had a population in excess of 250,000 in 1970 and the largest city, New York, had a population of 7.9 million. The Ohio cities were mostly small in population. In fact, more than half of the 40 cities had a population of less than 50,000, but more than 25,000. The largest city, Cleveland, had a population of 750,903 in 1970. The cities in the national sample represent 29 different states. The systems of government as policy-making institutions were more divergent among the national sample cities than among the Ohio cities. The public policy-crime rate relationships found in the 2 sets of sample will provide a cross-check for a more reliable interpretation of the policy impact on crime.

Problem-Centered Analysis

Policy impact analyses can be either *problem-centered* or *policy-centered.* Our approach is problem-centered. The problem-centered analysis of policy impact is illustrated in Figure 8–1 and the policy-centered analysis of policy impact is illustrated in Figure 8–2. The problem-centered analysis is to evaluate a variety of public policy measures and whether the policy measures have a particular desired impact on a specific problem. In our case, this approach is to evaluate whether various measures of control as well as social service policies have the effect of reducing crime rates.

In order to make a sensible evaluation of the impact of a policy measure on a specific problem, the objective of that policy measure must be clearly established in relation to that specific problem. We consider the ultimate objective of public policy in relation to the problem of crime is to reduce the crime rate, if crime cannot be eliminated altogether. In reality, however, various measures of public policy and governmental programs could have immediate objectives that are not specifically directed toward the reduction of crime rate although they deal with crime problems in one way or another. Nevertheless, the true effectiveness of any of those policy measures in dealing with crime problems can be ultimately tested by their ability to reduce crime rates. In short, the problem-centered analysis of policy impact on crime is designed to test as many appropriate policy variables as possible in order to identify those policy measures that have significant crime-reducing effect and to measure their significance.

In Figure 8–1, the square in the center represents a problem and the circles around the square represent individual policy measures. The ultimate objective of the analysis is in the search for more effective ways of solving the particular problem "a." For this purpose, the inquiry examines the effectiveness of existing policy measures. It is assumed that some of the existing policy measures may be more effective in solving a problem than others. Then, the strategy of policy development and coordination for the solution of that particular problem may give priority to those policy measures that bring about the desired impact in the solution of the problem. In our diagram, policies 1, 2, 3, and 4 show strong positive impacts on problem "a." while policies 5, 6, 7, and 8 show only weak relationships to the problem. Let us assume that policy emphasis is currently placed on policies 1, 2, 5, and 8. The policy strategy, then, must be readjusted in the way that the current emphasis on policies 1 and 2 should be continued, but the resources currently used for policies 5 and 8 must be shifted to policies 3 and 4, if their primary target is problem "a."

The policy-centered analysis of policy impact is a reversal process. In this approach, we attempt to measure the effect of a specific policy measure on a variety of related problems as shown in Figure 8–2. For example, the effect of

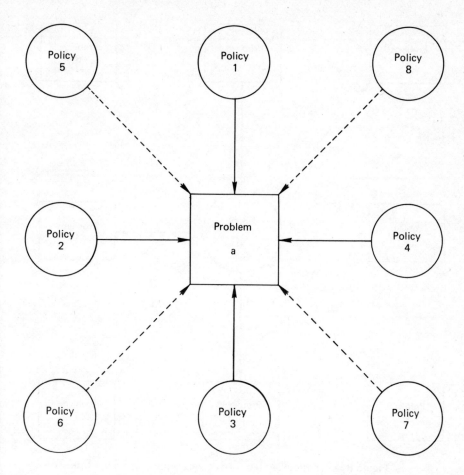

Figure 8—1. Problem-Centered Analytical Model of Policy Impact

urban renewal policy may be examined on a number of related problems such as the quantity of housing (housing stock), crime in the streets, residential segregation or integration, or quality of housing (percent housing standard).

Of those comparative studies noted in the beginning of this chapter, the studies of legislative reapportionment impact is a good example of policy-centered analysis of policy impact. Reapportionment of the state legislature is a structural policy and the impact analysis of reapportionment attempts to measure: (1) its effect on a variety of legislative decision-making such as expenditure decisions for various purposes, taxation decisions from various sources, and other legislative decisions; and (2) its impact on the realignment of political strength between the two major parties.[14]

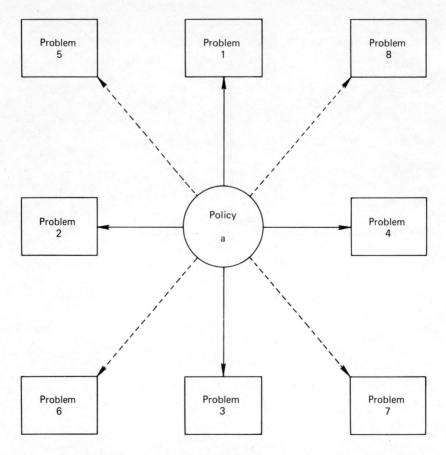

Figure 8–2. Policy-Centered Analytical Model of Policy Impact

EXPERIMENTAL PERSPECTIVE
OF PUBLIC POLICY

We often hear the complaint that social scientists are deprived of experimenting with public policy for the evaluation of its implications and for the formulation of the policy attuned to the reality. Policy experimentation is politically unpopular and unsupported, for it is costly, time-consuming, and most of all politically risky.[15] However, we argue here that experimentation in the sense that controlled and designed trial prior to formal adoption and implementation of the policy is not always indispensible for policy formulation or policy evaluation. The reason is that every public policy can be viewed as experimental, for public policies are always open to revisions through whatever feedback may be available.

It is true that the evaluation of the existing policies will not tell us what new policies, unrelated to those policies in effect, are needed. But this evaluation will show us what modifications in the existing policies are needed to strengthen those policies in such a way as to produce the desired impact. This evaluation, when adequately performed, will satisfy most of the evaluation need for policy formulation. Policy formulation seldom involves a new policy that is unrelated to the existing policies, but policy formulation is usually a matter of modifying the on-going policies. The findings of some recent studies that incrementalism is characteristic of policy-making at all levels of government provide empirical evidence. For example, budget policy-making is most likely to follow the pattern of budget policy in the preceding budget year.[16]

THE MODEL

The model for an empirical analysis of public policy impact on the crime rates of 2 sets of sample cities contains 3 principal components: (1) the crime rates as dependent variables; (2) the measures of public policy as test variables; and (3) the indicators of ecological environment as control variables. The model is schematically illustrated in Figure 8–3.

The interaction of the ecological forces is conceived to be the primary influence in the determination of the crime rates; namely, we consider

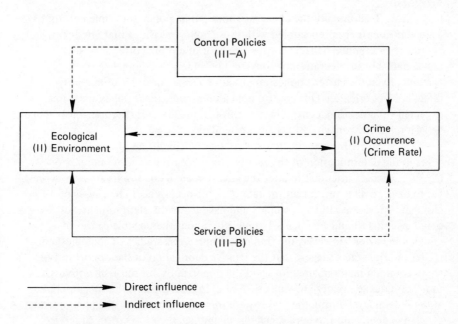

Figure 8–3. A Model for Analysis of Policy Impact on City Crimes

the ecological variables such as demographic, social, and economic variables as the primary predictors of the crime rate variance among the cities. We disregard in our model other possible influences such as psychological or genetic (physiological) influences, for example, as predictors of crime rates not because they are believed to be unimportant, but because they are more suitable for a micro analysis of crime.[17]

Studies of ecological correlates of crime variance within a city or among the cities indicate that various ecological variables are significantly correlated with crime rates. The findings of these studies are instructive for the purpose of measuring policy impact on crime. First, some ecological variables such as racial composition (percent Negro), ethnical composition (percent foreign born), personal income levels, level of educational attainment, crowdedness of housing, and so forth are found to be significantly correlated with one or more measures of the crime rates. Second, more importantly, these findings indicate that "the criminogenic forces" are not alike for all types of crimes.[18] The findings in the ecological correlates of crime make it clear that an undistorted assessment of policy impact on crime requires a systematic control for ecological variables. Therefore, our model, as shown in the schematic representation of Figure 8–3, recognizes the necessity to define the relationships between the ecological variables and the crime variables and to seek out those ecological variables that are influential in accounting for the variance of crime rates among the cities.

Traditionally the concerns about public policy for crime control have been almost entirely preoccupied with those policy measures that are directly restrictive of criminal behavior or the behavior of criminal offenders, such as police patrol or incarceration of convicted offenders or criminal suspects, for example. Even the current policy emphasis on crime control is dominantly direct-control oriented. Our control policies represent those policy measures expected to have crime-control effects through the direct restrictions on criminal behavior and the behavior of criminal offenders.

Since it is evident that environmental conditions are powerful influences in the determination of the rate of crime occurrence, those public policy measures that are intended to alter the environmental conditions are also expected to have possible impact on the rate of crime occurrence. The causes of criminal behavior are highly complex and have many different dimensions. We only have modest and fragmented knowledge about the possible causes of criminal behavior. However, the findings of numerous studies of ecological correlates of crime rates suggest that the relative deprivation of the opportunity to enjoy common material amenities and the opportunity for self-realization is a root cause of the rapidly growing crime rate. In fact, most of the social policies at the federal level during the 1960s were formulated to attack the phenomenon of relative deprivation to cure social ills, including crime.[19] Our social service policies represent those policy measures that are expected to affect, though indirectly, the rate of crime occurrence through the alteration of opportunity structure in the ecological environment.

Thus, our model is designed to test the effect of both control and social service policies on the rate of crime occurrence, while controlling for the appropriate ecological variables. Now we shall turn to the description of the individual variables comprising the 3 components of our model: (1) crime rates; (2) public policy measures; and (3) the indicators of ecological environment.

CRIME RATES (DEPENDENT VARIABLES)

The crime data are derived from the 1970 issue of the *Uniform Crime Report* of the Federal Bureau of Investigation. In our analysis, we only include the 7 categories of serious crimes—homicide, forcible rape, robbery, aggravated assault, burglary, larceny, and auto theft. Two minor alterations are made to the original data, exclusion of negligent manslaughter from homicide and exclusion of the cases involving less than $50,000 from larceny.

The decision to use the FBI crime data is not without the knowledge that the reliability and accuracy of these data have been questioned for good reasons. First, the FBI statistics are considered to report offenses substantially below the rate uncovered by surveys. Second, the comparability of the data among different cities is questionable, for the classification and reporting systems of criminal offenses do vary among the city police departments. It is often the case that an offense reported as assault at one place is entirely possible to be reported something less serious elsewhere.[20]

In spite of these and other alleged shortcomings, the FBI data are used here, for they are still the single source of cross-sectional data available and thus provide the most economic way of obtaining such data.

The crime rates are measured in terms of the number of offenses in each category per 100,000 population. There are, of course, other ways to construct crime rates—that is using a "victim-specific index." Instead of computing crime rates in relation to total population, for example, burglary rates may be computed in relation to the number of opportunities for burglarization, such as the number of commercial establishments or the number of homes, and so forth. Similarly, auto theft rates may be computed in relation to the number of registered cars in the community.[21] We did not follow this procedure not because it seemed undesirable but because it was too difficult to obtain the data necessary to estimate the chances for victimization.

The mean and standard deviation of each of the 7 crime rates are shown in Table 8–1 for the 2 sets of the sample.

PUBLIC POLICY VARIABLES (TEST VARIABLES)

Policy variables are developed for both sets of sample cities. For the cities of the national sample, 37 policy measures are developed. Twenty-one of them are

Table 8–1. Seven Crime Rate Variables: Means and Standard Deviations for National and Ohio Samples

Crime Variables	National Sample		Ohio Sample	
	Mean	Standard Deviation	Mean	Standard Deviation
1. Willful Homicide	16.9	10.5	6.3	7.4
2. Forced Rape	39.8	19.6	16.1	12.0
3. Robbery	455.7	361.3	158.4	153.6
4. Aggravated Assault	307.2	185.0	120.8	103.6
5. Burglary	1,881.2	697.4	949.8	461.0
6. Larceny	1,349.1	475.7	980.8	980.8
7. Auto Theft	1,077.3	491.1	555.4	493.3

control policy measures and the remaining 16 are social service policy measures. For the 40 Ohio cities, 21 policy measures are devised including 7 control policies and 14 social service policy measures.

Control Policies

Table 8–2 lists the control policy measures and the mean and standard deviation of each of the policy measures for the 2 sets of sample. When a particular policy variable does not show its value either in the column of the national sample or in the column of the Ohio sample, it means that the specific policy variable is not developed for that particular sample. This tabular arrangement has been made to eliminate the necessity of listing the policy variables (as well as other variables comprising the 3 components of our model) separately for each of the 2 sets of our samples.

The control policies are classified into a number of categories: police policies, court policies, corrections policies, total criminal justice policy, and localism of criminal justice system. The control policy measures for the Ohio cities are not as fully developed as those for the national sample cities. Only police policies are developed for the Ohio cities, because the data for other control policies are either not available or when available they are incomplete for small cities, particularly those cities with a population of less than 50,000. Even for the nation's largest cities, policy data desirable for meaningful comparison are often not available. Data on the level of training or length of experience for police officers is often available from individual police departments rather than published sources of statistical information. Such judicial policy data as the conviction rate of criminal defendants by type of criminal offenses or the type or severity of penalty for the defendants convicted of similar offenses are also unavailable in any of the published sources although records for such information may be available from individual courts.

The control policy measures are mostly local policies. However, some

Table 8–2. Control Policy Measures and Their Means and Standard Deviations for National and Ohio Samples

Policy Variables		National Sample		Ohio Sample	
Description	Abbreviation Used in Tables	Mean	Standard Deviation	Mean	Standard Deviation
1. Police Policies					
A. P.C. Expenditures for Police Protection, 69–70 ($)	Police Expenditures	29.65	14.34	18.84	6.82
B. Patrolman's Salary Entrance, 1970 ($)	Salary Entrance	7,836	1,167	7,571	790
C. Patrolman's Salary Maximum, 1970 ($)	Salary Maximum	9,308	1,303	8,692	882
D. Police Dept. Employees per 100,000 Population, 1970	Total Police Employees	275	121	165	48
E. Sworn Police Officers per 100,000 Population, 1970	Sworn Officers	234	108	147	42
F. Total Motor Vehicles Used by Police per 100,000 Population, 1970	All Police Vehicles	58	26	—	—
G. Police Cars per 100,000 Population, 1970	Police Cars	46	24	35	10
H. Police Motorcycles and Scooters per 100,000 Population	Minor Police Vehicles	12	8	6	3

Table 8–2. (cont.) Control Policy Measures and Their Means and Standard Deviations for National and Ohio Samples

Policy Variables		National Sample		Ohio Sample	
Description	Abbreviation Used in Tables	Mean	Standard Deviation	Mean	Standard Deviation
2. Court Policies					
A. P.C. Expenditures for Courts, 69–70 ($)	Court Expenditures	5.26	3.94	—	—
B. Pretrial Incarceration, 1970 (%)	Pretrial Incarceration	50.2	16.5	—	—
3. Corrections Policies					
A. P.C. Expenditures for Corrections, 69–70 ($)	Corrections Expenditures	5.08	5.85	—	—
B. Monthly Pay per Prison Employees, 1970 ($)	Prison Employee Pay	624	142	—	—
C. Number of Prison Employees per 100 Inmates, 1970	Employee— Inmate Ratio	24	32	—	—
D. Inmates as a Percent of the Capacity of the Prison (%)	Prison Crowdedness	89.2	25.9	—	—
E. Comprehensiveness Index of Prison Facilities, 1970 (%)	Prison Facilities	75.9	15.5	—	—
F. Corrections Employees per 100,000 Population, 1970	Corrections Employees	44	34	—	—

4. Total Criminal Justice Policy					
A. P.C. Expenditures for all Criminal Justice Functions, 69–70 ($)	Total Justice Expenditures	39.47	22.08	—	—
5. Local Assignment of State-Local Criminal Justice System					
A. Local Percent of State-Local Expenditures for All Criminal Justice Functions, 68–69 (%)	Localism— Total	71.6	7.9	—	—
B. Local Percent of State-Local Expenditures for Police Protection, 68–69 (%)	Localism— Police	83.9	6.3	—	—
C. Local Percent of State-Local Expenditures for Courts, 68–69 (%)	Localism— Courts	76.0	16.5	—	—
D. Local Percent of State-Local Expenditures for Corrections, 68–69 (%)	Localism— Corrections	32.2	17.9	—	—

of the local policies such as expenditures for police protection and other criminal justice functions partly represent federal or state policies so far as these spending measures include grants-in-aid funds from federal or state government.

Some of the policy variables present rather complex measurement problems. Since the local government system in a city area varies from place to place, the criminal justice systems operating within each city area also vary. This governmental system variation must be taken into consideration when local criminal justice policies in a municipal area are to be measured on a comparable basis for cross-sectional comparison. For example, in New York City all local functions for police, court, and correction are the responsibility of the city government. In contrast, in the City of Akron, the municipal police maintain an exclusive jurisdiction within the municipal boundaries, but local judicial functions and correctional functions are a shared responsibility between the county and municipal governments. This problem is resolved by allocating the city share of the county provided services for courts and correction based on the city–county proportion of population.[22]

Social Service Policies

Social service policies shown in Table 8–3 are grouped into 2 categories: measures of opportunity policy and measures of environment policy. The opportunity policies are generally future-oriented in their temporal dimension of delivery of intended benefits. Except for 2 education policy variables, all the other measures of opportunity policy are federally assisted programs and their principal targets are the poor, unemployed, and disadvantaged. Therefore, the 4 federally assisted programs are measured in two ways—per capita and per poor person—in computing the level of expenditures for these programs.

Six measures of service policies for environment are devised. Four of the policies mainly deal with housing—low-rent public housing or urban renewal— and are all federally funded programs. The remaining two programs, sanitation and recreation, are primarily locally-funded. The implementation of these service policies for environment can be expected to deliver immediate benefits in the case of more decent housing and more pleasant and constructive use of leisure time, while the service policies for opportunity—such as job training—are planned for future benefits.

ECOLOGICAL VARIABLES
(POSSIBLE CONTROL VARIABLES)

Ecological variables are included in our model for two major reasons: (1) to examine the ecological correlates of urban crime; and (2) to provide for appropriate statistical control for undistorted measurement of policy impact on crime. A pool of ecological variables is developed for each set in our sample; namely, 35 variables for the national sample and 27 for the Ohio sample. All of these variables are listed in Table 8–4, and they represent various dimensions of human ecological system in urban communities. They include: (1) demographic dimension (such as size and density, population composition, and population shift); (2) income and living standards; (3) education; (4) housing; and (5) physical structure of the community.

Except for a few, these variables are derived from the 1970 and 1960 census data. Property valuation data used for the description of physical characteristics of the community were derived from the 1967 Census of Governments data, while the retail sales data for the measurement of consumerism were derived from the Census of Business of 1967, for example.

Some of our variables are different from those used in earlier studies that attempted to ascertain the ecological correlates of city crime rates. They include: (1) population shift variables; (2) a measure of consumerism represented by per capita retail sales (what we really wanted to use for this measure was consumer loans outstanding per capita, but we failed to locate the data); (3) measures of income concentration for families and unrelated individuals; (4) variables describing the physical make-up of the community by ascertaining the percent assessed valuation of various types of property; and (5) Negro residential segregation index.[23]

Thus, our ecological variables represent various dimensions of socio-economic environment. Some of these variables were examined in earlier studies and were found to have significant criminogenic influence. Many others are tested here for the first time to ascertain their relevance to criminal behavior. We believe it imperative to assemble a wide variety of ecological variables for our purpose. A relatively small number of variables, selected on an *a priori* logic and applied uniformly to the 7 crime variables, are not likely to produce a set of strong predictor variables for each one of the crime variables because the 7 crimes are distinct in their nature despite their shared commonality with one another.[24]

To the extent that the crime variables are distinct in their nature, the ecological variables that account for their uniqueness are likely to be distinct. On the contrary, to the extent that the crime variables share commonality with one another, the ecological variables that account for their commonality are also likely to be common. The diversity of our ecological variables is designed to enable the selection of a set of more appropriate ecological predictor variables for each of the crime rates.

THE TECHNIQUES FOR ANALYSIS

Our analysis here is performed in two stages. First, we identify and select the ecological variables that are significantly correlated with crime measures. Since the ecological variables correlated with different crime measures are not alike, we selected the important ecological variables for each of the crime variables separately. Second, we assessed the impact of each of the control and service policy

Table 8–3. Social Service Policy Measures and Their Means and Standard Deviations for National and Ohio Samples

Policy Variables		National Sample		Ohio Sample	
Description	Abbreviation Used in Tables	Mean	Standard Deviation	Mean	Standard Deviation
1. Opportunity Policies					
A. Federal Spending for Headstart Program per Poor Person, Total of 1968, 69 and 70 ($)	Headstart Per Poor	29.79	30.69	12.60	21.60
B. Federal Spending for Headstart Program per Capita, Total of 1968, 69 and 70 ($)	Headstart Per Capita	4.53	5.21	1.69	2.59
C. OEO Spending per Poor Person, Total of 1968, 69 and 70 ($)	OEO Per Poor	105.25	221.41	26.26	16.75
D. OEO Spending Per Capita, Total of 1968, 69, and 70 ($)	OEO Per Capita	15.74	35.97	2.66	2.67
E. Federal Spending for Manpower Training Program per Poor Person, Total of 1968, 69 and 70 ($)	Manpower Per Poor	359.56	574.11	96.73	103.12
F. Federal Spending for Manpower Training Program per Capita, Total of 1968, 69 and 70 ($)	Manpower Per Capita	52.69	94.14	11.63	13.58
G. Federal Spending for Small Business per Poor Person, Total of 1968, 69 and 70 ($)	Small Business Per Poor	67.68	78.46	24.41	31.16

H. Federal Spending for Small Business per Capita, Total of 1968, 69 and 70 ($)	Small Business Per Capita	9.94	12.48	2.69	3.15
I. Expenditures for Local Public Schools per Capita, 69–70 ($)	P.C. School Expenditures	160.94	36.70	792.12*	153.18
J. Number of Public School Pupils per Teacher, 1970	Pupil–Teacher Ratio	21	10	24	2
2. Environment Policies					
A. Low-Rent Public Housing Units per 1,000 Occupied Housing Units, 1970	Public Housing	29	20	25	28
B. FHA Mortgage Insurance per Capita, Total of 1967, 68 and 69 ($)	FHA Mortgage	41.12	27.13	—	—
C. Federal Grants for Urban Renewal Approved per Capita, up to 1970 ($)	Urban Renewal Approved	121.43	96.53	63.87	77.10
D. Federal Grants for Urban Renewal Disbursed per Capita, up to 1970 ($)	Urban Renewal Disbursed	61.58	55.17	22.17	35.01
E. P.C. Expenditures for Sanitation Other than Sewage, 1969–70 ($)	Sanitation Expenditures	10.42	5.55	—	—
F. P.C. Expenditures for Parks and Recreation, 1969–70 ($)	Leisure Expenditures	17.47	9.96	7.70	6.28

*Per Pupil Expenditures

Table 8–4. Ecological Variables and Their Means and Standard Deviations for National and Ohio Samples

Ecological Variables		National Sample		Ohio Sample	
Description	Abbreviation Used in Tables	Mean	Standard Deviation	Mean	Standard Deviation
1. Demographic Variables					
A. Size and Density					
a. Total Population in Thousands, 1970	Total Population	824.0	1,190.0	111.5	157.4
b. Population per Square Mile, 1970	Population Density	7,298.3	4,829.3	5,217.9	2,455.4
B. Population Composition					
c. Percent Population Non-White, 1970	% Non-White	25.4	16.1	11.2	12.2
d. Percent Population Under Age 18, 1970	% Below 18 Yrs.	32.0	3.7	—	—
e. Percent Families Headed by Female with Own Children under Age 18, 1970	% Female-Headed Families	9.1	2.4	6.1	2.3
f. Percent Primary Male Individuals of Total Population, 1970	% Primary Male	3.5	1.3	2.3	0.8
g. Percent Population Teenagers (13–19), 1970	% Teenagers	9.1	0.8	12.9	0.7
C. Population Shift					
h. Percent Change in Total Population, 1960–70	Population Change	106.7	20.7	104.1	12.5
i. Percent Change in White Population, 1960–70	White Change	98.9	24.7	101.6	14.2
j. Percent Change in Non-White Population, 1960–70	Non-White Change	145.4	45.3	193.3	141.2

2. Income and Living Standards					
a. Median Family Income ($), 1970	MFI	9,472.41	1,109.2	10,567.68	2,441.70
b. Percent Families Below Poverty Income, 1970	% Families Poor	11.3	3.6	7.5	3.6
c. Percent Population Below Poverty Income, 1970	% Population Poor	15.1	4.1	10.1	4.7
d. Percent Unrelated Individuals Below Poverty Income, 1970	% Individuals Poor	33.5	5.3	34.0	8.4
e. Percent Families with $15,000 or More Annual Income, 1970	% Families Affluent	20.1	5.2	22.4	12.0
f. Index of Income Concentration—Family 1970	IIC Family	0.36	0.03	—	—
g. Index of Income Concentration—Unrelated Individuals, 1970	IIC Individuals	0.48	0.02	—	—
h. Median Value of Owner-Occupied Housing ($) 1970	Housing Value	16,221.71	5,371.80	17,505.00	6,138.49
i. Median Monthly Rent ($) 1970	Monthly Rent	90.86	18.47	93.00	30.69
j. Per Capita Retail Sales (Proxy of Consumerism), 1967	Retail Sales	1,879.27	395.85	—	—
3. Education					
a. Median School Years Completed by Persons 25 Years Old and Above, 1970	Adult Education Attainment	11.7	0.8	12.0	0.9
b. Percent Adults with Less than High School Completion, 1970	Adult H.S. Dropouts	48.7	9.2	25.1	7.5

Table 8-4. (cont.)

Ecological Variables		National Sample		Ohio Sample	
Description	Abbreviation Used in Tables	Mean	Standard Deviation	Mean	Standard Deviation
c. Percent Adults with Less than 5 Years of Schooling, 1970	Adult Illiteracy	6.0	2.7	3.3	1.8
d. Percent 14–17 Years Old, Not in School, 1970	H.S. Dropouts	7.6	2.0	–	–
e. High School Dropouts (Age 14–15), 1970	Fresh–Sopho. Dropouts	–	–	3.2	3.0
f. High School Dropouts (Age 16–17), 1970	Jr.–Sr. Dropouts	–	–	7.7	4.5
4. Housing Variables					
a. Percent Housing Owner-Occupied, 1970	Homeowner-ship	48.9	13.6	63.8	11.5
b. Percent Housing With More than One Person per Room, 1970	Housing Crowdedness	8.8	4.0	5.6	2.1
c. Percent Housing Lacking Some or All Plumbing, 1970	Substandard Housing	3.7	1.7	2.9	1.8
d. Percent Change in Owner-Occupancy, 1960–70	Change in Owner-Occupancy	109.2	20.1	–	–
e. Percent Change in Rent-Occupancy, 1960–70	Change in Rent-Occupancy	112.5	29.1	–	–
f. Percent Change in Rental Housing, 1960–70	Change in Rental Housing	102.2	36.2	–	–
g. Percent Change in Housing Crowdedness, 1960–70	Change, Housing Crowdedness	88.6	28.5	–	–
h. Negro Residential Segregation Index, 1970	NRSI	78.0	11.2	–	–

5. Physical Structure of the Community		
a. Percent Assessed Value of Single-Family Housing 1967	Single-Family Housing	48.4	14.5
b. Percent Assessed Value of Multi-Dwellings, 1967	Multi-Dwellings	12.9	9.0
c. Percent Assessed Value of Commercial and Industrial Property, 1967	Commercial-Industrial-Property	34.7	9.3

measures on the variance of crime rates after controlling for the selected ecological variables. For both of these operations, we used step-wise multiple regression analysis.[25]

The regression model used for the identification and selection of the influential ecological variables is:

$$Yc_1 = A + b_1 X_1 + \ldots + b_n X_n + e_1$$

Where Yc_1 represents the estimated (or computed) value of crime rate; A represents constant; X_1 through X_n represent the ecological variables regressed against the crime variable; b_1 through b_n represent the regression slopes for the ecological variables X_1 through X_n; and e_1 represents the error term. Through the step-wise regression procedure, the most significant ecological variable (X_1) is first picked and regressed against the crime variable (Y) and then X_2, X_3, and so forth in the order of the strength of the variables. This process creates as many regression equations as there are the ecological variables strong enough to be picked and included in the regressions. Of these, the one equation in which all of the ecological variables in the regression are significant simultaneously is identified and the ecological variables included in that regression are selected as the major criminogenic variables for the control purpose.[26]

We insist here that every control variable must have a statistically significant bearing on the dependent variable. This is the point where the way we use the regression procedure differs from the ways the regression technique is usually employed for statistical tests in other studies. Unless the control variables are statistically significant, the statistical controls, while provided to make possible a more accurate measurement of the relationship of the test variable to the dependent variable, are most unlikely to improve accuracy in the measurement of the relationship.[27] The reason is simply that controlling "wrong" variables is more likely to produce a statistical artifact than eliciting a substantive truth.

The regression model for the assessment of the policy impact while controlling for the criminogenic variables is identical with that used for the selection of the criminogenic variables. However, the regression model in this case includes only those significant criminogenic variables and one policy variable whose impact is assessed. This regression model is expressed as follows:

$$Yc_2 = A + b_1 X_1 + \ldots + b_n X_n + b_{pi} X_{pi} + e_2$$

where X_{pi} represents the policy variable tested.

The regression model used here is an additive model, not a multiplicative (or interactive) model for two reasons. First, our effort is not merely to create the best fitting equation, but to test the impact of policy variables on crime variance based on a rigid significance test. Second, because of this rigid selection criterion of the variables for inclusion in the regressions, the variables (whether they be crime, policy, or ecological ones) included in the regressions are expected to have a high degree of linearity in their inter-relationships.[28]

NOTES TO CHAPTER EIGHT

1. The works representing comparative policy analysis are too numerous to list all of them here. To cite just a few, see Alan K. Campbell and Seymour Sacks, *Metropolitan America: Fiscal Patterns and Governmental Systems* (New York: The Free Press, 1967); Thomas R. Dye, *Politics, Economics, and the Public* (Chicago: Rand McNally, 1966); and Ira Sharkansky, *The Politics of Taxing and Spending* (Indianapolis: The Bobbs–Merrill, 1969).

2. Ira Sharkansky, *ibid.*, chapter 6.

3. Thomas R. Dye, "Malapportionment and Public Policy in the States," *Journal of Politics*, XXVII (August, 1965) and his *Politics, Economics, and the Public;* Alan Pulsipher and James Weatherby, "Malapportionment, Party Competition, and the Functional Distribution of Government Expenditures," *American Political Science Review*, LXII (December, 1968), pp. 1207–1219; and H. George Frederickson and Yong Hyo Cho, "Legislative Apportionment and Fiscal Policy in the American States," a paper delivered at the Annual Meeting of the American Political Science Association, September, 1970, Los Angeles, California.

4. See, for example, Frank D. Bean and Robert G. Cushing, "Criminal Homicide, Punishment, and Deterrence: Methodological and Substantive Reconsideration," *Social Science Quarterly* (November, 1971), pp. 277–289; Charles R. Title, "Crime Rates and Legal Sancion," *Social Problems*, 16 (Spring, 1969), pp. 409–423; and Louis N. Gray and J. David Martin, "Punishment and Deterrence: Another Analysis of Gibbs' Data," *Social Science Quarterly*, 50 (September, 1969), pp. 389–395; Jack P. Gibbs, "Crime, Punishment, and Deterrence," *Social Science Quarterly*, 48 (March, 1968), pp. 515–530.

5. "Government Expenditures and Public Services in the American States," *American Political Science Review* (December, 1967), pp. 1066–1077.

6. Frank D. Bean, et. al., *op. cit.;* Charles R. Title, *op. cit.;* Louis N. Gray and J. David Martin, *op. cit.;* Jack P. Gibbs, *op. cit.;* and Ira Sharkansky, *op. cit.*

7. The only exception that I know of is my own study: "A Multiple Regression Model for the Measurement of the Public Policy Impact on Big City Crime," *Policy Sciences*, 3 (1972), pp. 435–455.

8. Marvin E. Wolfgang, *Patterns of Criminal Homicide*, (Philadelphia: University of Pennsylvania Press, 1958); David J. Pittman and William Handy, "Patterns in Criminal Aggravated Assault," *Journal of Criminal Law, Criminology and Police Science*, Vol. 55, No. 4 (1964); and John A. O'Donnell, "Narcotic Addiction and Crime," *Social*

Problems, Vol. 13, No. 4 (1966), pp. 374–85. The studies using individuals as unit of analysis of criminal behavior are too numerous to list all of them here.

9. There are also many studies using census tracts as unit of analysis for intra-city comparison. They include: Sarah L. Boggs, "Urban Crime Patterns," *American Sociological Review,* Vol. 30, No. 6 (1966), pp. 899–908; Clifford R. Shaw and Henry D. McKay, *Juvenile Delinquency and Urban Areas,* Revised Edition, (Chicago: University of Chicago Press, 1969); David J. Bordua, "Juvenile Delinquency and 'Anomie': An Attempt at Relation," *Social Problems,* Vol. 6, No. 3 (Winter 1958), pp. 230–238; and Richard Quinney, "Crime, Delinquency, and Social Areas," *Journal of Research in Crime and Delinquency,* Vol. 1, No. 2 (1964), pp. 149–54; Calvin F. Schmid, "Urban Crime Areas: Part I," *American Sociological Review,* Vol. 25, No. 4 (1960), pp. 527–42 and "Urban Crime Areas: Part II," *American Sociological Review,* Vol. 25, No. 5 (1960), pp. 655–78.

10. William F. Ogburn, "Factors in the Variation of Crime Among Cities," *Journal of the American Statistical Association,* Vol. 30 (March, 1935), pp. 12–34; Karl Schuessler, "Components of Variation in City Crime Rates," *Social Problems,* Vol. 9 (Spring 1962), pp. 314–327; Karl Schuessler and Gerald Slatin, "Sources of Variation in United States City Crime, 1950 and 1960," *Journal of Research in Crime and Delinquency,* Vol. 1 (July, 1964), pp. 127–148; and Tae Gun Lee, "Socio-Economic Correlates of the Urban Crime: Case of Large Cities in Ohio," Urban Studies Seminar Paper (Department of Urban Studies, University of Akron, 1973).

11. Richard Quinney, "Structural Characteristics, Population Areas, and Crime Rates in the United States," *Journal of Criminal Law, Criminology and Police Science,* Vol. 57, No. 1 (1966), pp. 45–52; Charles R. Title, "Crime Rates and Legal Sanctions," *Social Problems;* Bean and Cushing, "Criminal Homicide, Punishment, and Deterrence . . . "; and Thomas F. Pettigrew and Rosalind B. Spier, "The Ecological Structure of Negro Homicide," *The American Journal of Sociology,* Vol. 67, No. 6 (May, 1962), pp. 621–29 among others.

12. The 49 cities are Akron, Atlanta, Baltimore, Birmingham, Boston, Buffalo, Chicago, Cincinnati, Cleveland, Columbus, Dallas, Denver, Detroit, El Paso, Fort Worth, Honolulu, Houston, Indianapolis, Jacksonville, Kansas City, Long Beach, Los Angeles, Louisville, Memphis, Miami, Milwaukee, Minneapolis, Nashville-Davidson, Newark, New Orleans, New York, Norfolk, Oakland, Oklahoma City, Omaha, Philadelphia, Phoenix, Pittsburgh, Portland, St. Louis, St. Paul, San Antonio, San Diego, San Francisco, San Jose, Seattle, Toledo, Tulsa, and Washington, D.C.

13. The 40 Ohio cities are Akron, Alliance, Barberton, Canton, Cincinnati, Cleveland, Cleveland Heights, Columbus, Cuyahoga Falls, Dayton, East Cleveland, Elyria, Euclid, Findlay, Garfield Heights, Hamilton, Kettering, Lakewood, Lancaster, Lima, Lorain, Mansfield, Maple

Heights, Marion, Massillon, Middletown, Newark, Norwood, Parma, Portsmouth, Sandusky, Shaker Heights, South Euclid, Springfield, Steubenville, Toledo, Upper Arlington, Warren, Youngstown, and Zanesville.

14. For the impact of reapportionment on the competitive strength of the two major parties, see Robert S. Erickson, "The Partisan Impact of State Legislative Reapportionment," *Midwest Journal of Political Science,* Vol. 15, No. 1 (February, 1971), pp. 57–71.

15. For a discussion on the difficulty in policy experimentation, see Lee Bawden and William Harrar, "The Use of Experimentation in Policy Formulation and Evaluation," a paper presented at the 1972 National Conference of the American Society for Public Administration, Statler-Hilton Hotel, New York City, March 21–25, 1972.

16. For federal experiences, see Aaron Wildavsky, *The Politics of the Budgetary Process* (Boston: Little, Brown and Co., 1964); for state–local experiences, Ira Sharkansky, *The Politics of Taxing and Spending* (Indianapolis: The Bobbs-Merrill Co., 1969), chapter V; and for municipal experiences, John P. Crecine, "A Simulation of Municipal Budgeting: The Impact of Problem Environment," in Ira Sharkansky (ed.) *Policy Analysis in Political Science* (Chicago: Markham Publishing Co., 1970); and his *Government Problem Solving: A Computer Simulation of Municipal Budgeting* (Chicago: Rand McNally, 1968). Most of all, Charles E. Lindblom made perhaps the greatest contribution to the development of the theory of incremental policy making. See his, "The Science of Muddling Through," *Public Administration Review* (Spring 1959), pp. 79–88; and "Decision-Making in Taxation and Expenditure," in *Public Finances: Needs, Resources and Utilization* (Princeton: National Bureau of Economic Research, 1961), pp. 295–336.

17. Violent and aggressive behavior has been studied and explained as biological or physiological phenomenon. For example, a physiological explanation of violence suggests a particular component in the neural systems, when activated by particular stimuli, generates aggressive behavior. See K.E. Moyer, "The Physiology of Violence," *Psychology Today,* Vol. 7, No. 2 (July, 1973), pp. 35–38.

18. See, for example, Calvin F. Schmid, "Urban Crime Areas: Part I," *American Sociological Review,* 25 (August, 1960), pp. 527–542; Calvin F. Schmid, "Urban Crime Areas: Part II," *American Sociological Review,* 25 (October, 1960), pp. 655–678; Roland J. Chilton, "Continuity in Delinquency Area Research: A Comparison of Studies for Baltimore, Detroit and Indianapolis," *American Sociological Review,* 29 (February, 1964), pp. 71–83; Judith A. Wilks, "Ecological Correlates of Crime and Delinquency," in the President's Commission on Law Enforcement and Administration of Justice, *Task Force Report: Crime and Its Impact—An Assessment* (Washington: U.S. Government Printing Office, 1967); Karl Schuessler and Gerald Slatin, "Sources of Variation in U.S. City

Crime, 1950 and 1960," *Journal of Research in Crime and Delin-quency,* 1 (July, 1964), pp. 127–148; Karl Schuessler, "Components of Variation in City Crime Rates," *Social Problems,* 9 (Spring, 1962); and Richard Quinney, "Structural Characteristics, Population Areas, and Crime Rates in the United States," *The Journal of Criminal Law, Criminology, and Police Science,* 57 (1966), pp. 45–52.

19. See, for example, President Lyndon B. Johnson's 1967 Message on Crime. Reprinted in *Crime and Justice in America* (Washington, D.C.: Congressional Quarterly Service, August, 1967), pp. 54–61.

20. See, for example, Marvin E. Wolfgang, "Urban Crime," in James Q. Wilson (ed.), *Metropolitan Enigma* (Garden City: Doubleday & Company, Inc., 1970), pp. 270–311; Sophia M. Robinson, "A Critical View of the Uniform Crime Reports," *Michigan Law Review,* 64 (April, 1966), pp. 1031–1054; and especially, the President's Commission on Law Enforcement and Administration of Justice, *The Challenge of Crime in a Free Society* (Washington: U.S. Government Printing Office, 1967), pp. 20–22. See also the Chapter 2 of this volume for a more detailed discussion of the deficiencies of the FBI Crime Statistics.

21. See Wolfgang, *ibid.,* p. 294.

22. For example, to compute total local correctional expenditures per capita for the City of Akron, we first computed the city expenditure for correction per capita. Then we computed the county expenditure for correction per capita, using the total population in the county including the city population. Assuming that city use of the county provided services for correction is equal to other residents elsewhere within the county, the two per capita expenditure figures for correction are combined to develop total local expenditures for correction in the City of Akron. Similar procedures have been followed wherever multiple government units provide a given service in the city area included in our sample.

23. Several versions of Negro residential segregation index have been developed by various researchers. The particular index used here for our purpose was computed following the formula devised by Pierre deVise in "Chicago's Widening Color Gap," paper presented at the South Side Planning Board, held at the Illinois Institute of Technology, May 19, 1971. For other versions of Negro segregation index, see Karl Taeuber and Alma Taeuber, *Negroes in Cities* (Chicago: Aldine Publishing Co., 1965); and Frederic B. Glantz and Nancy J. Delaney, "Changes in Nonwhite Residential Patterns in Large Metropolitan Areas, 1960 and 1970," *New England Economic Review* (March/April, 1973), pp. 2–13.

24. Forcible rape and robbery, for example, are distinct in that the satisfaction the offenders seek from the victims is different—that is, one is for sexual satisfaction and the other for material gains. But they share a commonality, the imposition of the offender's will upon the victim by violent and coercive means.

25. The computer program used for this operation is "Stepwise Multiple Regression Analysis," *SPSS,* Version of March 13, 1971.
26. Everyone of the criminogenic variables selected for each crime variable is simultaneously significant at 0.05 level or above based on the *F* value of the variable and the degree of freedom of the regression equation. Some ecological variables so selected are common for more than one crime measure, while some others being unique for a particular crime variable.
27. Some statistically insignificant independent variables are often retained in a regression as control variables on the ground that these variables are conceptually relevant. Even though they are considered to have a conceptual relevancy in an *a priori* logic, when a statistical or empirical evidence does not back it up, their conceptual relevancy remains yet to be proved.
28. For the discussion on the performance of additive and multiplicative models in regression analysis, see Walter Dean Burnham and John Sprague, "Additive and Multiplicative Models of the Voting Universe: The Case of Pennsylvania: 1960–1968," *American Political Science Review,* LXIV (June, 1970), pp. 471–490; Frank D. Bean and Robert G. Cushing, *op. cit.;* and Hubert M. Blalock, *Social Statistics,* (New York: McGraw Hill, 1960), p. 313.

Chapter Nine

Urban Ecology and the Crime Rates

Criminal behavior is a highly complex, multi-dimensional phenomenon. Criminal causality has long been a serious subject of scholarly research for many social and behavioral scientists including sociologists, psychologists, and anthropologists. There are a vast variety of theories that attempt to explain criminal behavior. However, we do not intend here to make a full review of theories on criminal behavior; we will only outline a few of these theories to provide a background for our ecological perspective of criminal behavior.

Our principal objective here is to identify those ecological variables that are statistically significant in accounting for the crime rate variance among our sample cities. The ecological variables so identified will be used as control variables for the measuring of the public policy impact on criminal behavior in the subsequent two chapters. In addition, this operation will enable us to re-examine the ecological correlates of crime rates with the most current data available.

BIOLOGICAL THEORIES

In biological theories of crime, the cause of criminal behavior is attributed to various biological characteristics such as genetic inheritance, physical traits, or neural systems. For example, one most widely known biological theory of crime is the view that the type of body build is associated with criminal behavior. Goring, Kretchner, Sheldon, and Hooton, for example, classified body build into 3 types: (1) mesomorphic (muscular), (2) endomorphic (fat), and (3) ectomorphic (skeletal). The mesomorphic are claimed most likely to become delinquents.[1]

PSYCHOLOGICAL THEORIES

Psychic conditions and personality traits are most often the underlying concepts for a variety of psychological theories of criminal behavior. Freudian psychology has a strong influence on psychological and psychoanalytic perspectives of criminality. Freudians view criminality psychoanalytically and crime is considered as a product of inner psychic conflict and symbolic manifestation of such conflict: e.g., "a man kills his wife because in doing so he is symbolically killing his mother."[2]

Personality traits are mainly used for describing and labelling criminal behavior and criminal personality in psychiatric or psychiatric-social studies of criminal behavior. In psychiatry, criminal behavior is considered as a behavioral manifestation of personality disorder or psychopathic personality. Criminals are classified according to their behavior into such categories as "antisocial (psychopathic), dissocial, and neurotic," for example.[3] Such classification or labelling is, however, not explanatory of criminal behavior or criminal personality, but merely descriptive of it.

SOCIOLOGICAL THEORIES

Criminal behavior has long been one of the major fields in sociology and many interesting theories have been generated as a result. Sociological theories use such concepts as social norms, social interaction, cultural values, roles, and social status, and so forth, for the explanation of social behavior in general and criminal behavior in particular. The more prominent or widely known theories include theory of differential association and theory of differential opportunity, among others.

The theory of differential association views that crime is a learned behavior in association with or in imitation of others as postulated by Gabriel Tarde in 1912.[4] This theory has been further elaborated by many subsequent studies.[5] However, the validity of the differential association theory has been disputed for two main reasons: (1) Glueck argues that "criminal association often follows, rather than precedes, criminal behavior, and thus, . . . criminals associate with criminals because they are criminals rather than . . . criminals are criminals because they associate with criminals";[6] and (2) criminals identify with criminal as well as noncriminal values.[7]

The theory of differential opportunity attributes crime to the inequity in the opportunity structure of the society; namely, there is a discrepancy between the culturally defined ends (or goals) and the socially structured means (or modes) of attaining them. Robert Merton, Albert Cohen, and Richard Cloward and Lloyd Ohlin are some of the sociologists associated with the development of this theory.[8]

One of the fundamental assumptions underlying most of the theories of criminal behavior or criminality is that there are criminals and noncriminals. The criminals and noncriminals are distinct in one or more aspects of the following: Biological inheritance of genes; the physical build of the body; mental or psychic conditions; the modes of socialization; social norms; or cultural value systems, for example. This assumption does not seem to represent the reality accurately. The reason is two-fold: (1) it is certainly questionable if the differences between the "criminals" and "noncriminals" are greater than similarities; and (2) it is equally questionable if criminals tend to behave criminally while noncriminals tend to behave noncriminally because they are so predisposed. Rather, what appears to be more realistic is that criminal behavior may be viewed as a *probability behavior* for any persons instead of a *certainty behavior* for particular persons.

Halleck's theory of behavior seems to be most helpful to enhance the clarity of this argument. Halleck views behavior as an adaptation to an environment. The adaptation takes two forms of responses: (1) alloplastic responses, which change the external environment; and (2) autoplastic responses, which change the internal environment (mental life). Criminal activities are viewed as alloplastic responses.[9]

Thus, a behavior is a product of two interacting variables: environment and people responding to the environment for adaptation. The environment is likely to differ in the types or intensity of criminogenic influence, while people are likely to differ in their propensity to respond to the environment depending on their necessity for adaptation. Then, it becomes possible to assume that the interaction patterns between environment and population of given characteristics are likely to be reliable predictors of the probability of criminal behavior. This assumption can be accommodated in the ecological approach to urban analysis, although this particular conceptual implication has never been clear in the ecological approach to crime analysis.

Robert Park and his associates first applied the biological concept of ecology to social studies. They postulated that cities are composed of "natural areas" that are distinct in physical, social, and cultural characteristics.[10] The concentric zone thesis advanced by Burgess was an elaboration of the ecological concept of natural areas of the city.[11] Burgess formulated a scheme to divide a city into five concentric zones with Zone I in the core of the city on the one extreme and Zone V in the urban fringe beyond the city limits on the other extreme. The five zones are as follows: Zone I, business and industrial district; Zone II, the area in transition from slum residence to business and industry; Zone III, the residential area of industrial workers; Zone IV, the residential area of exclusive single family dwellings and high priced apartments; and Zone V, the commuters' zone, lying beyond the city limits.

The social area analysis that gained prominence in the 1950s and thereafter is a continuation and refinement of the ecological concept of natural areas. The social area analysis attempts to identify distinct sub-areas within a city based on a number of socio-economic characteristics. The Shevky–Bell technique is the best known and a most often used device for the development of typology of urban neighborhoods based on their socio-economic status (i.e., family, ethnic, and economic status).[12] Now we will turn to a brief review of ecological analysis of urban crime before presenting our own findings.

ECOLOGICAL ANALYSES OF URBAN CRIME

An ecological analysis of criminal behavior is necessarily a comparative and statistical study that attempts to predict the variance in crime rates among different geographical units by ascertaining the statistical correlations between crime rate variables and socio-economic variables that represent the ecological characteristics of the areas. In a most perceptive review of ecological literature of crime analysis, Judith Wilks classified the ecological literature into 4 categories dependent on geographical areas used as analytical units and among which the difference of crime rates is compared. They are: (1) rural—urban comparison; (2) intra-city comparison; (3) inter-city comparison; and (4) inter-regional comparison.[13]

Our review here will be limited to selected studies of intra-city and inter-city comparison.

Intra-City Comparison

Clifford R. Shaw and Henry D. McKay pioneered the application of the concept of social ecology to the analysis of crime.[14] Clifford and McKay's findings are classical that the rate of delinquency is highest in the core of the city where physical deterioration is most serious and socio-economic indicators show a high degree of economic deprivation and social disorganization, while the rate of delinquency is lowest in the periphery of the city where physical deterioration, economic deprivation, and social disorganization are nearly absent.

Lander's study of Baltimore, Bordua's study for Detroit, in comparison with the Baltimore study, and Chilton's study for Indianapolis in comparison with the Baltimore and Detroit studies represent a cumulative effort of social area analysis of Urban Crime.[15]

Lander developed a juvenile delinquency rate with the data obtained from the Juvenile Court of Baltimore and a set of socio-economic variables with the data derived from the 1940 census reports for census tracts. A series of statistical analyses (i.e. linear zero order correlation, partial correlation, curvilinear correlation, multiple regression, and factor analysis) were made between the delinquency rate and the socio-economic variables such as education, rent, overcrowding, substandard housing, percent population non-white, and percent population foreign born. Lander's study found that the proportion of owner-occupancy of housing and the proportion of non-white in the population were statistically more important predictors of delinquency rates than such variables as percent population foreign born, average educational level, average rent, and proportion of overcrowded or substandard housing. Lander's interpretation of his findings attributed delinquency to anomie:

> Delinquency is fundamentally related to the anomie and not specifically to the socioeconomic conditions of an area. The delinquency rates in a stable community will be low in spite of its being

characterized by bad housing, poverty, and propinquity to the city center. On the other hand, one would expect a high delinquency rate in an area characterized by normlessness and social instability. In such sections there is a deficiency in the traditional social controls which maintain conventional behavior in a stable community.[16]

Bordua included two additional socioeconomic variables (median family income and percent of unrelated individuals) for his examination of the relationships between delinquency rate and socioeconomic variables among the census tracts in Detroit. Bordua's findings were generally comparable with those of Lander's though not identical. Bordua, like Lander, found owner-occupancy of housing being powerful as a predictor of the delinquency rate. Unlike Lander, Bordua found that education and overcrowding variables were statistically important predictors of delinquency rates. Bordua, however, disagreed with Lander's conclusion that attributed delinquency to anomie. He argued that anomie cannot cause delinquency. Rather, delinquency is a species of anomie.[17]

More recent and more elaborate studies of social area analysis of crime include Richard Quinney's Lexington study and Calvin Schmid's Seattle study.[18] Quinney developed 3 dependent variables (crime variables) for the census tracts of the Lexington metropolitan area; i.e., (1) adult crime rate; (2) juvenile delinquency rate; and (3) the juvenile delinquency–adult crime ratio based on the 1960 police arrest records. Quinney also developed 3 categories of social area variables: (1) economic status, measured by educational level and the proportion of blue-collar workers in the labor force; (2) family status, measured by the proportion of women in the labor force, fertility ratio, and the proportion of single-structure housing units; and (3) racial status, represented by the percentage of population non-white.

Quinney's findings demonstrate the following relationships between social area characteristics and crime and delinquency:

(1) Crime rates are negatively correlated with economic status and positively correlated with racial status, but not correlated with family status;

(2) Delinquency rates are negatively correlated with economic status and family status and positively correlated with racial status; and

(3) The proportion of delinquency to crime (delinquency/crime ratio) is positively correlated with economic status and negatively correlated with family status and racial status.[19]

Schmid's Seattle study is highly elaborate in the breakdown of crime variables (20) and includes a large number of socioeconomic variables (18). By factor analyzing the 20 crime variables and 18 socio-economic variables assembled for the 93 census tracts of the city of Seattle, Schmid for the first time recognized the multiplicity in the dimensions of criminality and social characteristics and identified some of these dimensions. The 8 rotated orthogonal factors derived from the analysis are illustrative of that multi-dimensional complexity of crime and social area characteristics. For example, Factor I showed that those socio-economic variables representing low social cohesion and low family status were heavily loaded with such crime variables as auto theft, theft from auto, indecent exposure, shop lifting, nonresidential robbery, and check fraud. Factor 4 showed that high population mobility was heavily loaded with such crime variables as check fraud, shop lifting, burglary of residence by night, attempted suicide, burglary of residence by day, auto theft, and theft from auto. Schmid's study, as other similar studies, demonstrated a close statistical relationship between crime rates and socio-economic characteristics, but more importantly this study made it clear that there are distinct dimensions in the association pattern between crime variables and socio-economic characteristics.

Inter-City Comparison

The inter-city analysis of ecological correlates of crime is logically an extension of intra-city analysis so that a city as a whole is to be considered as a social area unit instead of a neighborhood within a city. However, the studies of inter-city comparison are few in number. For example, William Ogburn examined the statistical relationships between the so-called general crime rate, a composite of 6 categories of serious crime (murder, rape, robbery, aggravated assault, burglary, and larceny), and 24 socio-economic variables among the cities of 3 size groups (large, from 250,000 to 578,000 in population; medium, from 100,000 to 168,000 in population; and small, from 36,000 to 58,000 in population).[20] Ogburn found that there were clusters of variables that influenced crime rates regardless of city size. Two of these were crime-deterring factors: the first contained such variables as large family size, religious participation, and employment in manufacturing; and the second cluster contained average monthly rent and wage increases. The third cluster, a crime-producing factor, was related to the sex ratio of the population; namely, the higher the proportion of male population, the higher the city's crime rate.

Nearly three decades after the path-breaking study by Ogburn, Karl Schuessler and Gerald Slatin provide the most recent studies of inter-city crime analysis.[21] Schuessler's 1962 study examined the relationships between 7 crime rate variables (murder, robbery, aggravated assault, burglary, grand larceny, petty larceny, and auto theft) and 20 selected socio-economic variables among 105 cities with a population of 100,000 or more in 1950. It is noteworthy that Schuessler treated each crime category as a separate variable instead of creating a composite index by combining different crime rates.

Schuessler found that the rates of different offenses are not identically related to what were thought to be major predictor variables. Only 2 variables (the percentage of the labor force employed in manufacturing and the percentage of males foreign born) out of the 20 ecological variables were consistently and inversely correlated with all of the offense rates. Three other variables (the percentage of dwelling units crowded, the percentage of families with two or three members, and percentage of non-white) were all positively correlated with all of the offense rates.[22] The results of factor analysis also demonstrated the multiplicity in the dimensions of the relationships between crime variables and socio-economic variables, as shown by Schmid in his Seattle study.

Schuessler–Slatin study examined the relationships between criminal offense rates and socio-economic variables among the cities with a population of 100,000 or more at two points in time, 1950 and 1960. They used 7 offense rates and 28 ecological variables for the 1950 analysis and 26 ecological variables for the 1960 analysis. They found that the variables tended to maintain approximately the same rank order in both periods and that factorial results were also nearly alike for the both periods. The factor analysis identified 2 key criminogenic factors—an anomic factor and a minority factor. Property offenses were found to be heavily loaded on the anomic factor, while offenses against the person were found to be heavily loaded on the minority factor.

The crime studies discussed above and other ecological studies of criminal behavior are different in many important specifics such as: (1) the ways the crime variables are measured often vary; some develop a single crime index by combining various crime types, while others formulate separate variables for the different crime types; (2) the specific ecological variables included in the studies vary from one study to another at least in part; (3) the statistical techniques employed for the analysis of the data are not always identical; or (4) the sociological concepts used for the interpretation of the statistical findings are often not in agreement.

Such differences notwithstanding, one important finding stands out throughout these studies. There are a number of ecological variables that are powerful predictors of crime rate variance among the census tracts within a city or among the different cities. For example, such variables as the percentage of non-white population, overcrowded housing, homeownership, percent population foreign born, population mobility, family structure, educational level, and income level, in a certain combination or individually, tended to show either a high correlation with certain crime variables or tended to load heavily with one or more crime measures. Though specific findings often vary from study to study, the ecological studies have clearly demonstrated that the variance of crime rates or delinquency rates is, in a significant way, a function of the socio-economic characteristics of the neighborhoods or the cities.

CRIME AND ECOLOGICAL INFLUENCE: LARGE U.S. CITIES

Now we turn to our own findings of ecological correlates of crime rates among the 49 largest cities in the United States and among the 40 largest cities in the state of Ohio. We first present the findings of the 49 U.S. cities, followed by those of the 40 Ohio cities and then the comparison of the findings of the 2 samples.

Tables 9–1 through 9–7 report the results of the stepwise multiple linear regression analysis of the 35 socio-economic variables upon each of the 7 crime variables. The socio-economic variables included in the tables are all statistically significant at least at the confidence level of 95 percent and above according to the F value shown in the tables. All of the tables are set up as follows: (1) the far left hand column lists the significant socio-economic variables including their computer code numbers. Five statistical relationships between each crime rate variable and the selected socio-economic variables are shown in the next 5 columns. They are coefficient of simple correlation (r), regression coefficient (B), standardized regression coefficient (Beta), the percent of the variance in the crime rate variable accounted for by each of the socio-economic variables included in the regression (ΔR^2), and the F value in the far right column. At the bottom of each table, we present multiple correlation coefficient (R), coefficient of multiple determination (R^2), and the intercept (constant).

Table 9–1 shows the relationships of homicide rate to four selected ecological variables; i.e., percent of families headed by female with own children under age 18, percent adults without high school completion, per capita retail sales, and percent non-white in the population. All of these variables are positively correlated with the homicide rate and together they account for 68.8 percent of the variance in the homicide rate among the 49 cities. These findings suggest that the homicide rate is significantly higher in those cities where family disorganization is extensive, the level of adult educational attainment is lower, the propensity to consume is stronger, and a larger proportion of the population is non-white.[23]

Shown in Table 9–2 are the relationships of the rate of forcible rape to 4 selected ecological variables. Although the total variance explained by the 4 variables is modest (40.5 percent), the individual variables selected generally confirm the findings of earlier studies. A high proportion of adult males living

Table 9–1. Relationship Between Willful Homicide Rate and Selected Ecological Variables: 49 Largest U.S. Cities, 1970

	r	B	Beta	ΔR^2	F
VAR049–% Female-Headed Family	.649	.949	.219	.421	2.4
VAR089–% Adults, H.S. Dropouts	.614	.451	.393	.099	11.7
VAR063–P.C. Retail Sales	.227	.092	.344	.100	12.5
VAR047–% Non-White	.633	.234	.359	.068	7.5
R				.829	
R^2				.688	
Intercept (constant)				−36.963	

Table 9–2. Relationship Between Forcible Rape Rate and
Selected Ecological Variables: 49 Largest U.S. Cities, 1970

	r	B	Beta	ΔR^2	F
VAR050–% Primary Male	.402	12.854	.853	.161	13.9
VAR084–% Change in Rental Housing	.278	.161	.297	.115	4.8
VAR048–% Population Under 18	−.148	2.444	.464	.084	4.1
VAR083–% Population Below Poverty	.222	1.017	.214	.044	2.5
R		.636			
R^2		.405			
Intercept (constant) . .		−115.437			

Table 9–3. Relationship Between Robbery Rate and Selected
Ecological Variables: 49 Largest U.S. Cities, 1970

	r	B	Beta	ΔR^2	F
VAR049–% Female-Headed Family	.636	57.100	.384	.404	6.2
VAR046–Population Density	.604	.322	.430	.146	11.6
VAR047–% Non-White	.595	6.962	.311	.055	5.3
VAR050–% Primary Male	.424	84.021	.303	.026	5.9
VAR054–% Homeownership	−.433	8.707	.328	.044	4.5
R		.822			
R^2		.675			
Intercept (constant) . .		−1200.480			

alone contribute most to the high rate of forcible rape.[24] A greater increase in rental housing is also a significant contributor to a high rate of rape. A more rapid increase in rental housing may be considered as the evidence of increasing instability in the community's population structure and of increasing population mobility. In the earlier studies, both neighborhood instability and population mobility factors were found to be strong criminogenic influences.[25] Often the young have been blamed for being perpetrators of a variety of crimes. The high correlation between the percent population under age 18 and the rate of rape supports such argument. A high proportion of population below poverty income level also contributes significantly to the high rate of rape. Thus, the significant predictors of forcible rape represent diverse dimensions of ecological conditions.

Five variables are selected as ecological predictor variables for the rate variance of robbery and they are shown in Table 9–3. The percentage of families headed by female with own children under age 18 and percent population non-white, both of which were significant explanatory variables for the rate variance of homicide, are again significant predictors for the rate variance of robbery. The percentage of primary male, which was the most powerful explanatory variable for the variance of rape, is also significant for robbery. The other two variables are population density and homeownership, and the latter was considered as a crime-deterring influence,[26] but here it is positively correlated with the rate of robbery. The positive regression coefficient (B) of homeownership may be resulted because of its multicolinearity with the other 4 independent variables in the regression. The coefficient of simple correlation for homeownership ranged from −.594 with percent female headed family, −.564 both with population density and percent primary male to −.381 with percent non-white.

Table 9–4 indicates that the variance of aggravated assault is primarily a function of social and economic deprivation. The lower level of educational attainment by adults (median school years completed by persons 25 years old and above), a greater inequality in family income distribution, and increase in overcrowded housing all contribute significantly to the higher rate of aggravated assault. Per capita retail sales do not indicate the ability to consume by the lower-income families, therefore, when income distribution is more unequal and the general level of consumption in the community is relatively higher, the sense of deprivation for the lower-income groups may become more intensified. The 4 variables combined account for 50.7 percent of total variance in the assault rate.

As shown in Table 9–5, the burglary rate is most influenced by percent primary male in the population, percent non-white, percent homeowner-

Table 9–4. Relationship Between Aggravated Assault Rate and Selected Ecological Variables: 49 Largest U.S. Cities, 1970

	r	B	Beta	ΔR^2	F
VAR088–Median Education	−.534	−131.731	−.534	.286	18.8
VAR086–Family Income Inequality	.398	2217.785	.346	.106	8.0
VAR095–% Change, Overcrowded Hsing.	.237	1.866	.288	.080	5.7
VAR063–P.C. Retail Sales	.082	.881	.189	.035	2.4
R		.712			
R^2		.507			
Intercept (constant) . . .		716.565			

Table 9–5. Relationship Between Burglary Rate and Selected Ecological Variables: 49 Largest U.S. Cities, 1970

	r	B	Beta	ΔR^2	F
VAR050–% Primary Male	.477	352.067	.658	.228	16.4
VAR047–% Non-White	.405	15.568	.360	.118	6.0
VAR054–% Homeownership	−.204	16.778	.328	.050	3.8
VAR090–% Adults, Illiterate	.205	62.161	.237	.046	2.8
R		.665			
R^2		.442			
Intercept (constant) . . .		−946.297			

ship, and adult illiteracy rate (percent adults with less than 5 years of schooling). The 4 variables combined account for 44.2 percent of the variance in the burglary rate among the cities.

The relationships of 4 ecological variables to larceny rate are shown in Table 9–6. The ecological correlates of larceny mostly contradict the expected relationships between environmental variables and criminal behavior. For example, the percent change in rental housing and percent of multi-dwellings are inversely correlated with larceny although the fast increase in rental housing and more multi-dwellings should be considered as a factor contributing to the instability of the community, thus contributing to a higher rate of larceny. Percent population under age 18 is also inversely correlated with larceny in spite of the widely accepted suspicion that the youth population tends to be prime perpetrators of larcenous offenses. Only the index of inequal distribution of family income is positively correlated with larceny as expected.

The four variables shown in Table 9–7 account for 59.1 percent of the variance in the auto theft rate. The percent primary male is the most powerful influence on auto theft. Teenagers are believed to be the principal perpetrators of auto theft in view of their high arrest rate for the crime. But the arrest rate does not seem to reflect the extent of teenagers' involvement in auto theft.

Table 9–6. Relationship Between Larceny Rate and Selected Ecological Variables: 49 Largest U.S. Cities, 1970

	r	B	Beta	ΔR^2	F
VAR048—% Population Under 18	−.429	−53.308	−.418	.184	8.2
VAR094—% Change in Rental Hsing.	−.399	−4.958	−.377	.114	7.7
VAR086—Family Income Inequality	.246	5027.729	.305	.056	4.7
VAR060—% Multi-Dwellings	−.016	−13.927	−.265	.056	3.2
R		.640			
R^2		.409			
Intercept (constant) . . .		1916.965			

Table 9–7. Relationship Between Auto Theft Rate and Selected Ecological Variables: 49 Largest U.S. Cities, 1970

	r	B	Beta	ΔR^2	F
VAR061—% Commercial-Industrial Property	.635	20.317	.385	.404	8.4
VAR050—% Primary Male	.453	160.179	.425	.094	12.4
VAR094—% Change in Rental Hsing.	.339	3.416	.252	.067	4.6
VAR088—Median Education	−.359	−125.866	−.192	.027	2.2
R		.769			
R^2		.591			
Intercept (constant) . . .		935.195			

The teenagers' arrest rate appears to be a lot higher than the extent of actual involvement, perhaps because the teenagers are more vulnerable to arrest when they steal a car than adults. Finally, a high level of adult education is correlated with a low rate of auto theft.

The Configuration Pattern of Ecological Influences on Crime Rates

The results of our analysis presented in Tables 9–1 through 9–7 are schematically illustrated in Figure 9–1 to display the configuration pattern of each of the 7 crime variables and the 16 of the 35 ecological variables included in the 7 regression equations. The crime variables are shown in squares and the ecological variables are shown in circles. The straight arrows indicate the linkage of the ecological variables to crime variables. The number that appears on each arrow line represents the Beta coefficient (standardized regression coefficient) of that ecological variable in relation to the particular crime measure while controlling for other ecological variables in the regression. The number that appears within each square (R^2) represents the percent of the variance in that crime variable accounted for by the ecological variables linked to that crime variable.

The configuration pattern visually demonstrates (1) what particular ecological variable is related to what crime variable and to how many different crime variables; and (2) which 2 crime variables have in common what particular ecological variable or how many ecological variables. For example, percent primary male (V–50) is related to as many as 4 different crime variables (C_5, C_3, C_2, and C_7) and percent non-white (V–47) is related to three different crime measures (C_5, C_3, and C_1), while such variables as percent of adults who are high school dropouts (V–89) and population density (V–46) are related to only a single crime variable, homicide (C_1) and robbery (C_3), respectively. Robbery (C_3) and burglary (C_5) have in common as many as 3 different ecological variables; percent non-white (V–47), percent homeownership (V–54), and percent primary male (V–50), whereas homicide (C_1) and robbery (C_3) have in common 2 ecological variables; percent non-white (V–47) and percent families headed by female (V–49).

This schema thus tells us the ecological context of the interrelationships between the crime variables. For example, homicide (C_1) is most closely related to robbery (C_3), while homicide (C_1) is not related to auto theft (C_7), forcible rape (C_2), or larceny (C_6), when viewed from the ecological perspective of criminal behavior.

The Influence Scale of Ecological Variables

An influence index is constructed to measure the criminogenic influence of each of the ecological variables for each of the crimes and for all of the crimes. This influence index is constructed in such a way as to make it possible to compare the relative strength of each ecological variable's influence on all

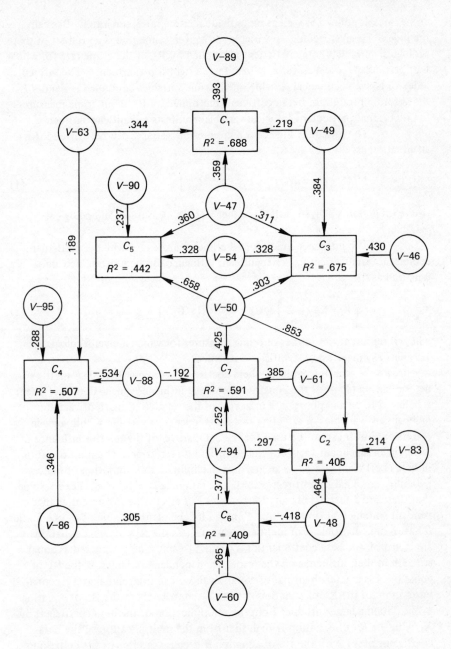

Figure 9–1. The Configuration Pattern of Crime Rates and Ecological Variables: 49 Largest U.S. Cities

crime rates combined as well as on individual crime rates, separately. Basically, the index of a given ecological variable for a given crime rate is a product of that ecological variable's beta coefficient multiplied by R^2 of the crime rate for which that particular ecological variable manifests a significant influence. The influence index of a given ecological variable on all crime variables combined is a sum of the absolute product of beta coefficient multiplied by R^2 of all crime measures for which that particular ecological variable manifests a significant influence.

The influence index for a given crime variable can be written into an equation as:

$$I \ (V_i \cdot C_i) = [\beta(C_i \cdot V_i) \cdot R^2 \ (C_i)]$$ (1)

where i represents a given variable, either a crime measure or an ecological variable.

The influence index for all crime measures for which a particular ecological variable manifests a significant influence can be written into an equation as:

$$I \ (V_i \cdot C_k) = \Sigma \ [\beta(C_k \cdot V_i) \cdot R^2 (C_k)]$$ (2)

where k represents any types of crime measures for which a given ecological variable (V_i) manifests a significant influence.

We chose to multiply beta coefficient with coefficient of multiple determination (R^2) for the construction of the influence index. Beta coefficient is believed to be an appropriate indicator of the relative strength of various independent variables in affecting the same dependent variable within a given regression, but it cannot be used for the comparison of the relative influence of different independent variables among different regressions. The multiplication of beta coefficient and R^2 is an attempt to eliminate this limitation of noncomparability among different regressions. The rationale is as follows: Let's assume that there are 2 regression equations, A and B. Let's further assume that an independent variable (X_1) in equation A and an independent variable (X_2) in equation B have a beta coefficient of identical value. Unless the R_2s of the 2 equations are identical, the beta coefficient of X_1 and X_2 cannot be considered as equal strength in their influence on the respective dependent variables. If the R_2 of equation A is greater than that of equation B, we can interpret that X_1 contributes more to the R^2 of equation A than X_2 contributes to the R^2 of equation B. We obtain a larger product from the multiplication of the beta coefficient of X_1 with the R^2 of equation A than that from the multiplication of the beta coefficient of X_2 with the R^2 of equation B because the R^2s of the equations are different although the beta coefficient of X_1 and X_2 are identical. Thus, the multiplication of beta coefficient and R^2 resolves this particular comparability problem.

The influence index score of any ecological variables can be computed from the formulas shown in Equations (1) and (2) either for a particular crime measure or for all crime measures. To compute the index score of the variable, percent primary male (V–50), for all crime measures, for example: where $i = 50$, substituting 50 for i in Equation 2, then

$$I \, (V\text{--}50 \cdot C_k) = \Sigma \, [\beta \, (C_k \cdot V\text{--}50) \cdot R^2 \, (C_k)] \qquad (3)$$

since V–50 is affecting the crime measures, C_2, C_3, C_5, and C_7, then Equation 2 becomes as follows:

$$
\begin{aligned}
I \, (V\text{--}50 \cdot C_k) \;\; &= \Sigma \, [\beta \, (C_k \cdot V\text{--}50) \cdot R^2 \, (C_k)] \\[6pt]
&= [\beta (C_2 \cdot V\text{--}50) \cdot R^2 \, (C_2)] + [\beta (C_3 \cdot V\text{--}50) \cdot R^2 \, (C_3)] \\[6pt]
&\quad + [\beta (C_5 \cdot V\text{--}50) \cdot R^2 \, (C_5)] + [\beta (C_7 \cdot V\text{--}50) \cdot R^2 \, (C_7)] \\[6pt]
&= [.853 \times .405] + [.303 \times .675] \\[6pt]
&\quad + [.658 \times .442] + [.425 \times .591] \\[6pt]
&= 1.092
\end{aligned}
$$

The influence score of each of the 16 ecological variables for each and all of the 7 crime variables is presented in Table 9–8. For example, the influence of percent non-white on homicide (the second line of the homicide column) is almost twice as strong as the influence of income inequality on larceny (the nineth line of the larceny column). The total index score in the last column shows that percent primary male is the most powerful influence, while percent population below poverty income is the least powerful influence of all the ecological variables selected and included in the 7 equations.

CRIME AND ECOLOGICAL INFLUENCE: OHIO CITIES

The ecological variables significantly correlated with crime variables among the 40 largest Ohio cities are presented in Tables 9–9 through 9–14 exactly in the same format as done for the sample of U.S. cities above. One crime variable, larceny, was found unrelated with any of the ecological variables examined here. Therefore, we did not proceed to further analyze larceny for the Ohio cities.

Table 9–9 shows that three demographic variables (percent non-white, total population, and percent change in white population) are the dominant predictors of homicide rate. This finding is generally in accord with the

Table 9–8.   Index of Ecological Influence on Crime: 49 Largest U.S. Cities

	Homicide (C_1) $[\beta(C_1, V_i) \cdot R^2 (C_1)]$	Forcible Rape (C_2) $[\beta(C_2, V_i) \cdot R^2 (C_2)]$	Robbery (C_3) $[\beta(C_3, V_i) \cdot R^2 (C_3)]$
I. Demographic Variables			
V–49. % Families Headed by Female	.151	–	.259
V–47. % Non-White	.247	–	.210
V–50. % Primary Male	–	.345	.205
V–48. % Pop. Under 18	–	.188	–
V–46. Population Density	–	–	.290
II. Income & Living Standards			
V–63. P.C. Retail Sales	.237	–	–
V–83. % Pop. Below Poverty	–	.086	–
V–86. Income Inequality–Family	–	–	–
III. Education			
V–89. % Adults High School Dropouts	.270	–	–
V–88. Adult Education Level	–	–	–
V–90. % Adults Illiterate	–	–	–
IV. Housing			
V–94. % Change in Rental Housing	–	.120	–
V–54. % Homeownership	–	–	.221
V–95. Change in Overcrowded Housing	–	–	–
V. Physical Structure			
V–60. % Multi-Dwellings	–	–	–
V–61. % Comm. & Indus. Property	–	–	–

findings of earlier studies.[27] The 3 demographic variables together account for as much as 74.3 percent of the variance in the homicide rate among the 40 cities.

The variance of forcible rape was also dominantly influenced by 4 demographic variables; total population, percent non-white, population density, and percent primary male as shown in Table 9–10. All but population density are positively correlated with the forcible rape rate. Percent primary male was also found to be the most powerful predictor for the 49 largest cities in the nation.

Table 9–11 reports the relationships of 4 ecological variables (3 demographical and 1 education) to robbery rate. They together account for 86.5 percent of the variance in the robbery rate. Of the 3 demographic variables, percent families headed by female and the size of total population of the community are positively correlated with the robbery rate, while the change rate of white population is inversely correlated with the crime variable as expected. The education variable (high school dropout rate of the youth), however, shows a

Aggravated Assault (C_4) $[\beta(C_4, V_i) \cdot R^2 (C_4)]$	Burglary (C_5) $[\beta(C_5, V_i) \cdot R^2 (C_5)]$	Larceny (C_6) $[\beta(C_6, V_i) \cdot R^2 (C_6)]$	Auto Theft (C_7) $[\beta(C_7, V_i) \cdot R^2 (C_7)]$	Total $\Sigma [\beta(C_k, V_i) \cdot R^2 (C_k)]$
–	–	–	–	.410
–	.159	–	–	.616
–	.291	–	.251	1.092
–	–	.171	–	.359
–	–	–	–	.290
.096	–	–	–	.333
–	–	–	–	.086
.175	–	.125	–	.300
–	–	–	–	.270
.271	–	–	.113	.384
–	.105	–	–	.105
–	–	.154	.149	.423
–	.145	–	–	.366
.146	–	–	–	.146
–	–	.108	–	.108
–	–	–	.228	.228

relationship to the robbery rate that seems inconsistent with the expectation: namely, the higher the dropout rate, the less the robbery rate. This apparent inconsistency cannot be resolved within the present context of analysis.

Only two ecological variables showed a significant relationship with aggravated assault, as shown in Table 9–12. They are percent families headed by female and population density, and the level of their influence on the crime variable is modest with an R^2 of .308.

Table 9–13 shows that burglary is most influenced by 5 variables. Three of the 5 (percent families headed by female, high school dropouts, and the change rate of white population) are identical with the predictor variables of robbery. This finding indicates that burglary and robbery are greatly in common in their ecological context. As noted earlier in this chapter, it has been widely believed that the teenagers are the most crime-prone of all the age groups in the population. The police arrest records have frequently supported such arguments. The finding here that the percent of male teenagers in the population

Table 9–9.   Relationship Between Willful Homicide Rate and Selected Ecological Variables: 40 Ohio Cities, 1970

	r	B	Beta	ΔR^2	F
VAR10–% Non-White	.733	.275	.452	.538	20.7
VAR08–Total Population	.711	.020	.421	.158	18.3
VAR15–% Change of White Population 1960–70	−.483	−.121	−.232	.048	6.7
R		.862			
R^2		.743			
Intercept (constant) . .		13.329			

Table 9–10.   Relationship Between Forcible Rape Rate and Selected Ecological Variables: 40 Ohio Cities, 1970

	r	B	Beta	ΔR^2	F
VAR08–Total Population	.670	.033	.438	.449	13.9
VAR10–% Non-White	.630	.297	.300	.116	3.8
VAR09–Population Density	.024	−.001	−.298	.053	7.3
VAR13–% Primary Male	.605	4.323	.293	.034	3.5
R		.807			
R^2		.652			
Intercept (constant) . . .		6.910			

Table 9–11.   Relationship Between Robbery Rate and Selected Ecological Variables: 40 Ohio Cities, 1970

	r	B	Beta	ΔR^2	F
VAR12–% Female-Headed Family	.790	37.195	.556	.625	40.9
VAR18–Total Population	.744	.419	.430	.125	32.1
VAR28–High School Dropouts	.185	−10.984	−.320	.048	19.4
VAR15–% Change, White Population	−.548	−3.276	−.302	.068	17.7
R		.930			
R^2		.865			
Intercept (constant) . .		301.453			

is significantly and positively correlated with the burglary rate also supports the validity of such argument as far as the experience of the Ohio cities goes.

Table 9–14 shows the relationships of 4 ecological variables to auto theft as follows: the greater the proportion of non-white in the population, the larger the total population size of the community, the higher the median value of owner-occupied housing, and the faster the rate of decline of total population, the higher the rate of auto theft is.

Table 9–12. Relationship Between Aggravated Assault Rate and
Selected Ecological Variables: 40 Ohio Cities, 1970

	r	B	Beta	ΔR^2	F
VAR12–% Female-Headed Family	.478	24.165	.536	.229	14.7
VAR09–Population Density	−.180	−.012	−.287	.079	4.2
R		.555			
R^2		.308			
Intercept (constant) . .		35.786			

Table 9–13. Relationship Between Burglary Rate and Selected
Ecological Variables: 40 Ohio Cities, 1970

	r	B	Beta	ΔR^2	F
VAR12–% Female-Headed Family	.766	175.600	.875	.587	86.5
VAR09–Population Density	−.198	−.061	−.323	.128	12.2
VAR37–% Male Teenagers	.220	226.824	.188	.041	4.4
VAR28–High School Dropouts	.291	−22.975	−.223	.020	5.9
VAR15–% Change, White Population	−.475	−6.619	−.203	.030	5.3
R		.898			
R^2		.807			
Intercept (constant) . . .		−183.214			

Table 9–14. Relationship Between Auto Theft Rate and Selected
Ecological Variables: 40 Ohio Cities, 1970

	r	B	Beta	ΔR^2	F
VAR10–% Non-White	.657	18.064	.446	.432	16.0
VAR08–Total Population	.626	1.195	.382	.118	12.8
VAR22–Med. Value of Owner- Occupied Housing	.144	.033	.406	.074	15.4
VAR14–% Change, Total Population	−.343	−12.791	−.324	.078	9.2
R		.838			
R^2		.701			
Intercept (constant) . . .		979.635			

The crime rates of the Ohio cities tend to be most often and most
strongly influenced by demographic variables such as percent non-white, total
population size of the community, family disorganization, and population shift,
among others. It is also evident that the extent of ecological influence on crime
is more discernible for the Ohio cities than for the U.S. cities within the limits of
the variables employed here in view of the differences in the R^2s except for
larceny.

The Configuration Pattern of Ecological
Influence on Crime Rates

Figure 9–2 is the schematic presentation of the 10 ecological variables found to be statistically significant predictors for 1 or more crime variables. The total population size of the community (V–8) has the most wide-ranging influence affecting 4 measures of crime, homicide (C_1), forcible rape (C_2), robbery (C_3), and auto theft (C_7). Percent non-white (V–10), percent families headed by female (V–12), and percent change in white population (V–15) show the next most wide-ranging influence affecting 3 crime measures each.

This schema also indicates that robbery (C_3) and burglary (C_5) are most closely interrelated by sharing 3 common ecological variables (V–12, V–15, and V–28). Homicide (C_1) and robbery (C_3), homicide and forcible rape (C_2), homicide and auto theft (C_7), forcible rape (C_2) and auto theft (C_7), and aggravated assault (C_4) and burglary (C_5) are sharing 2 common ecological variables each. Some of the crime variables, such as auto theft and aggravated assault or auto theft and burglary, do not share any common ecological variables.

The Influence Scale of Ecological Variables

Table 9–15 presents the influence index of ecological variables for each crime variable separately and all crime variables combined. The total index indicates that family disorganization and the population size of the community are the most powerful influence on the major crimes in the Ohio cities, followed by the non-white percent of population, the change rate of white population and population density, and so forth.

COMPARISON AND SUMMARY

The pattern of ecological correlates of crime shows both similarities and differences between the U.S. cities and Ohio cities. The ecological variables are important predictors of crime for both groups of the cities. However, the R^2s suggest that the ecological influence of crime is better identifiable for the Ohio cities than for the U.S. cities out of the ecological variables examined here. The findings for the both sets of the cities also demonstrate that some of the ecological variables bearing significant influence on crime are common to more than one crime measure and some others are unique for one particular crime variable. This is indicative of the commonality and uniqueness in the nature of various crimes as evidenced by their ecological contexts.

As far as the specific variables go, the ecological context of criminal behavior is more different than similar between the 2 sets of the cities. The selected ecological variables for the U.S. city crimes generally represent diverse dimensions of urban ecology such characteristics as population, income, education, housing, and physical structure of the community. In contrast, the selected ecological variables for the Ohio city crimes represent almost entirely a single

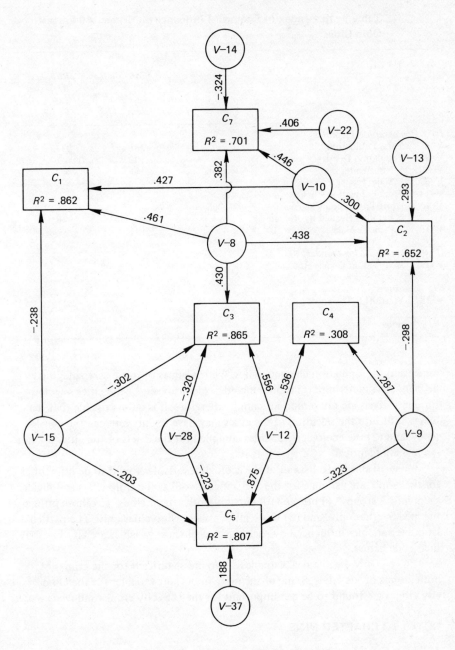

Figure 9–2. The Configuration Pattern of Crime Rates and Ecological Variables: 40 Largest Ohio Cities

Table 9–15.   Index of Ecological Influence on Crime: 40 Largest Ohio Cities

	Homicide (C_1) $[\beta(C_1, V_i) \cdot R^2(C_1)]$	Forcible Rape (C_2) $[\beta(C_2, V_i) \cdot R^2(C_2)]$	Robbery (C_3) $[\beta(C_3, V_i) \cdot R^2(C_3)]$
I. Demographic Variables			
V–8. Total Population	.397	.286	.372
V–9. Population Density	–	.190	–
V–10. % Non-White	.368	.196	–
V–37. % Male Teenagers	–	–	–
V–14. Total Population Change	–	–	–
V–15. White Population Change	.205	–	.261
V–12. % Families Headed by Remale	–	–	.481
V–13. % Primary Male	–	.191	–
II Income & Living Standards			
V–22. Med. Val. of Owner-Housing	–	–	–
III. Education			
V–28. Youth H.S. Dropouts	–	–	.277
IV. Housing	–	–	–

dimension of population characteristics. While sources of this discrepancy may be many, the more important ones include: (1) both sets of the cities selected for our analysis are not a random sample, therefore, it is quite possible that the biases built into the selection of the cities may have unduly reduced the consistency; and (2) the ecological variables compiled for the 2 sets of the cities are not completely identical.

Table 9–16 lists all of the ecological variables found to be influential for the crime rate variance for the U.S. cities as well as the Ohio cities and divides them into 3 groups: (1) those influential in both sets of cities, (2) those influential in U.S. cities only, and (3) those influential in Ohio cities only. The particular crime variables influenced by each of the ecological variables are also listed by their code names.

Only 4 ecological variables are found significant for the crimes of both groups of the cities. Some of the more important variables for the Ohio city crimes are found to be not important for the U.S. city crimes and *vice versa*.

NOTES TO CHAPTER NINE

1.   Ruth Cavan, *Criminology,* 2nd edition (New York: Crowell Co., 1955), pp. 688–697; Edwin H. Sutherland and Donald R. Cressy, *Principles of Criminology,* 7th edition (Philadelphia: Lippincott Co., 1966),

Aggravated Assault (C_4) $[\beta(C_4, V_i) \cdot R^2(C_4)]$	Burglary (C_5) $[\beta(C_5, V_i) \cdot R^2(C_5)]$	Larceny (C_6) $[\beta(C_6, V_i) \cdot R^2(C_6)]$	Auto Theft (C_7) $[\beta(C_7, V_i) \cdot R^2(C_7)]$	Total $\Sigma[\beta(C_k, V_i) \cdot R^2(C_k)]$
–	–		.268	1.323
.088	.261		–	.539
–	–		.313	.877
–	.152		–	.152
–	–		.227	.227
–	.164		–	.630
.165	.706		–	1.352
–	–		–	.191
–	–		.285	.285
–	.180		–	.457
–	–		–	–

pp. 122–143; and C. Ray Jeffery, *Crime Prevention Through Environmental Design*, (Beverly Hills: Sage Publications, 1971), pp. 95–96.

2. Jeffery, *Crime Prevention Through Environmental Design* (Beverly Hills: Sage Publications, 1971), p. 97.

3. Jeffery, *ibid.*, p. 98.

4. Gabriel Tarde, *Penal Philosophy* (Boston: Little, Brown and Co., 1912).

5. See, for example, Albert J. Reiss, Jr. and Albert Lewis Rhodes, "An Empirical Test of Differential Association Theory," *Journal of Research in Crime and Delinquency*, Vol. 1, No. 1 (1964), pp. 5–18; Edwin H. Sutherland and Donald R. Cressy, *Principles of Criminology*, 7th ed., (Philadelphia: Lippincott Co., 1966); and Martin R. Haskell and Lewis Yablonsky, *Crime and Delinquency* (Chicago; Rand McNally, 1970).

6. Sheldon Glueck, "Theory and Fact in Criminology," *British Journal of Criminology* (October, 1956), p. 95 as cited in C. Ray Jeffery, *Crime Prevention Through Environmental Design*, p. 102.

7. Solomon Kobrin, "The Conflict of Values in Delinquent Areas," *American Sociological Review* (October, 1951), pp. 653–661; Gresham Sykes and David Matza, "Techniques of Neutralization: A Theory of Delinquency," *American Journal of Sociology* (December, 1957), pp. 664–670.

Table 9-16.   Ecological Variables and Crime Rates: Comparison of U.S. and Ohio Cities

Crime Variables (U.S. Cities)	→	Ecological Variables	→	Crime Variables (Ohio Cities)
		U.S. and Ohio Cities		
C_3, C_2, C_5, C_7	→	% Primary Male (V–50)	→	C_2
C_3, C_1, C_5	→	% Non-White (V–47)	→	C_1, C_2, C_7
C_3, C_1	→	% Female-Headed Family (V–49)	→	C_3, C_4, C_5
C_3	→	Population Density (V–46)	→	C_2, C_4, C_5
		U.S. Cities Only		
C_2, C_6, C_7	→	% Change Rental Housing (V–94)		
C_2, C_6	→	% Population Under 18 (V–48)		
C_3, C_5	→	Home Ownership (V–54)		
C_1, C_4	→	Retail Sales (V–63)		
C_4, C_6	→	Family Income Inequality (V–86)		
C_4, C_7	→	Adult Education (V–88)		
C_6	→	Multi-Dwelling (V–60)		
C_7	→	Comm.-Indus. Property (V–61)		
C_2	→	% Pop. Below Poverty (V–83)		
C_1	→	Adult H.S. Dropout (V–89)		
C_5	→	Adult Illiteracy (V–90)		
C_4	→	Change Hsg. Crowdedness (V–95)		
		Ohio Cities Only		
		Total Population (V–8)	→	C_1, C_2, C_3, C_7
		Change White Population (V–15)	→	C_1, C_2, C_3, C_5
		Youth H.S. Dropout (V–28)	→	C_3, C_5
		Male Teenagers (V–37)	→	C_5
		Housing Value (V–22)	→	C_7
		Change Total Population (V–14)	→	C_7

8. Robert K. Merton, "Social Structure and Anomie," *American Sociological Review*, Vol. 3, No. 5 (1938), pp. 672–682; Albert Cohen, *Delinquent Boys: The Culture of the Gang* (New York; Free Press, 1955); and Richard A. Cloward and Lloyd E. Ohlin, *Delinquency and Opportunity: A Theory of Delinquent Gang* (Glencoe, Ill.: The Free Press, 1960).

9. Seymour L. Halleck, *Psychiatry and the Dilemmas of Crime* (New York: Hoeber Medical Books, 1967).

10. Robert E. Park, Ernest W. Burgess, and Roderick D. McKenzie, *The City* (Chicago: University of Chicago Press, 1925).

11. Ernest W. Burgess (ed.), *The Urban Community* (Chicago: University of Chicago Press, 1926).

12. Eshref Shevky and Wendell Bell, *Social Area Analysis* (Stanford: Stanford University Press, 1955).

13. Judith A. Wilks, "Ecological Correlates of Crime and Delinquency," The President's Commission on Law Enforcement and Administration of Justice, Task Force Report; *Crime and Its Impact—An Assessment* (Washington, D.C.: U.S. Government Printing Office, 1967), pp. 138–156.

14. "Social Factors in Juvenile Delinquency: A Study of the Community, the Family, and the Gang in Relation to Delinquent Behavior," for the National Commission on Law Observance and Enforcement, *Report on the Causes of Crime*, Vol. II, No. 13, 1931; and *Juvenile Delinquency and Urban Areas: A Study of Rates of Delinquency in Relation to Differential Characteristics of Local Communities in American Cities,* revised edition (Chicago: University of Chicago Press, 1942, 1969).

15. Bernard Lander, *Towards an Understanding of Juvenile Delinquency: A Study of 8,464 Cases of Juvenile Delinquency in Baltimore* (New York: Columboa University Press, 1954); David J. Bordua, "Juvenile Delinquency and 'Anomie': An Attempt at Relation, *"Social Problems,* Vol. 6 (Winter, 1958), pp. 230–238; and Roland J. Chilton, "Continuity in Delinquency Area Research: A Comparison of Studies for Baltimore, Detroit, and Indianapolis," *American Sociological Review,* 29 (Feb., 1964), pp. 71–83.

16. Lander, *ibid.,* p. 89.

17. Bordua, *op. cit.,* p. 237.

18. Richard Quinney, "Crime, Delinquency, and Social Areas," *The Journal of Research in Crime and Delinquency,* Vol. 1 (July, 1964), pp. 149–154; and Calvin R. Schmid, "Urban Crime Areas: Part I," *American Sociological Review,* Vol. 25 (1960), pp. 527–542 and "Urban Crime Areas: Part II," *ASR,* Vol. 25 (1960), pp. 655–678.

19. Quinney, *ibid.,* p. 154.

20. William F. Ogburn, "Factors in the Variation of Crime Among Cities," *Journal of the American Statistical Association,* 30 (March, 1935), pp. 12–45.

21. Karl Schuessler, "Components of Variation in City Crime Rates," *Social Problems,* 9 (Spring, 1962), pp. 314–327; and Karl Schuessler and Gerald Slatin, "Sources of Variation in United States City Crime, 1950 and 1960," *Journal of Research in Crime and Delinquency,* 1 (July, 1964), pp. 127–148.

22. Schuessler, *ibid.,* p. 316.

23. Except for non-white, the other three variables have never been specifically tested in earlier studies. Many of the earlier studies found that non-white proportion of the population had a strong correlation with crime in general and violent crime in particular. See, for example, Quinney, *op. cit.* (racial factor); and Schuessler and Slatin, *op. cit.* (minority factor).

24. This variable is sometimes called low family status factor and found to be a powerful predictor of sex crimes. See Calvin F. Schmid, *op. cit.,* for example.

25. See Schmid., *ibid.,* Lander (Baltimore study), *op. cit.;* and Bordua (Detroit study), *op. cit.,* among others.

26. See, for example, Lander (Baltimore study), *ibid.*

27. For example, Schuessler and Slatin suggest that violent crimes (offenses against the person such as homicide) are a product of minority factor and Quinney found that racial status was positively correlated with crime and delinquency. See Schuessler and Slatin, *op. cit.;* and Richard Quinney, *op. cit.*

Chapter Ten

Policy Impact on Crime: Control Policies

The public policy impact on the crime rate pattern among the sample cities was tested through a step-wise multiple regression procedure described in Chapter 8. The regression analyses generated 364 regression equations for the 2 groups of the cities. They include: (1) 147 control policy equations for the 49 largest U.S. cities; (2) 21 control policy equations for the 40 largest Ohio cities; (3) 112 social service policy equations for the 49 U.S. cities; and (4) 84 social service policy equations for the 40 Ohio cities. In the present chapter, we present some salient results of control policy analysis. The results of social service policy analysis shall be presented in Chapter 11. We will first discuss the results of control policy analysis for the 49 cities of national sample, followed by the presentation of the findings for the 40 cities of the Ohio sample.

Our tabular presentation of policy impact equations includes 5 statistics that define the relationships between each of the policy measures and each of the crime rate variables. They are: simple correlation coefficient (r), regression coefficient, partial correlation coefficient, R^2 change (the percent of the variance in the crime variable accounted for by the policy measure), and F value. Also shown at the bottom of each table is the list of the significant ecological variables controlled for the measurement of "net" relationships between a policy measure and a crime variable.

Since there are too many equations to present all of them in our tables, we arbitrarily selected only those equations whose F value is in excess of 1.00 for the inclusion in the tables to conserve the space. However, the F value should be substantially higher for a policy measure to be independently significant in its relationship to a crime variable.[1] Even when the crime—policy relationship is statistically significant as evidenced by the F value, it is statistically unjustifiable to interpret the significance of the relationship as the evidence of the existence of a policy-to-crime causal relationship. The reason is that the policy variables used for our analysis are not experimental in a statistical sense though they may be viewed as experimental in a political sense.

THE 49 U.S. CITIES

None of the control policy measures are correlated with 2 crime variables, burglary and larceny, strong enough to produce an F value of 1.00 for the 49 U.S. cities. Therefore, no control policy equations are reported here for the 2 crime variables.

Homicide

Table 10-1 reports the relationships of selected control policy measures to willful homicide rate while controlling for 4 ecological variables. Homicide is a crime of passion, mostly committed in a private setting (most often in the kitchen or the bedroom) by persons who knew the victims intimately.[2] For this reason, the prevention and control of homicide through public policy may be considered ineffective. However, out of the 21 control policy measures tested, 3 corrections policy measures are significantly correlated with homicide rate. They are pay for prison employees (an indicator of professionalism in prison personnel systems), the employee—inmate ratio in the prisons, and prison crowdedness. When the prison employees are paid better and the prison personnel is more heavily staffed, the homicide rate tends to be significantly lower. On the contrary, when the local prisons are overcrowded, the homicide rate in the city tends to be significantly higher. These relationships however, do not necessarily support a conclusion that overcrowded prisons would increase homicide rate, while a greater degree of professionalism and more generous staffing of prison personnel would reduce homicide rates. The interpretation may also be reversed as follows: (1) prisons are overcrowded because crimes, including

Table 10-1. Relationship of Control Policies to Willful Homicide, Controlling for the Major Ecological Variables: 49 Largest U.S. Cities, 1970

Control Policies	Simple r	Regression Coefficient	Partial r	R^2 Change	F
Police Policies					
P-22 Police Expenditure	.388	-.128	-.238	.018	1.98
P-29 Sworn Officers	.423	-.015	-.203	.013	1.42
Correction Policies					
P-67 Pay for Prison Employees	-.064	-.119	-.249	.019	2.19
P-68 Employee—Inmate Ratio	-.159	-.550	-.290	.026	3.04
P-64 Prison Crowdedness	.269	.092	.381	.045	5.62
P-69 Prison Facilities	.091	-.074	-.180	.010	1.11
Localism—State Centralism					
P-42 Localism—Police	.025	-.181	-.178	.010	1.08

Note: The ecological variables controlled are: % Female-Headed Family; % Adults High School Dropout; P.C. Retail Sales; and % Non-White.

homicide in the community, are so numerous; (2) a community may be able to pay its prison employees more generously because it needs so few prison employees since it has so few inmates due to a low crime rate; and (3) a community may be able to keep the employee–inmate ratio high because the crime rate, including homicide in the community, is low and therefore the number of inmates in the local prison is so small.[3]

Two measures of police policy (per capita police expenditures and sworn police officers per 100,000 population) show a considerable strength, though not statistically significant, in their relationships to homicide rates. Namely, the higher the level of police expenditures and the larger the number of sworn police officers relative to population, the homicide rate tends to be lower. These relationships tend to render a conceptual support to a posibility of the positive effects that police policies may have on homicide.[4] However, our findings shown in Table 10–1 do not offer strong enough an evidence to expect that an improvement in police policies, by way of increasing the allocation of public resources to police operations or expanding police manpower, would contribute to the reduction of the homicide rate.

Forcible Rape

Forcible rape is also a crime often committed in a private setting by persons who knew the victim. Amir reports that as many as "48 percent of the identified victim–offender relationships conformed to our definition of 'primary' relationships" in his study of 646 victims and 1,292 offenders recorded in the police files of the Philadelphia Police Department.[5] As shown in Table 10–2, only one policy measure (the local percent of state and local expenditures for police) was inversely and significantly correlated with forcible rape at the 90 percent confidence level. Police salary at the entrance level and per capita expenditures for corrections are also inversely correlated though not significant.

Table 10–2. Relationship of Control Policies To Forcible Rape Controlling the Major Ecological Variables: 49 Largest U.S. Cities, 1970

Control Policies	Simple r	Regression Coefficient	Partial r	R^2 Change	F
Police Policies P–26 Salary–Entrance	.113	−.374	−.190	.021	1.23
Correction Policies P–24 Correction Expenditure	.159	−.515	−.172	.018	1.01
Localism P–42 Localism–Police	−.043	−.619	−.247	.036	2.15

Note: The ecological variables controlled are: % Primary Male; % Change in Rental Housing; % Population under 18; and % Population Below Poverty

So far as our findings indicate, control policy measures are generally unrelated to forcible rape.

Robbery

Several control policy measures are correlated with robbery at a considerable level of strength (partial r = 0.200 and above), but only 2—police scooters and motorcycles as well as per capita expenditures for all justice functions—are significantly correlated. As shown in Table 10–3, these 2 policy measures are positively correlated with robbery rate, implying that more scooters and motorcycles for police departments and higher levels of expenditures for the entire local criminal justice operations lead to significantly higher robbery rates. The other policy variables reported in Table 10–3 also have a positive correlation with the robbery rate.

It makes no sense, however, to think that more police vehicles and more financial resources committed to criminal justice operations as well as other measures of control policy would contribute to the increase in robbery rate. This finding seems to indicate a pattern of policy response to the rising crime rate in the communities. What is not apparent, but detectable, is this. When the robbery rate along with other crimes goes up, the public pressure for more police protection and tougher criminal justice operations ensues. Policy decisions responding

Table 10–3.   Relationship of Control Policies to Robbery Controlling the Major Ecological Variables: 49 Largest U.S. Cities, 1970

Control Policies	Simple r	Regression Coefficient	Partial r	R^2 Change	F
Police Policies					
P–22 Police Expenditure	.757	7.039	.255	.015	1.52
P–28 Total Employees	.740	.666	.211	.013	1.33
P–29 Sworn Officers	.727	.748	.218	.014	1.43
P–33 Scooters and Motorcycles	.565	1086.172	.360	.029	3.11
Court Policies					
P–23 Court Expenditure	.612	13.356	.200	.011	1.15
Correction Policies					
P–24 Correction Expenditure	.598	9.652	.236	.014	1.48
P–69 Prison Crowdedness	.373	1.667	.219	.011	1.17
Total Justice Policy					
P–25 Total Justice Expenditure	.759	4.622	.293	.021	2.21
Localism					
P–Localism–Courts	.176	2.672	.250	.011	1.10

Note: The ecological variables controlled are: % Female-Headed Families; Population Density; % Non-White; % Primary Male; and % Homeownership.

to public pressure of this nature increase expenditures for criminal justice operations and expand facilities, equipment, and manpower for law enforcement, but reduction in robbery rate does not follow. E.S. Savas, the former First Deputy Administrator in the Office of the Mayor of New York, makes a telling point about what happens when more resources are poured into police operations. He argues that hiring more police officers may not necessarily improve the crime-fighting capability of the criminal justice system in view of the New York City experiences. Savas points out:

> . . . between 1940 and 1965, the number of policemen in New York City increased by 50 percent (from 16,000 to 24,000), but the *total* number of hours worked by the entire force in 1965 was actually *less* than in 1940. The increase in manpower was completely eaten up by a shorter work week, a longer lunch break, more vacation days, more holidays, and more sick leave.[6]

Aggravated Assault

Six control policy measures are moderately correlated with aggravated assault, but prison crowdedness is the only variable whose correlation is significant nearly at the 95 percent confidence level. The positive correlation suggests that the more crowded the local prisons are, the higher the rate of aggravated assault in the community. The implications of this finding are undoubtedly complex and ambiguous. It may mean that crowded prisons are indicative of poor policy support for prison facilities and poor prison facilities are unsuitable for rehabilitative services for the inmates, thus not being able to break down the vicious cycle of recidivism and the rising crime rate, including criminal assault. Or it may mean that the prisons are overcrowded merely because there are too many crimes in the community, many suspects for which are arrested, tried, convicted, and incarcerated.

Other control policies reported in Table 10–4 indicate that a higher level of control policies is associated with a higher rate of criminal assault. This finding again suggests that raising the policy level does not reduce the crime rate contrary to the simplistic expectations often manifested by the "law-and-order" proponents.

Auto Theft

As shown in Table 10–5, 2 of the control policy measures are significantly correlated with auto theft rate. The 2 policy measures (police scooters and motorcycles and pay for prison employees), however, demonstrate a contradictory effect on that crime rate: the larger the number of scooters and motorcycles, the higher the auto theft rate, whereas the higher the level of pay for prison employees, the lower the auto theft rate.

Table 10–4. Relationship of Control Policies to Aggravated Assault Controlling the Major Ecological Variables: 49 Largest U.S. Cities, 1970

Control Policies	*Simple* r	*Regression* *Coefficient*	*Partial* r	R² *Change*	*F*
Police Policies					
P–22 Police Expenditure	.406	2.022	.202	.020	1.40
P–28 Total Employees	.444	.266	.221	.024	1.69
P–33 Scooters and Motorcycles	.331	389.747	.190	.018	1.24
Court Policies					
P–23 Court Expenditure	.328	6.351	.178	.016	1.08
Correction Policies					
P–64 Prison Crowdedness	.284	1.377	.260	.033	2.39
Total Justice Policies					
P–25 Total Justice Expenditure	.391	1.300	.206	.021	1.46

Note: The ecological variables controlled are: Median Adult Education; Family Income Inequality; % Change in Overcrowded Housing; and P.C. Retail Sales.

Table 10–5. Relationship of Control Policies to Auto Theft Controlling the Major Ecological Variables: 49 Largest U.S. Cities, 1970

Control Policies	*Simple* r	*Regression* *Coefficient*	*Partial* r	R² *Change*	*F*
Police Policies					
P–33 Scooters and Motorcycles	.329	1271.042	.266	.029	2.52
Correction Policies					
P–67 Pay for Prison Employees	.146	−8.144	−.259	.027	2.37

Note: The ecological variables controlled are: % Commercial and Industrial Property; % Primary Male; % Change in Rental Housing; and Median Adult Education.

SUMMARY

The test results of the control policy effect on crime rates among the 49 largest U.S. cities warrant the following 2 generalizations: (1) so few of the control policy measures display a measurable effect on 1 or more of the crime rates; and (2) some policy measures demonstrate a positive effect in the sense that the higher the policy level, the lower the crime rate, while some others reveal a negative effect in the sense that the higher the policy level, the higher the crime rate as well.

As shown in Figure 10–1, only 6 of the 21 control policy measures

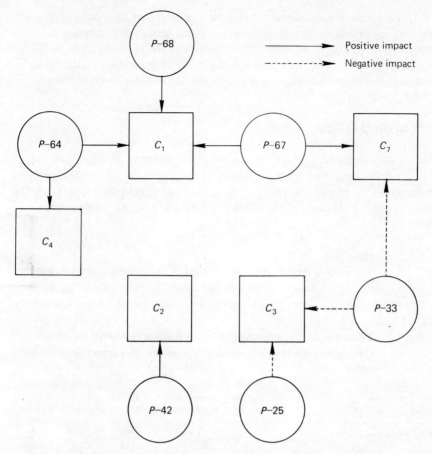

Figure 10–1. The Configuration Pattern of Crime Rates and Control Policy Measures: 49 Largest U.S. Cities

are significantly correlated with one or more crime rates. Three of the 6 significant control policy measures are corrections policy measures and they all demonstrate a positive effect on crime rate: prison crowdedness(P–64) on homicide rate (C_1) and aggravated assault (C_4); pay for prison employees (P–67) on homicide rate (C_1) and auto theft (C_7); and employee–inmate ratio (P–68) on homicide (C_1). In contrast, a police policy measure and the expenditure level for total justice operations display a negative impact on crime rate.

Is it centralism or decentralism that is more effective as a way of organizing public service delivery system? This question has long been a subject of heated debate for the students of public management.[7] We examined four variables measuring the degree of centralism or decentralism in law enforcement and criminal justice. Our findings do not offer a decisive evidence to shed a new light on the time-worn controversy. Only one measure, the local percent of state and local expenditures for police protection (local decentralism measure of police operations) is positively and significantly correlated with forcible rape rate (C_2). In short, the evidence of the crime-reducing effect of the control policy measures is disappointingly negligible as far as the experience of the 49 largest cities in the United States indicates.

THE 40 OHIO CITIES

For the 40 selected Ohio cities, the control policy measures tested include only 7 police policy measures. They are police expenditures, salary–entrance, salary–maximum, total employees, sworn officers, police cars, and police scooters and motorcycles.[8] The impact of these 7 policy measures is tested for six crime variables.[9]

Homicide

Table 10–6 reports the relationships of police policy measures to homicide rate. The findings indicate that the higher the maximum salary for the police officers and the larger the number of police scooters and motorcycles per

Table 10–6. Relationship of Police Policies to Willful Homicide Controlling the Major Ecological Variables: 40 Largest Ohio Cities, 1970

Police Policies	Simple r	Regression Coefficient	Partial r	R^2 Change	F
P–50 Salary–Entrance	.315	.001	.203	.010	1.49
P–51 Salary–Maximum	.334	.002	.311	.025	3.75
P–55 Scooters and Motorcycles	.383	.430	.346	.031	4.75

Note: The ecological variables controlled are: % Non-White; Total Population; and % Change in White Population.

Table 10–7. Relationship of Police Policies to Forcible Rape Controlling the Major Ecological Variables: 40 Largest Ohio Cities, 1970

Police Policies	Simple r	Regression Coefficient	Partial r	R^2 Change	F
P–48 Police Expenditure	.401	–.632	–.347	.042	4.66
P–52 Total Employees	.504	–.116	–.437	.066	8.01
P–53 Sworn Officers	.507	–.100	–.353	.043	4.83
P–54 Police Cars	.089	–.129	–.173	.010	1.05

Note: The ecological variables controlled are: Total Population; % Non-White; Population Density; and % Primary Male.

100,000 population in the community, the more likely the homicide rate is to be significantly higher. These findings simply do not offer any evidence that an expansion in police policies will help arrest the trends of the rising homicide rate.

Forcible Rape

The findings reported in Table 10–7 suggest that 3 measures of police policies are highly significant restraints on forcible rape. Greater levels of public resources committed to police protection and larger police departments (total employees as well as sworn officers) in communities result in a significantly lower rate of forcible rape.

Robbery

The relationships of police policy measures to robbery reported in Table 10–8 are exactly the reverse of the police policy–forcible rape relationships. When the police expenditure level is higher, total employees and sworn officers are larger in number, and scooters and motorcycles are more numerous, the robbery rate tends to be measurably higher.

Aggravated Assault

The relationships of police policy measures to aggravated assault reported in Table 10–9 are the same as the pattern of the police policy-to-robbery relationships except that the correlations between police policies and aggravated assault are not quite as strong.

Burglary

Only one variable, police cars per 100,000 population, is moderately but not significantly correlated with burglary as shown in Table 10–10. Burglary may be considered as the type of crime that is more receptive to police activities for crime prevention and crime deterrence. For example, more police manpower for patrol, more motor vehicles for mobility, and more resources for a more effective electronic communications system, and so forth may be believed to be helpful in deterring or preventing break and entry at commercial as well as resi-

Table 10–8. Relationship of Police Policies to Robbery Controlling the Major Ecological Variables: 40 Largest Ohio Cities, 1970

Police Policies	Simple r	Regression Coefficient	Partial r	R^2 Change	F
P–48 Police Expenditure	.767	4.597	.367	.018	5.28
P–52 Total Employees	.835	.610	.250	.008	2.27
P–53 Sworn Officers	.813	.711	.268	.010	2.62
P–55 Scooters and Motorcycles	.431	7.812	.407	.022	6.75

Note: The ecological variables controlled are: % Female-Headed Families; Total Population; High School Dropouts by Youth; and % Change in White Population.

Table 10–9. Relationship of Police Policies to Aggravated Assault Controlling the Major Ecological Variables: 40 Largest Ohio Cities, 1970

Police Policies	Simple r	Regression Coefficient	Partial r	R² Change	F
P–50 Salary–Entrance	–.012	.021	.170	.020	1.07
P–52 Total Employees	.482	.712	.262	.047	2.65
P–53 Sworn Officers	.451	.627	.205	.029	1.57
P–55 Scooters and Motorcycles	.305	6.720	.241	.040	2.22

Note: The ecological variables controlled are: % Female-Headed Families and Population Density.

Table 10–10. Relationship of Police Policies to Burglary Controlling the Major Ecological Variables: 40 Largest Ohio Cities, 1970

Police Policies	Simple r	Regression Coefficient	Partial r	R² Change	F
P–54 Police Cars	.309	4.116	.182	.006	1.13

Note: The ecological variables controlled are: % Female-Headed Families; Population Density; % Male Teenagers; High School Dropouts by Youth; % Change in White Population.

Table 10–11. Relationship of Police Policies to Auto Theft Controlling the Major Ecological Variables: 40 Largest Ohio Cities, 1970

Police Policies	Simple r	Regression Coefficient	Partial r	R² Change	F
P–48 Police Expenditure	.751	19.889	.293	.026	3.20
P–53 Sworn Officers	.692	3.117	.243	.018	2.13
P–55 Scooters and Motorcycles	.286	19.554	.222	.015	1.77

Note: The ecological variables controlled are: % Non-White; Total Population; Median Value of Owner-Occupied Housing; and % Change, Total Population.

dential places. Surprisingly, however, our findings offer no evidence that the resources, manpower, or motorized mobility for the police force would deter or prevent burglary.

Auto Theft

Two measures of police policies—police expenditures and sworn officers—are significantly and positively correlated with the auto theft rate as shown in Table 10–11. As in the cases of homicide, robbery, and aggravated assault, a higher level of control policies is associated with a higher rate of auto theft.

SUMMARY

Most of the police policy measures tested demonstrate a significant correlation with various crime rates among the 40 largest Ohio cities. Figure 10–2 schematically presents the pattern of relationships between 5 police policy measures and 5 crime variables found to be significant. The policy implications of these findings are disturbing but instructive. More police manpower, more motorized mobility for the police, higher salary for the police officers, or simply more money for the police activities has been the course of policy action most often taken to counteract the rising tide of crime rate in our cities. What seems evident from our findings, however, is that the better financed, better staffed, better equipped, and better paid police forces are not likely the right response to the call for the reduction of crime rates.

COMPARISON OF THE CONTROL POLICY IMPACT: U.S. AND OHIO CITIES

The police policies are the only control policy measures common to the both sets of cities analyzed for comparison. As shown in Table 10–12, only 1 police policy measure (scooters and motorcycles) shows an important influence for some crime rates in both groups of cities. Other measures of police policy, however, bear no important influence on the crime rate pattern of the 49 U.S. cities. Although most of the police policy measures are significant predictors of various crime rate variables for the Ohio cities, it is evident that police policies do not have a crime-reducing influence.

A recent experiment in the effect of police patrol on crime rate confirms the validity of our findings that police policies are unlikely to have a crime-reducing impact. The effectiveness of preventive patrol was tested in a year-long study sponsored by the Police Foundation in Kansas City, Missouri from October 1, 1972, to September 30, 1973. The preliminary results of the study indicated that the variance in patrol intensity in matched areas with no regular patrol cars, 1 patrol car and 4 or 5 patrol cars made no corresponding difference in the levels of reported crime.[10]

Unlike police policies, corrections policies demonstrate a strong influence on the crime rate pattern of the 49 U.S. cities. When corrections personnel are more numerous and better paid and the local prisons are less crowded in a community, the crime rates there are also found to be significantly lower. Of course, these relationships do not necessarily imply a causality but offer an alternative for the reordering of the priorities within the area of control policy such as a shift in policy emphasis from police protection to corrections. This

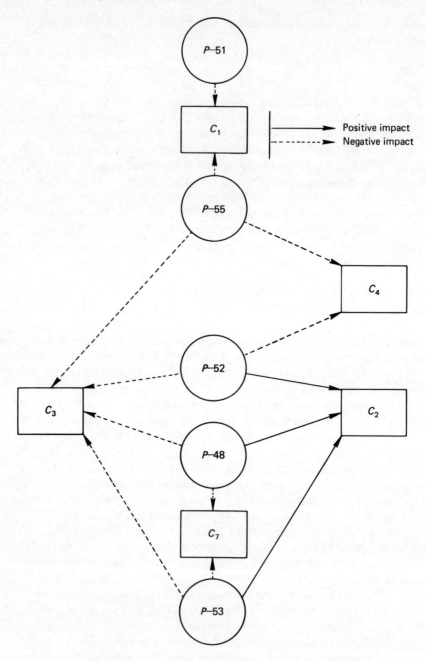

Figure 10–2.   The Configuration Pattern of Crime Rates and Control Policy Measures: 40 Largest Ohio Cities

Table 10–12. Control Policy Measures and Crime Rates: Comparison of U.S. Cities and Ohio Cities

Crime Variables	Control Policy Measures	Crime Variables
U.S. Cities		*Ohio Cities*
	U.S. and Ohio Cities	
C_7, C_3 ←	(P–33) Police Scooters and Motorcycles (P–55) →	C_1, C_3, C_4
	Ohio Cities Only	
	(P–22) Police Expenditures →	C_2, C_3, C_7
	(P–27) Salary–Maximum →	C_1
	(P–28) Total Employees →	C_2, C_3, C_4
	(P–29) Sworn Officers →	C_2, C_3, C_7
	U.S. Cities Only	
C_7, C_1 ←	(P–67) Pay for Prison Employees	
C_1 ←	(P–68) Employee–Inmate Ratio	
C_4, C_1 ←	(P–64) Prison Crowdedness	
C_3 ←	(P–25) Total Justice Expenditure	
C_2 ←	(P–42) Localism–Police	

shift in policy emphasis has already been adopted by the LEEA in its grants-distribution policies.[11] Many states and local communities have recognized the importance of innovative corrections policies and they have recently initiated various progressive programs, particularly for young offenders.[12] Nevertheless, the pattern of expenditure distribution clearly indicates that only a minor share of total expenditures for criminal justice is used for corrections programs.[13]

NOTES TO CHAPTER TEN

1. Considering the degree of freedom of our regression equations (the number of variables in the equations ranging from 4 to 6, including ecological, policy, and crime variables and 40 observations for the Ohio cities and 49 observations for the U.S. cities), the regression coefficient or partial correlation coefficient of a policy measure to be significant at the 90 percent confidence level ($P = 0.10$), at the 95 percent confidence level ($P = 0.05$), and at the 99 percent confidence level ($P = 0.01$), the corresponding F values should be approximately 2.00, 2.45, and 3.50 respectively.

2. Marvin E. Wolfgang, "A Sociological Analysis of Criminal Homicide," in Bruce J. Cohen (ed.), *Crime in America,* (Itasca, Illinois: F.E. Peacock Publishers, Inc., 1970), pp. 52–60; and Alex D. Pokorny, "A Comparison of Homicides in Two cities," in Bruce J. Cohen, *Crime in America,* pp. 60–69.

3. Bean and Cushing faced a similar dilemma in their interpretation of the relationship of the certainty index of punishment to a lower crime rate. See their "Criminal Homicide, Punishment, and Deterrence: Methodological and Substantive Reconsideration," *Social Science Quarterly* (November, 1971), pp. 277–289.

4. Although homicide *per se* is a crime of passion usually committed in a private setting to which law enforcement authority is seldom accessible for preventive action, a better equipped and better staffed police force may be able to maintain personnel capability to mediate family fights, which may result in homicide, or to check concealed weapons, which could be used for manslaughter, more thoroughly. Such police capability may indirectly contribute to the reduction of the chance for possible homicidal actions.

5. Menachem Amir, "Forcible Rape," in Bruce J. Cohen (ed.), *Crime in America,* pp. 82–90. The quotation is from p. 88.

6. E.S. Savas, "Municipal Monopoly," *Harper's Magazine,* (December, 1971), pp. 55–60. The quotation is from p. 57.

7. Specifically for law enforcement and criminal justice, some writers argue that centralized organization is one of the prerequisites for effective operations. See, for example, June Romine and Daniel L. Skoler, "Local Government Financing and Law Enforcement, *The American County* (May, 1971), pp. 17–43 among others.

8. For a more detailed description of these policy variables, see Chapter 8 of this volume.
9. The larceny rate was excluded from our policy impact test because of the failure of identifying adequate control variables. None of the ecological variables examined at the first stage regression procedures were found significant predictors for the larceny rate.
10. "A Police Study Challenges Value of Anticrime Patrol," *The New York Times,* November 11, 1973, p. 1 and 67.
11. Douglas Harmon, "Law Enforcement Assistance: Who Gets, What, Where, When and How?" *The Municipal Yearbook, 1971,* (Washington, D.C.: International City Management Association, 1971), pp. 53–59.
12. See Chapter 3 of this volume.
13. See Chapters 4 and 6 of this volume.

Chapter Eleven

Policy Impact on Crime:
Social Service Policies

As discussed in Chapter 9, crime in the cities is mainly considered as a function of the urban ecology that is characterized by demographic status, income and living standards, education, and housing, and so forth. Our ecological perspective of social analysis views that the interactive combinations of the 2 sets of variables, demographic and socio-economic, constitute the primary source of influence that governs social behavior pattern including criminal behavior.

Social service policy is a principal instrument of the government for the intervention in the interactive process of the ecological forces. A wide-ranging variety of social legislation—enacted during the New Deal under the Roosevelt Administration in the 1930s, during the Fair Deal under Truman, the New Frontiers under Kennedy, and the Great Society under Johnson—manifests the trends of cumulative expansion in the social policy intervention by federal government. The social policy intervention is expected to weaken the criminogenic influence in the socioeconomic conditions because the main thrust of the social service policies is lodged in moderating the extreme inequities in the social and economic opportunity structure. Therefore, social service policies are expected to have an indirect crime-reducing impact.

We report here the test results of social service policy impact on city crime rates for the U.S. cities and Ohio cities. For the 49 U.S. cities, the effect of 16 social service policy variables is examined on each of the 7 crime rate variables. For the 40 Ohio cities, we tested the effect of 14 social policy measures on 6 crime rate variables.[1] The social service policy measures are further classified into 2 categories—social service policies for opportunities (the opportunity policies) and those for environment (the environment policies).

The opportunity policies represent those policy measures that are aimed at improving the opportunities for a better life for the socially and economically deprived segment of the population. These policies place their primary emphasis on the enhancement of marketable skills as well as cultural and intellectual development. Included in this policy category are a plethora of OEO programs, manpower development and training program, small business development, and public school policies. Viewed from temporal perspective, the nature of these opportunity policies is future-oriented in the sense that the payoffs of the policy benefits are not likely to be immediate.

The environment policies represent those policy measures that attempt to improve the environmental quality of urban life. Included in this policy category are such hardware-oriented policies as low-rent public housing, FHA mortgage insurance, urban renewal, municipal sanitation service, and municipal parks and recreation programs. Both categories of the policies are similar in the sense that they attempt to reduce the extreme inequities in the opportunity structure and the living environment and standards. But the nature of these inequities is different: the environment policies are delivery mechanisms for essentials and amenities of urban living to the poor in the form of tangible goods and services; whereas the opportunity policies are instruments employed for strengthening cultural, social, and economic foundations for the deprived and disadvantaged so that they may have a more equitable share of social and economic opportunities.

The format of presentation of the results of the social service policy impact analysis is identical with the one used for the presentation of control policy impact. First, we report the findings of the 49 U.S. cities analysis, then that of the 40 Ohio cities analysis, and finally the comparison of the two.

THE 49 U.S. CITIES

Homicide

Table 11–1 indicates that all but one of the environment policy measures are significantly correlated with homicide rates while none of the opportunity policy measures are even moderately correlated with it. The higher the ratio of low-rent public housing to occupied housing units, the higher the

Table 11–1. Relationship of Service Policies to Willful Homicide Controlling the Major Ecological Variables: 49 Largest U.S. Cities, 1970

Service Policies	Simple r	Regression Coefficient	Partial r	R^2 Change	F
For Environment					
P–36 Public Housing	.429	−12.462	−.292	.027	3.08
P–78 FHA Mortgage	−.099	.080	.324	.033	3.86
P–79 Urban Renewal Approved	.175	−.028	−.403	.051	6.40
P–80 Urban Renewal Disbursed	.267	−.047	−.357	.040	4.83
P–38 Leisure Expenditure	−.109	−.255	−.412	.053	6.75

Note: The ecological variables controlled are: % Female-Headed Families; % Adults High School Dropouts; P.C. Retail Sales; and % Non-White.

expenditure level for urban renewal (approved and disbursed), and the higher the municipal expenditure level for leisure activities such as parks and recreation, the lower the homicide rate is in a community. On the contrary, the higher the mortgage insurance extended by FHA to the metropolitan area in which the particular sample city is located, the higher the homicide rate is in that city.

These findings are susceptible to more than one interpretation of the policy implications for criminal behavior. First, the fact that the environment policies are strongly correlated with homicide rate, while the opportunity policies are not, may be considered as an empirical evidence supportive of a class culture theory of criminal behavior. Edward C. Banfield advanced a theory that lower-class individuals have a greater propensity to commit crime in his controversial book, *The Unheavenly City.* Cultural class difference is characterized by the difference in the perception of temporal span: the lower the cultural class of an individual, the more present-oriented his temporal perception and *vice versa.* Banfield writes:

> The more present-oriented an individual, the less likely he is to take account of consequences that lie in the future. Since the benefits of crime tend to be immediate and its costs (such as imprisonment or loss of reputation) in the future, the present-oriented individual is *ipso facto* more disposed toward crime than others.[2]

Although Banfield suggested the thesis of cultural class and temporal-orientation mainly as a determinant of the propensity to commit *property* crimes, the hypothesis may also be relevant for the interpretation of our findings here. Murder within the family (about 25 percent of total homicide in 1972) makes up the single largest group of the victim—offender relationships. Usually homicide within the family is a result of family arguments, which are most often a result of financial problems within the family.

When low-rent public housing is more readily available and publicly provided recreation facilities are more easily accessible to lower-class individuals, we may assume that the resulting impact may contribute to the reduction of the homicide rate—that is, such essentials and amenities as public housing and public recreation programs provided by the environment policies may reduce the chances of family arguments related to housing accommodations and leisure time activities, since delivery of these benefits is likely to be immediate. Thus, reduced chances for family arguments, particularly those for the lower-class families who are the main clientele group of low-rent public housing and public recreation facilities, may be assumed to bring about the corresponding reduction in the circumstances under which criminal homicide is likely to be provoked.

Second, public housing in general and low-rent public housing in particular are criticized and degraded for being less than suitable for human habitation and for being a breeding ground of crime. Yet, the presence of more low-rent public housing in the community is strongly correlated with lower homicide rate (and lower robbery rate as shown in Table 11—3). Residents of public housing may find that life there is more normal and stable than as viewed by learned critics from outside.[3]

Third, the finding that the higher the FHA mortgage insurance in the metropolitan area as a whole, the higher the homicide rate in the central city of that metropolitan area may be considered as empirical evidence supporting the theory of homicidal subculture of the black minority. For example, Wolfgang found an unusually high rate of criminal homicide among the blacks in Philadelphia and attributed this phenomenon to a *"subculture of violence"* of the blacks who "suffer from residential and general cultural isolation from the rest of the community."[4] If, indeed, the subculture theory is valid, the FHA mortgage insurance will reinforce the black ghetto subculture. The reason is that the beneficiary of the FHA mortgage insurance is mainly white, middle-class home buyers in the suburbs, thus accentuating the residential and cultural isolation of the black lower class in the central city ghettoes.

Fourth, urban renewal is chiefly aimed at blighted areas, residential and otherwise. The stated objectives of urban renewal are many, the most important of which being "decent housing for every American family," as stated in the preamble of the U.S. Housing Act of 1949. Urban planners and city administrators have also argued slum clearance and the replacement of the physically blighted properties with new housing construction, office buildings, and other productive land use for commercial, industrial, or civic purposes would reduce crime and fire hazards. Although critics of urban renewal have been unmerciful and relentless by characterizing it as a slum removal or a negro removal among others, our finding indicates that urban renewal is likely to have a restraining impact on the tendencies of criminal homicide.

Forcible Rape

As shown in Table 11—2, none of the social service policy measures are significantly correlated with forcible rape, although 2 measures of the opportunity policy and 1 measure of the environment policy are moderately correlated with it. The findings reported in Table 11—2 renders a conceptual support to the possibility that the higher levels of expenditures for OEO programs, manpower development and training programs, municipal sanitation, may contribute to a lower rate of forcible rape.

Robbery

As Table 11—3 shows, the relationships of the opportunity policy measures to robbery rate are the exact reverse of the relationships of the environment policy measures to robbery. The opportunity policy measures are positively correlated with the robbery rate, while the environment policy measures are inversely correlated with it. When the level of expenditures for OEO programs

Table 11–2. Relationship of Service Policies to Forcible Rape Controlling the Major Ecological Variables: 49 Largest U.S. Cities, 1970

Service Policies	Simple r	Regression Coefficient	Partial r	R^2 Change	F
For Opportunities					
P–72 OEO/Poor	.103	–.016	–.210	.026	1.52
P–73 OEO/Capita	.120	–.095	–.204	.025	1.43
P–74 Manpower/Poor	.083	–.006	–.205	.025	1.45
P–75 Manpower/Capita	.111	–.036	–.201	.024	1.41
For Environment					
P–37 Sanitation Expenditure	–.069	–.577	–200	.024	1.37

Note: The ecological variables controlled are: % Primary Male; % Change in Rental Housing; % Population Under 18; and % Population Below Poverty Income.

Table 11–3. Relationship of Service Policies to Robbery Controlling the Major Ecological Variables: 49 Largest U.S. Cities, 1970

Service Policies	Simple r	Regression Coefficient	Partial r	R^2 Change	F
For Opportunities					
P–70 Headstart/Poor	.458	1.490	.203	.012	1.27
P–71 Headstart/Capita	.537	11.623	.240	.019	1.99
P–72 OEO/Poor	.496	.280	.260	.022	2.28
P–73 OEO/Capita	.524	1.822	.271	.023	2.47
P–74 Manpower/Poor	.494	.112	.272	.023	2.49
P–75 Manpower/Capita	.530	.690	.266	.022	2.33
P–76 Small Business/Poor	.362	.650	.144	.015	1.52
P–77 Small Business/Capita	.437	4.693	.183	.019	1.96
For Environment					
P–36 Public Housing	.278	–401.606	–.334	.022	2.29
P–80 Urban Renewal Disbursed	.274	–.834	–.207	.011	1.09
P–38 Leisure Expenditure	.050	–4.868	–.241	.015	1.56

Note: The ecological variables controlled are: % Female-Headed Families; Population Density; % Non-White; % Primary Male; and % Homeownership.

and manpower development and training programs are higher, the robbery rate tends to be significantly higher, whereas when the low-rent public housing units are more numerous, the rate of robbery tends to be measurably lower. The inverse correlations of the environment policy measures are consistent with the policy correlates of homicide rate discussed above. The positive correlations of the opportunity policy variables, however, may be considered as another evidence supporting the crime theory advanced by Banfield. The opportunity policy measures such as headstart programs, the entire OEO activities, manpower training, or small business development, are highly unlikely to deliver the policy benefits immediately. Therefore, these policies are hardly likely to gratify the present-oriented needs of lower-class individuals although they would be expected to satisfy their needs eventually if successful. Banfield stated:

> Most stealing is done by persons who want small amounts now. For them a job that must be worked at regularly and that pays *only at the end of the week* is not a real alternative to stealing. Even if the wage rate is high, such a job is of no interest to one who wants only a few dollars—enough, say, to buy a couple of six-packs of beer and a carton of cigarettes—but wants them now—this very day, perhaps this very hour. What is needed to reduce stealing, then, is not so much high employment and rising incomes as it is greater opportunity for people who live in the present to get small sums when they want them. Paying unskilled workers by the day instead of the week would help matters some.[5]

If the assumption that the opportunity policies are generally incapable of reducing crime, including robbery, is valid, it would be logical to expect to find no correlations between the opportunity policy variables and the robbery rate after controlling for the ecological variables. However, the fact is that 2 of the opportunity policy programs are significantly correlated with robbery and 2 more programs are moderately correlated with it. This finding does not imply that the opportunity policies contribute to a higher rate of robbery. Rather, this apparent inconsistency seems to suggest that the federal fund allocation policy for the OEO programs, manpower development and training programs, and other similar programs has been more favorable to those cities where urban problems are more serious including crime, poverty, and unemployment.[6]

Aggravated Assault

None of the social service policy measures are significantly correlated with aggravated assault. However, 4 of the opportunity policy variables and 2 of the environment policy variables are moderately correlated with criminal assault at an F value of above 1.00 as shown in Table 11–4. Just as for robbery, the opportunity policy measures are positively correlated with assault, while the environment policy measures are inversely correlated with it.

Burglary

Only 3 of the environment policy measures are moderately correlated with burglary as reported in Table 11–5. The level of FHA mortgage insurance in the metropplitan area is nearly significant at the 90 percent confidence level, thus suggesting the possibility that residential isolation of black minorities in the central city resulting from the federal housing financing policy may accentuate the tendency of burglary in the central city.

Table 11—4.   Relationship of Service Policies to Aggravated Assault Controlling the Major Ecological Variables: 49 Largest U.S. Cities, 1970

Service Policies	Simple r	Regression Coefficient	Partial r	R^2 Change	F
For Opportunities					
P—72 OEO/Poor	.222	.116	.183	.017	1.15
P—73 OEO/Capita	.261	.685	.174	.015	1.03
P—76 Small Business/Poor	.196	.344	.182	.016	1.13
P—77 Small Business/Capita	.307	2.238	.182	.016	1.13
For Environment					
P—37 Sanitation Expenditure	.200	−4.879	−.186	.017	1.18
P—38 Leisure Expenditure	−.066	−2.502	−.186	.017	1.19

Note: The ecological variables controlled are: Median Adult Education; Inequal Distribution of Family Income; % Change in Overcrowded Housing; and P.C. Retail Sales.

Table 11—5.   Relationship of Service Policies to Burglary Controlling the Major Ecological Variables: 49 Largest U.S. Cities, 1970

Service Policies	Simple r	Regression Coefficient	Partial r	R^2 Change	F
For Environment					
P—78 FHA Mortgage	.180	4.871	.235	.031	1.93
P—37 Sanitation Expenditure	.070	−24.025	−.211	.025	1.53
P—38 Leisure Expenditure	.026	−10.800	−.189	.020	1.23

Note: The ecological variables controlled are: % Primary Male; % Non-White; % Home-ownership; and % Adults Illiterate.

Larceny

The ecological influence pattern and the public policy implications for larceny shown in Table 11—6 are markedly different from the other crime rate variables studied here. First, its correlations with some of the ecological variables are irratic.[7] Second, its correlations with some of the policy variables are inconsistent, too. For example, pupil—teacher ratios in the local public schools—the only policy variable significant for the larceny rate—is inversely correlated with larceny, implying that the larger the number of pupils per teacher, the lower the larceny rate. To put it differently, a city that is higher in its quality indicator of school policy is also likely to have a higher rate of larceny. Again, the environment policy measures, such as low-rent public housing and urban renewal variables, are positively correlated with the larceny rate contrary to the pattern of their relationships to other crime rate variables.

Table 11–6. Relationship of Service Policies to Larceny Controlling the Major Ecological Variables: 49 Largest U.S. Cities, 1970

Service Policies	Simple r	Regression Coefficient	Partial r	R² Change	F
For Opportunities					
P–40 Pupil–Teacher Ratio	–.131	–12.157	–.307	.056	3.45
For Environment					
P–36 Public Housing	.058	368.349	.180	.019	1.11
P–79 Urban Renewal Approved	.143	.673	.172	.018	1.01
P–38 Leisure Expenditure	.080	–7.686	–.189	.021	1.22

Note: The ecological variables controlled are: % Population Under 18; % Change in Rental Housing; Inequal Distribution of Family Income; and % Multi-Dwellings.

Table 11–7. Relationship of Service Policies to Auto Theft Controlling the Major Ecological Variables: 49 Largest U.S. Cities, 1970

Service Policies	Simple r	Regression Coefficient	Partial r	R² Change	F
For Environment					
P–38 Leisure Expenditure	–.124	–12.684	–.355	.052	4.77

Note: The ecological variables controlled are: % Commercial and Industrial Property; % Primary Male; % Change in Rental Housing; and Median Adult Education.

Auto Theft

Only a single policy measure—expenditures for leisure programs—is significantly correlated with auto theft, as reported in Table 11–7. The higher the level of per capita expenditures for municipal parks and recreation, the lower the rate of auto theft is in that city. This finding renders a credence to the often-made-argument that auto theft is a pastime for many idle, unoccupied teenagers seeking pleasure-riding, and constructive recreation programs may help keep such "adventure-seeking" youngsters from delinquent activities.

SUMMARY

Figure 11–1 is a schematic summary of the preceding seven tables. Ten of the 16 social service policy measures are significantly correlated with 1 or more of the 4 crime rate variables (willful homicide, robbery, larceny, and auto theft). The most striking of the findings is that all the policy measures showing a positive impact on a crime variable are the environment policy measures and all the policy measures displaying a negative impact are the opportunity policy measures.[8]

When the comparative experiences of the 49 largest cities in the

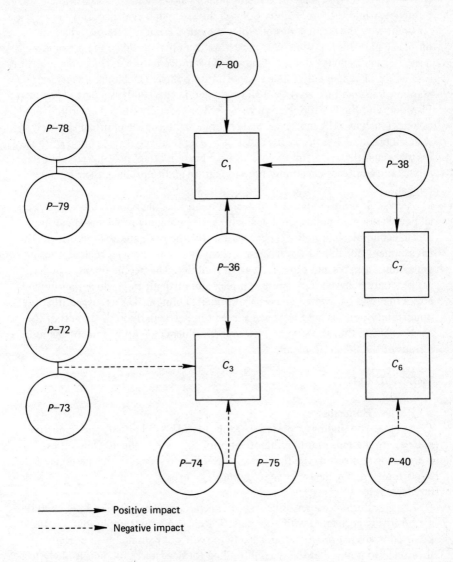

Figure 11–1. The Configuration Pattern of Crime Rates and Social Service Policy Measures: 49 Largest U.S. Cities

United States alone are considered, we find a distinct pattern of the policy–crime relationships—that is, the environment policies alone tend to have a crime-reducing influence, while the opportunity policies show no such evidence. It is not apparent why the 2 categories of policy measures demonstrate such distinct influence patterns for crime tendencies. We can only speculate the possible reasons, such as policy duration and the substantive nature of the policy measures.

The federally funded opportunity policies (including Headstart, OEO, Manpower, Small Business) were all originated in the 1960s as a part of the New Frontiers and the Great Society programs. The federally funded environment policies (such as FHA mortgage, low-rent public housing, and urban renewal) were all originated in the 1930s and 1940s. The relatively short period of time during which the opportunity policies have been in effect may suggest that the opportunity policies need more time to mature and to produce their intended impact.[9]

It is also important to bear in mind that the opportunity policies are all people-oriented policies and deal with such intangible problems as cultural, social, economic, and political deprivations for the poor and the minorities. The environment policies, however, are primarily hardware policies such as housing, sanitation, or parks and other recreation facilities. The people-oriented policies are generally believed to be more complex and difficult to produce their intended effect than the hardware policies. This understanding makes us suspect that the opportunity policies have not been successful, particularly in the largest of the nation's cities, thus showing no measurable influence on crime, one of the more serious of the urban problems.

THE OHIO CITIES

Homicide

The findings reported in Table 11–8 show that only the opportunity policies are the important predictors of homicide rate in the 40 Ohio cities. This is a striking contrast to the findings of the U.S. cities analysis, where none of the opportunity policy measures were found to be even moderately correlated with homicide rate.

Both measures of headstart expenditures (per poor and per capita) are positively correlated with homicide. These correlations imply that a better financed headstart program is not likely to reduce the homicide rate. Rather, they seem to imply that the federal funding for headstart programs is likely to be more generous to those cities where social problems are more rampant including a high rate of criminal homicide.

Forcible Rape

Low-rent public housing is the only policy variable significantly correlated with forcible rape as shown in Table 11–9. Contrary to the experiences of the largest U.S. cities, the Ohio cities' experiences tend to suggest that

Table 11–8. Relationship of Service Policies to Willful Homicide
Controlling the Major Ecological Variables: 40 Largest Ohio Cities,
1970

Service Policies	Simple r	Regression Coefficient	Partial r	R² Change	F
For Opportunity					
P–38 Headstart/Poor	.292	.046	.257	.017	2.48
P–39 Headstart/Capita	.372	.378	.249	.016	2.31
P–40 OEO/Poor	.523	.068	.231	.014	1.98
P–41 OEO/Capita	.729	.539	.213	.012	1.66

Note: The ecological variables controlled are: % Non-White; Total Population; and %
Change in White Population.

Table 11–9. Relationship of Service Policies to Forcible Rape
Controlling the Major Ecological Variables: 40 Largest Ohio Cities,
1970

Service Policies	Simple r	Regression Coefficient	Partial r	R² Change	F
For Opportunity					
P–41 OEO/Capita	.494	−.918	−.214	.016	1.63
P–58 Pupil–Teacher Ratio	.335	1.038	.191	.013	1.29
For Environment					
P–59 Public Housing	.558	.075	.243	.021	2.13
P–49 Leisure Expenditure	.324	−.258	−.193	.013	1.31

Note: The ecological variables controlled are: Total Population; % Non-White; Population
Density; and % Primary Male.

public housing is likely to contribute to a higher rate of forcible rape. Of course,
it is a widely held belief that crime is heavily concentrated in public housing com-
plexes and the opponents of public housing often use crime as one of the reasons
for their objection to new construction of public housing.[10]

Robbery

The relationship of social service policy measures to robbery in the
Ohio cities is remarkably similar to that for the U.S. cities. As shown in
Table 11–10, the opportunity policy correlates are positive, while the environ-
ment policy correlates are inverse.

Aggravated Assault

The social service policy correlates of aggravated assault are generally
comparable with those of robbery. As Table 11–11 indicates, 5 of the opportunity policy measures are positively correlated with criminal assault while a single
environment policy variable—urban renewal-approved—is inversely correlated

Table 11–10.   Relationship of Service Policies to Robbery Controlling the Major Ecological Variables: 40 Largest Ohio Cities, 1970

Service Policies	Simple r	Regression Coefficient	Partial r	R^2 Change	F
For Opportunities					
P–38 Headstart/Poor	.285	.728	.271	.010	2.69
P–39 Headstart/Capita	.410	7.917	.339	.015	4.40
P–40 OEO/Poor	.558	1.263	.273	.010	2.73
P–41 OEO/Capita	.810	11.817	.300	.012	3.36
P–58 Pupil–Teacher Ratio	.226	−7.355	−.187	.005	1.23
For Environment					
P–47 Urban Renewal Disbursed	.597	−.528	−.220	.006	1.72
P–49 Leisure Expenditure	.406	−2.669	−.250	.008	2.27

Note: The ecological variables controlled are: % Female-Headed Families; Total Population; High School Dropouts by Youth; and % Change in White Population.

Table 11–11.   Relationship of Service Policies to Aggravated Assault Controlling the Major Ecological Variables: 40 Largest Ohio Cities, 1970

Service Policies	Simple r	Regression Coefficient	Partial r	R^2 Change	F
For Opportunities					
P–38 Headstart/Poor	.318	.747	.177	.022	1.16
P–40 OEO/Poor	.200	1.265	.225	.035	1.91
P–41 OEO/Capita	.407	8.172	.191	.025	1.36
P–42 Manpower/Poor	.560	.349	.316	.069	3.99
P–57 School Expenditure/Pupil	.058	.151	.254	.045	2.48
For Environment					
P–46 Urban Renewal Approved	.160	−.253	−.187	.024	1.31

Note: The ecological variables controlled are: % Female-Headed Families; and Population Density.

with it. However, only 2 of the opportunity policy variables—expenditures for manpower training per poor and school expenditures per pupil—are statistically significant. Nevertheless, the positive correlations are a clear enough indication that a higher level of spending for manpower training or a higher level of spending for local schools is unlikely to have a crime-reducing influence among the Ohio cities.

Burglary

As reported in Table 11–12, both the opportunity and the environment policy measures are positively correlated with burglary rate. When federal

Table 11–12. Relationship of Service Policies to Burglary Controlling the Major Ecological Variables: 40 Largest Ohio Cities, 1970

Service Policies	Simple r	Regression Coefficient	Partial r	R² Change	F
For Opportunities					
P–38 Headstart/Poor	.383	2.446	.245	.012	2.11
P–39 Headstart/Capita	.480	18.082	.204	.008	1.43
P–40 OEO/Poor	.256	3.545	.250	.012	2.21
P–44 OEO/Capita	.610	24.656	.226	.010	1.77
P–42 Manpower/Poor	.685	.681	.249	.012	2.19
P–43 Manpower/Capita	.792	9.481	.389	.029	5.87
P–44 Small Business/Poor	.061	−1.160	−.174	.006	1.03
For Environment					
P–46 Urban Renewal Approved	.541	.742	.225	.010	1.76
P–47 Urban Renewal Disbursed	.656	2.988	.368	.026	5.16

Note: The ecological variables controlled are: % Female-Headed Families; Population Density; % Male Teenagers; High School Dropouts by Youth; and % Change in White Population.

expenditures for headstart programs per poor person, federal expenditures for OEO programs per poor person, expenditures for manpower training programs per poor as well as per capita, and urban renewal expenditures per capita (disbursed) are higher, the burglary rate tends to be also higher. The urban renewal variable is, however, found to be inversely correlated with other crime rate variables.

Auto Theft

Both measures of the manpower policy, one of the urban renewal variables (disbursed), and municipal expenditures for leisure time activities are all powerful predictors of auto theft rate as shown in Table 11–13. The more resources are committed to manpower training, urban renewal, and leisure time activities, the more likely the auto theft rate tends to be significantly lower. The OEO expenditure variable does not follow this general pattern with a positive correlation with auto theft.

SUMMARY

Ten of the 14 social service policy variables are significantly correlated with 1 or more of the 6 crime rate variables. The pattern of their interrelationships is schematically illustrated in Figure 11–2. In general, those social service policies expected to enhance the future opportunities for the disadvantaged tend to show a negative impact on various crimes and those policies instrumental for the improvement of the environmental quality of urban life tend to show a positive

Table 11–13.   Relationship of Service Policies to Auto Theft Controlling the Major Ecological Variables: 40 Largest Ohio Cities, 1970

Service Policies	Simple r	Regression Coefficient	Partial r	R² Change	F
For Opportunities					
P–39 OEO/Capita	.640	47.709	.258	.020	2.42
P–42 Manpower/Poor	.270	−1.071	−.264	.021	2.56
P–43 Manpower/Capita	.429	−12.061	−.276	.023	2.79
For Environment					
P–47 Urban Renewal Disbursed	.348	−4.477	−.404	.049	6.64
P–49 Leisure Expenditure	.212	−20.436	−.403	.049	6.60

Note: The ecological variables controlled are: % Non-White; Total Population; Median Value of Owner-Occupied Housing; and % Change in Total Population.

impact on crimes. However, this generalization is not fully consistent. For example, federal expenditures for manpower training per poor (P–42)—an opportunity policy variable—shows a positive impact on auto theft (C_7), while displaying a negative impact on aggravated assault (C_4) and burglary (C_5). Per capita urban renewal expenditures (P–47)—a policy for environment—show a negative impact on burglary (C_5) and a positive impact on auto theft (C_7).

COMPARISON OF SOCIAL SERVICE POLICY IMPACT: U.S. CITIES AND OHIO CITIES

As listed in Table 11–14, 7 of the social service policy variables are strong predictors for 1 or more crime rate variables in both U.S. cities and Ohio cities. They include 3 of the environment policy measures and 4 of the opportunity policy measures. Three opportunity policy variables—headstart expenditures per capita and per poor and school expenditures per pupil—are salient influences on crimes in Ohio cities only. In contrast, 2 policy variables for environment—FHA mortgage and urban renewal (approved)—and 1 opportunity policy variable—pupil—teacher ratio—are important only for U.S. cities.

The social service policy measures are almost fully comparable for both city groups. Their influence on crimes in Ohio cities is, however, more wide-ranging than in the national sample cities, but the influence pattern in the Ohio cities is less consistent and more complex than the one for the national sample cities. In both sets of the sample, one generalization stands out: the people-related policies that strive to enhance the social and economic opportunities for the disadvantaged tend to show little evidence of crime-reducing impact, where-as the hardware-related policies that attempt to improve the quality of urban environment tend to show a strong evidence of crime-reducing impact.

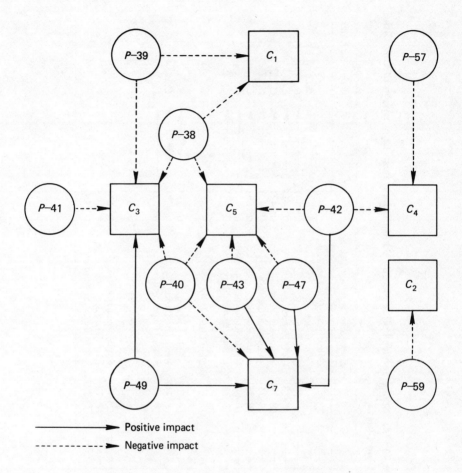

Figure 11–2. The Configuration Pattern of Crime Rates and
Social Service Policy Measures: 40 Largest Ohio Cities

Table 11–14.   Social Service Policy Measures and Crime Rates: Comparison of U.S. Cities and Ohio Cities

Crime Variables (U.S. Cities)		Social Service Policy Measures		Crime Variables (Ohio Cities)
		Common to U.S. Cities and Ohio Cities		
C_3	(P–72)	OEO/Poor	(P–40)	C_3, C_5, C_7
C_3	(P–73)	OEO/Capita	(P–41)	C_3
C_3	(P–74)	Manpower/Poor	(P–42)	C_4, C_5, C_7
C_3	(P–75)	Manpower/Capita	(P–43)	C_5, C_7
C_1, C_3	(P–36)	Public Housing	(P–59)	C_2
C_7, C_1	(P–80)	Urban Renewal Disbursed	(P–47)	C_5, C_7
C_7, C_1	(P–38)	Leisure Expenditure	(P–49)	C_3, C_7
		Ohio Cities Only		
	(P–70)	Headstart/Poor	(P–38)	C_1, C_3, C_5
	(P–71)	Headstart/Capita	(P–39)	C_1, C_3
	(P–39)	School Expenditure	(P–57)	C_4
		U.S. Cities Only		
C_6	(P–40)	Pupil–Teacher Ratio	(P–58)	
C_1	(P–78)	FHA Mortgage	(—)	
C_1	(P–79)	Urban Renewal Approved	(P–46)	

NOTES TO CHAPTER ELEVEN

1. Each of the specific policy measures is listed in Table 8–3 in Chapter 8.
2. Edward C. Banfield, *The Unheavenly City* (Boston: Little, Brown, and Co., 1970), p. 162.
3. Robert Coles' works on various groups of American poor in rural as well as urban areas shed a new light on the life of these economically and socially disadvantaged groups including, perhaps, those living in public housing. See, for example, the cover story of *Time*, February 14, 1972.
4. Marvin E. Wolfgang, "A Sociological Analysis of Criminal Homicide," in Bruce J. Cohen (ed.), *Crime in America*, pp. 52–60. The quotation is from p. 54.
5. Banfield, *The Unheavenly City*, pp. 175–6.
6. The pattern of CAP funds allocation among the states reveals a high correlation with the percentage of poor population which is urban. See Andrew T. Cowart, "Anti-Poverty Expenditures in the American States: A Comparative Analysis," *Midwest Journal of Political Science*, 13 (May, 1969), pp. 219–236.
7. For example, the percent increase in rental housing was inversely correlated with larceny contrary to a logical expectation although it was positively correlated with forcible rape and auto theft. See Tables 9–6, 9–2, and 9–7 of Chapter 9.
8. When a higher level of policy is associated with a lower level of crime, we call it as having a positive impact, while we call it a negative impact when a higher level of policy is associated with a higher rate of crime.
9. Since the Nixon Administration has virtually abandoned the Great Society programs, there is no possibility for testing the maturity hypothesis for the opportunity policies.
10. In the late 1950s, an alleged high crime incidence in public housing complex was one of the top reasons used by the Newark City Council in its opposition to the new construction of additional public housing units. See Harold Kaplan, *Urban Renewal Politics: Slum Clearance in Newark* (New York: Columbia University Press, 1963), p. 158.

Chapter Twelve

Conclusion: Alternatives for Policy Innovation

How effective is public policy in preventing or deterring crime in American cities? Do the existing measures of public policy offer possible solutions to the crime problems of the cities? In search of the answers to these questions, we analyzed the recent experience of the 49 largest cities in the United States and that of the 40 largest cities in the state of Ohio.

It is apparent from our findings that the public policy implications for the criminal tendency in our sample cities are highly complex and often ambiguous. However, one overall generalization stands out: the existing policy measures are rather unlikely to bring about a drastic reversal in the crime tendency in the cities. Simply, the evidence of crime-reducing effect of the policy measures is too modest to imply that the crime rate variance among the cities is primarily a function of the public policy variance. Here we will attempt to recapitulate the policy implications of our findings and to set forth some alternative approaches.

PUBLIC POLICY AND URBAN CRIME

Police Policy

Those measures of police policy that we tested in this study tend to show no evidence of crime-reducing effects. The lack of such evidence warrants a conclusion that police policy is not an effective means for reducing the crime rate, contrary to the belief of conventional wisdom. Conventional wisdom is disposed to the belief that strong law enforcement and criminal justice policies, particularly strong police, are better able to control crime. In fact, it is this belief that has always dominated the directions of crime control policy.

As the crime rate rises, the cities throughout the nation have rapidly increased their police budgets, police personnel, equipment, and facilities. The strengthening of such police policies, however, has not brought about the corresponding reduction in crime rate. Rather, the rate of some crimes is found to be significantly higher in those cities where the level of some measures of police policy is higher. It does not make sense to think that this relationship between police policy and crime rate is an indication that the police is an influence contributing to a higher crime rate. What seems to be more logical as an explanation of this relationship is as follows: When the crime rate rises, the political pressure also mounts in demand of more effective crime control measures. The resulting policy response is most likely to be the expansion of police policy, but an expansive police policy simply does not lower the crime rate.[1]

Some recent experiments of police policy tend to confirm our conclusion that police policy does not deter crime. The Police Foundation in cooperation with the Kansas City Police Department tested the effect of police patrol on crime rate in a year-long experiment from October 1, 1972, to September 30, 1973. Specifically, this experiment tested whether or not various intensities of police patrol differently affect the crime rate of patrolled areas whose ecological environments were comparable. Patrol cars were assigned to selectively matched areas of the city in 3 variations; no regular patrol car, 1 patrol car, and 4 or 5 patrol cars. A preliminary result of this test indicated that the difference in the patrol car assignment was found to make no difference in the level of reported crime during the test period.[2]

Team policing is considered as a new and innovative method for improving the crime-controlling ability of the police. A study, sponsored again by the Police Foundation, describes the concept of team policing in terms of operational elements and organizational supports as follows: operational elements—(1) geographical stability of patrol (that is, permanent assignment of teams of police to small neighborhoods), (2) maximum interaction among team members, and (3) maximum communication among team members and the community; organizational supports—(1) unity of supervision, (2) lower-level flexibility in policy-making, (3) unified delivery of services, and (4) combined investigative and patrol functions.[3]

The Police Foundation study is not focused on the assessment of the team-policing effect on crime rate. However, considering the fact that the team-policing method itself was devised to make the crime control of the police more effective, it is important to notice that the team-policing impact on crime reduction is uncertain at best. The comments by Chief Sardino on the team-policing experience of Syracuse offer an insight:

> The original purpose of the experiment was to demonstrate that the CCT (Crime Control Team) organizational concept was a more effective way to control crime. Early in the program the difficulty (if not impossibility) of demonstrating this premise became obvious.[4]

Our findings and the results of recent police experiments cited above clearly suggest that the excessive reliance of the current crime control policy on the police activities, particularly the police patrol, is unjustifiable and lacks rationality. A dominant proportion of the local criminal justice budget is devoted to the police activities.[5] Police patrol takes up a dominant share of police activity time budget.[6] Thus, the patrol-oriented police policy and the police-oriented criminal justice policy may offer psychological comfort to the citizens, but not effective crime reduction.

Judicial Policy

Two measures of judicial policy are tested in our study: per capita expenditures for courts and percent prison inmates not serving sentence (mostly pretrial incarceration). In spite of the particular importance of a fair and prompt trial in the American concept of justice, the courts have become a bottleneck of the criminal justice process in many cities. The backlogs in court dockets have made it impossible to provide prompt adjudication of cases. The arbitrary imposition of bail, practiced ubiquitously, tends to be discriminatory of the poor because they are often unable to post bail bonds and thus suffer incarceration even before trial and conviction. Again due to backlogs in dockets, the settlement of cases by plea bargaining seems to have replaced the standard judicial procedure of settling a case by trial.[7] These conditions are believed to have a deteriorating effect on the quality of justice, and thus impede the deterrence of crime.

The level of resources made available to the court system and the extent of pretrial incarceration represent only a small part of the multidimensional quality of the court policy. Neither of the 2 policy measures, however, demonstrate their importance as a deterrent of crime. Since our measures of court policy do not represent a broad range of judicial policy, this evidence is too inconclusive to say that judicial policies are not an effective deterrent of crime. But our findings certainly tempt us to conclude that while more resources in support of court operations and less discriminatory incarceration before trial may not necessarily help reduce the crime rate, such measures may improve the quality of justice.

Corrections Policy

Our measures of corrections policy represent a diverse dimension of prison policies, including prison personnel and prison facilities, although they fail to include any measures of the community-based corrections policies. The prison policy measures are the only areas of control policies tested here that consistently display strong evidence of crime-reducing effects. After all, it is the corrections system that is responsible for rehabilitating the criminal convicts and for breaking down the vicious cycle of recidivism.

The case for prison reform has been made repeatedly and sometimes dramatically by study commissions and individual experts.[8] A variety of innovative and experimental programs have been adopted by state and local correctional institutions. One of the more visible changes can be found in federal law enforcement grant policies. The federal emphasis of law enforcement grants to state and local governments shifted from police to corrections soon after the inauguration of the LEEA grant programs. As far as the allocation pattern of total criminal justice resources indicates, however, the corrections programs are still far from commanding the level of priority they deserve within the criminal justice system.[9]

Centralism—Decentralism

The effect of centralism vs. decentralism in management of organizations has long been an interesting issue to the students of public administration. We tested the implications of the local decentralism of criminal justice operations in controlling crime. The evidence we uncovered suggests that whether the organization of criminal justice operations in state-centralized or local-decentralized hardly makes any difference in the pattern of the crime rate variance.

Social Service Policies for Opportunity

The opportunity policy measures (such as Headstart, OEO, Manpower Training, Small Business, and those for public education) are designed as the vehicle through which a greater equity in the opportunity structure of the American society can be achieved for its poor and minorities. We assume that the improved equity in the opportunity structure is to help dissipate the crime-inducive influence in the society, thus making an indirect contribution to the prevention of crime. The results of our analysis, however, show little evidence to suggest that opportunity policy measures contribute to crime prevention in our sample cities.

There seems to be at least two important reasons that are helpful in explaining why our opportunity policy measures do not show a crime-preventive impact. First, our opportunity policy measures are funded by federal government and are recent in origin (of course, local public school policy is an exception). However, they are the kind of programs whose benefits are neither immediate nor certain. In this sense, our findings may imply that the benefits of our opportunity policy measures have not yet sufficiently materialized to make a measurable impact on the crime rate pattern. Second, the opportunity policy measures have been underfinanced and neglected from the early stages of their initiation because of the heavy drain on the federal treasury for the expensive and prolonged war in Vietnam. In the late 1960s, these programs reached the stage of virtual abandonment because of the lack of sufficient funds. For this reason, it is probable that the insufficient funding has caused the failure of these programs to produce their intended effect.

Social Service Policies for Environment

Unlike the opportunity policies, our environmental policy measures (such as low-rent public housing, FHA mortgage, urban renewal, municipal sanitation, and municipal leisure time programs) have long been established and their benefits are usually immediate rather than futuristic. Our measures of environmental policies are most consistent of all policy categories in demonstrating a significant crime-reducing influence.

POLICY ALTERNATIVES

Empirical and quantitative analysis of social problems such as our present study has its own pitfalls. The most dangerous of such pitfalls seems to be a possible indulgence in trivia merely because they are conducive to conceptualization, measurement, and interpretation. This is the danger that Dr. Rene Dubos referred to when he said, "The more measurable tends to drive out the more important."[10] The public policy measures we tested, the crime variables we analyzed, and the socio-economic variables we examined in this study are believed to represent most of the more important variables for our purposes. These variables are highly complex and often exceedingly subtle in their substantive nature. We made every effort possible to use the best data available and to use the best technique for their analysis. Our efforts and precaution, however, do not provide assurance of the accuracy of our findings, but they offer some important reasons to trust their reliability.

No matter how public policy may be manipulated, it will not be able to eliminate crime for it is but a small link in the big chain that binds together society, morality, government, and legality into an ordered and functioning system. Governmental policy cannot (or should not if it can) control the entirety of social environment in which crime is rooted, nor should it control the entire range of social behavior of the citizens of which criminal behavior is also a part, particularly under the American concept and idea of governance and public policy. It is rather natural to recognize the limitation of the role of public policy in crime control as demonstrated by the outcomes of our analyses here.[11] The reordering of the policy priorities will not bring a miracle of reversing the crime trends drastically, but it will bring about a better result in the prevention and deterrence of crime within the limits.

As became apparent in the preceding discussion of our findings, 2 policy areas deserve the highest priority. They are corrections policy and social service policy for environment. More resources should be devoted to corrections policies in general and the prison policies in particular. Included in the latter are the expansion of prison personnel, the furtherance of their professionalism, and the improvement of prison facilities, especially more space to prevent overcrowdedness. We urge a shifting of the emphasis of local resource allocations from police programs to corrections programs to create a balance in the criminal justice system. The political impulse to expand the police operations should be firmly restrained since the criminal justice system is overshadowed by police dominance, and the police policies appear to be ineffective as a deterrent of crime.

Local expenditures for criminal justice as a percent of total local expenditures have been increasing as discussed in Chapters 6 and 7 of this volume. Logic dictates us to consider the channeling of the increasing resources for criminal justice to corrections and other programs more effective in crime-reducing influence rather than using them for the police. Our emphasis to reorder the policy priorities does not necessarily imply cutting down on police operations, for the police do perform useful functions, such as law enforcement, social services, and order maintenance, even though these functions are evidently not effective in reducing crime.[12]

More resources should be allocated to social service programs designed to enhance the environmental quality of urban life. Specifically, program expansion is urged for low-rent public housing, urban renewal, and municipal parks and recreation. However, we do not suggest that resources be shifted from the social service policies for opportunity to the social service policies for environment. We believe that while the opportunity policies, particularly those initiated and financed by the federal government, have not been given a chance to prove their effectiveness, they are conceptually sound, technically innovative, and politically progressive in dealing with the more urgent problems in the cities.

We make a specific suggestion to change the orientation of FHA mortgage policy drastically. By favoring new homes for mortgage guarantee, the FHA mortgage policy is one of the principal forces responsible for the massive suburbanization movement in post-war years. Homeownership of central city residents may be encouraged by reversing the FHA mortgage preference; namely, older homes in the central cities should be given special preferences for mortgage guarantee rather than newer homes in the suburbs. Such a deliberate policy encouraging homeownership in the central cities may improve the stability of urban neighborhoods and may slow down the suburban exodus of middle-income families and thus strengthen the crime-repulsive influence in the central cities.

More importantly, a new perspective and a new strategy for crime policy seem indispensable to make the public policy measures more effective in controlling crime. For nearly all local governments, it is customary to confine the strategic consideration of crime policy to control policies only. However, to make the governmental intervention in crime problems more effective, what seems to be most urgently needed is the development of comprehensive crime policy strategy. Such strategy should be focused on the coordination and balance-making of multiple dimensions of such public policies as control policies and social service policies, as our present analysis illustrates.

BEYOND PUBLIC POLICY

Finally, we hasten to add a moralistic note on the issue of crime control, although this concern is outside the main province of this book. Essentially, crime is an act in violation of the law. No matter what the government may do in the form of control or service policies, the crisis of urban crime is unlikely to recede unless the authority of the law is enhanced. In a moralistic sense, the citizens must obey the law not necessarily because they are afraid of the consequence of breaking the law, but because they respect the moral authority of the law—that is to say, the belief that what is legal is also morally just and fair must compel the citizens to obey the law voluntarily. So viewed, the current crisis of crime reflects the deteriorated authority of the law. Some of the more direct reasons that account for the deterioration of the authority of the law may include: (1) the abuse of the law by the powerful and the rich; (2) the change in the perception of what is meant by the law; (3) the increasing anachronism in the statutory provisions, which render them unenforceable.

For example, the National Advisory Commission on Criminal Justice Standards and Goals concluded in its recent report that a major source of crime in the streets is corruption in government.[13] Corruption in government may take many different forms. Rigging the law behind the shield of power and influence by high governmental officials for their personal gains of political or economic advantages at the expense of public interest is bound to weaken the authority of the law in the eyes of the public. Other actions and inactions of governmental authority, either illegal or morally dubious, are bound to cause public distrust in government and public contempt of the law.[14]

The so-called "preconventional" morality appears to rise among the racial minorities (the blacks in particular) and the poor in the nation's cities.[15] It is evident, for example, the black minority in the urban ghettoes see the law of America as the law for the protection of the white and the rich as much as they see two societies in America; one white and one black, separate and unequal.[16] The belief of a substantial minority that the law of the land does not serve their interest as it does others is destined to create a massive erosion in the authority of the law.

Often, many of the criminal statutes are anachronistic and unenforceable. The case in point is the nation's drug laws and other statutes dealing with the so-called victimless crimes. For example, the penalty for the violation of marijuana laws in the state of Ohio is so severe that strict enforcement of the laws seems next to impossible. The possession of marijuana for sale, for instance, calls for a minimum sentence of 10 years of imprisonment and a maximum sentence of 20 years of imprisonment and the actual sale calls for doubling the sentence stipulated for the possession for sale.[17]

In short, a society may become free from the crisis of crime only when the legal order of the society and the ways the legal power is used in the society are believed to be morally just by its citizens. Then, the law of the society will possess the moral authority not because the law is merely *legal* and *punitive,* but because the law is *just* and *fair.* When the moral authority of the law is challenged in a society, the influence of its public policy cannot remain effective as a deterrent to crime.

NOTES TO CHAPTER TWELVE

1. There are other possible interpretations of this relationship. For example, it has often been suggested that whenever the police force is increased, the additional police officers available make it possible to keep the records of criminal statistics more accurately and more completely, thus reporting more of the crime incidence that was not attended to previously. A more cynical view suggests that police departments tend to inflate the crime statistics in order to justify the increase of the police budget for more personnel and equipment. Considering the possibility that the underreporting of criminal incidence is likely to be lessened under both of the circumstances, it is understandable to see that a higher level of police policy and a higher rate of crime are a concurrent phenomenon.

2. David Burnham, "A Police Study Challenges Value of Anticrime Patrol," *The New York Times* (November 11, 1973), p. 1, c. 5–6 and p. 67, c. 1.

3. Lawrence W. Sherman *et al, Team Policing: Seven Case Studies* (Washington, D.C.: Police Foundation, 1973), pp. 3–7.

4. Sherman *et al., ibid.,* pp. 37–38.

5. For a recent example, the estimated expenditures for criminal justice in New York City during the 1972–73 fiscal year show that expenditures for the police department accounted for 73.5 percent of $1,354 million expended for criminal justice. Police patrol alone accounted for 55.3 percent ($749 million) of the total. Lesley Oelsner, "Courts are Found Unable to Deter Crime in the City," *The New York Times* (April 15, 1973), p. 1, c. 1 and p. 54, c. 1–5.

6. The breakdown of police time spent on various activity categories of the Syracuse Police Department shows that patrol takes up most of the police time. See James Q. Wilson, *Varieties of Police Behavior: The Management of Law and Order in Eight Communities* (Cambridge, Mass.: Harvard University Press, 1968).

7. For example, in the New York City court system, only 8 percent of all cases were tried rather than settled by pleas in 1972. This was an improvement over the previous year when only 3 percent were tried. See Lesley Oelsner, *op. cit.*

8. See, for example, Karl Menninger, *The Crime of Punishment* (New York: The Vikings Press, 1968); and The President's Commission on Law Enforcement and Administration of Justice, Task Force Report,

Corrections (Washington, D.C.: U.S. Government Printing Office, 1967).

9. For example, all local governments in the United States are considered together, expenditures for corrections accounted for 12.9 percent of total expenditures for criminal justice during the 1970–71 fiscal year, a slight increase from 10.2 percent in the 1968–69 fiscal year. See Table 5–5 in Chapter 5 of this volume.

10. This quotation was cited from Herman S. Somers "Delivery and Financing of Health Care: Movement and Change," in *Exploring the Future of Health Care,* The Maxwell Summer Lecture Series (Syracuse University, 1973), p. 27.

11. This point was one of the central themes incisively treated by Edward C. Banfield, in his book,*The Unheavenly City,* This was also the point that provoked a great deal of hostile comments on the book.

12. Our follow-up analysis, however, indicates that the measures of police policy tend to show their effectiveness in increasing the rate of apprehension of the criminal suspects.

13. This particular conclusion drawn by the commission was editorialized by the *Akron Beacon Journal,* November 28, 1973, p. A6.

14. A case in point is the 1970 tragedy at Kent State University. The deaths of 4 students and several injuries by the National Guardmen's gunshots have never been fully investigated by the federal grand jury in spite of persistent public demands, including a petition for such an action to the President of the United States with 50,000 signatures. Only in December 1973—after more than three and a half years following the event—the Department of Justice of the United States announced its decision to impanel a grand jury to investigate the case.

15. The preconventional morality is defined as follows: "One whose morality is 'preconventional' understands a 'right' action to be one that will serve his purpose and that can be gotten away with; a 'wrong' action is one that will bring ill success or punishment." Cited from Edward C. Banfield, *The Unheavenly City,* p. 161.

16. See *Report of the National Advisory Commission on Civil Disorders* (New York: A Bantam Book, 1968).

17. The exceedingly harsh punishment for the violation of marijuana laws is obvious when the minimum sentence for marijuana law violation is compared with the minimum sentence for other crimes. The Ohio penal codes stipulate a 3-year minimum sentence for the following crimes: robbery by force, assault with the intent to kill, and maiming and disfiguring another. This information is drawn from Timothy H. Smith, "A Critical Analysis of Ohio Drug Policy Pertaining to Marijuana Laws," A Graduate Seminar Paper (The Department of Urban Studies, The University of Akron, 1973).

Bibliography

BOOKS

Abbott, David W., Louis H. Gold, and Edward T. Rogowsky. *Police, Politics, and Race.* New York: The American Jewish Committee, 1969.

Alper, Benedict Solomon. *Crime: International Agenda; Concern and Action in the Prevention of Crime and Treatment of Offenders, 1846–1972.* Lexington, Mass.: Lexington Books, 1972.

Amir, M. *Patterns in Forcible Rape.* Chicago: University of Chicago Press, 1971.

Anslinger, H.J. and William F. Tompkins. *The Traffic in Narcotics.* New York: Funk and Wagnalls Co., 1953.

Banfield, Edward C. *The Unheavenly City.* Boston: Little, Brown and Company, 1970.

Becker, Theodore Lewis and Vernon G. Murray (eds.). *Government Lawlessness in America.* New York: Oxford University Press, 1971.

Blackburn, Sara. *White Justice: Black Experience Today in America's Courtrooms.* New York: Harper & Row, 1971.

Blalock, Hubert M. *Social Statistics.* New York: McGraw-Hill, 1960.

Bordua, David J. (ed.). *The Police: Six Sociological Essays.* New York: Wiley & Sons, 1967.

Brager, George A. and Francis P. Purcell. *Community Action Against Poverty.* New Haven: College and University Press, 1967.

Burgess, Ernest W. (ed.). *The Urban Community.* Chicago: University of Chicago Press, 1926.

Cabe, June G. *The States and Criminal Justice.* Lexington: Council of State Governments, 1971.

Campbell, Alan K. (ed.). *The States and the Urban Crisis.* Englewood Cliffs: Prentice-Hall, 1970.

Campbell, Alan K. and Seymour Sacks. *Metropolitan America: Fiscal Patterns and Governmental Systems.* New York: The Free Press, 1967.

Campbell, James Sargent, Joseph R. Sahid, and David P. Stang (eds.). *Law and Order Reconsidered: Report of the Task Force on Law and Law*

Enforcement to the National Commission on the Causes and Prevention of Violence. New York: Praeger, 1970.

Cantril, Albert H. and Charles W. Roll, Jr. *Hopes and Fears of the American People,* A Potomac Associates Book. New York: Universe Books, 1971.

Cavan, Ruth. *Criminology,* 2nd Edition. New York: Crowell Company, 1955.

Cho, Yong Hyo. *Local Financing for Criminal Justice in Northeast Ohio: Patterns, Trends, and Projections.* Akron: Center for Urban Studies, University of Akron, 1972.

Clark, Joseph S., *et al.* (ed.). *Crime in Urban Society.* New York: Dunellen, 1970.

Clark, Ramsey. *Crime in America: Observations on Its Nature, Causes, and Prevention, and Control.* New York: Simon and Schuster, 1970.

Cleaver, Eldridge. *Soul On Ice.* New York: Delta, 1968.

Clinard, Marshall Barron. *Sociology of Deviant Behavior.* New York: Holt, Rinehart & Winston, 1963.

Clinard, M. and R. Quinney. *Criminal Behavior Systems: A Typology.* New York: Holt, Rinehart & Winston, 1967.

Cloward, Richard A. and Lloyd E. Ohlin. *Delinquency and Opportunity: A Theory of Delinquent Gangs.* Glencoe, Ill.: The Free Press, 1960.

Cohen, Albert. *Delinquent Boys: The Culture of the Gang .* New York: Free Press, 1955.

Cohen, Bruce J. (ed.). *Crime in America: Perspectives on Criminal and Delinquent Behavior.* Itasca, Ill.: F.E. Peacock Publishers, Inc., 1970.

Committee for Economic Development. *Reducing Crime and Assuring Justice.* New York: CED, 1972.

Committee for Economic Development. *Fiscal Issues in the Future of Federalism.* New York: CED, 1968.

Congressional Quarterly Service. *Crime and Justice in America.* Washington, D.C.: C.Q.S., 1967.

Congressional Quarterly Service. *Crime and the Law.* Washington, D.C.: C.Q.S., 1971.

Conrad, John Phillips. *Crime and Its Correction: An Interpretational Survey of Attitudes and Practices.* Berkeley: University of California Press, 1965.

Conrad, J.P. *Crime and Its Correction: International Survey of Attitudes and Practices.* Berkeley: University of California Press, 1967.

Cortés, Juan B. *Delinquency and Crime: A Biopsycho Social Approach: Empirical, Theoretical, and Practical Aspects of Criminal Behavior.* New York: Seminar Press, 1972.

Crecine, John P. *Government Problem Solving: A Computer Simulation of Municipal Budgeting.* Chicago: Rand McNally, 1968.

Cressy, Donald Ray. *Crime and Criminal Justice.* Chicago: Quadrangle Books, 1971.

Cressy, Donald R. *Principles of Criminology.* Philadelphia: Lippincott Co., 1966.

Dawidowicz, Lucy S. *The 1966 Elections: A Political Patchwork.* New York: The American Jewish Committee, April, 1967.

Douglas, Jack D. (ed.). *Crime and Justice in American Society.* Indianapolis: Bobbs-Merrills, 1971.

Downes, D.M. *The Delinquent Solution: A Study in Subcultural Theory.* New York: Free Press, 1966.

Dye, Thomas R. *Politics, Economics, and the Public.* Chicago: Rand McNally, 1966.

Eysenck, H.J. *Crime and Personality.* Boston: Houghton Mifflin, 1964.

Fleisher, Belton, *Economics of Delinquency.* Chicago: Quadrangle Press, 1966.

Gardner, Erle Stanley, *Cops on Campus and Crime in the Streets.* New York: Morrow, 1970.

Gardiner, John A. *The Politics of Corruption: Organized Crime in an American City.* New York: Russell Sage Publications, 1970.

Gerber, Rudolph J. *Contemporary Punishment: Views, Explanations, and Justifications.* University of Notre Dame Press, 1972.

Gibbons, Don C. *Changing the Lawbreaker: The Treatment of Delinquents and Criminals.* Englewood Cliffs: Prentice-Hall, 1965.

Glaser, Daniel. *Crime in the City.* New York: Harper & Row, 1970.

Glaser, Daniel. *Adult Crime and Social Policy.* Prentice-Hall, 1972.

Glaser, Daniel. *The Effectiveness of a Prison and Parole System.* Indianapolis: Bobbs-Merrill, 1964.

Halleck, Seymour L. *Psychiatry and the Dilemmas of Crime.* New York: Hoeber Medical Books, 1967.

Haskell, Martin R. and Lewis Yablonsky. *Crime and Delinquency.* Chicago: Rand McNally, 1970.

Hills, Stuart L. *Crime, Power, and Morality; Criminal Law Process in the United States.* Scranton: Chandler Pub., 1971.

Hood, Roger G. *Key Issues in Criminology.* London: Weidenfeld & Nicolson, 1970.

Hopkins, Ernest Jerome. *Our Lawless Police: A Study of the Unlawful Enforcement of Law.* New York: Da Capo, 1972, copyright 1931.

James, Howard. *Crisis in the Courts.* New York: D. McKay Co., 1971.

Jeffery, Clarence Ray. *Crime Prevention Through Environmental Design.* Beverly Hills: Sage Publications, 1971.

Johnston, Norman Bruce. *The Sociology of Punishment and Correction.* New York: John Wiley, 1970.

Jones, Howard. *Crime and the Penal System.* London: University Tutorial Press, 1965.

Jones, Howard. *Crime in a Changing Society.* Penguin Books, 1969.

Kaplan, Harold. *Urban Renewal Politics: Slum Clearance in Newark.* New York: Columbia University Press, 1963.

Kerper, Hazel B. *Introduction to Criminal Justice System.* St. Paul: West Pub. Co., 1972.

Kirkham, J.F., G. Levy, and W.J. Crotty. *Assassination and Political Violence.* New York: Bantam, 1970.

Klonoski, James Richard and Robert I. Mendelsohn (eds.). *The Politics of Local Justice.* Boston: Little, Brown and Co., 1970.

Knudten, Richard D. (ed.). *Crime, Criminology, and Contemporary Society.* Homewood, Ill.: Dorsey Press, 1970.

Lander, Bernard. *Towards an Understanding of Juvenile Delinquency: A Study of 8,464 Cases of Juvenile Delinquency in Baltimore.* New York: Columbia University Press, 1954.

Leonard, Vivian Anderson. *Police Crime Prevention.* Springfield, Ill.: Thomas, 1972.

Lewin, Stephen. *Crime and Its Prevention.* New York: Wilson, 1968.

Lindesmith, Alfred R. *The Addict and the Law.* Bloomington: Indiana University Press, 1965.

Lineberry, William P. (ed.). *Justice in America: Law, Order, and the Courts.* New York: H.W. Wilson Co., 1972.

Lópes, Rey y Arrojo, Manuel. *Crime: An Analytical Appraisal.* New York: Praeger, 1970.

Lowenberg, Henry A. *Until Proven Guilty.* Boston: Little, Brown and Co., 1971.

Mannheim, Herman. *Comparative Criminology.* Boston: Houghton Mifflin, 1965.

Marris, Peter and Martin Rein. *Dilemmas of Social Reform.* New York: Atherton Press, 1967.

Mays, John Barron. *Crime and Its Treatment.* London: Longman, 1970.

McClintock, Frederick Hemming. *Crime in England and Wales.* London: Heinemann Educational, 1968.

Menninger, Karl. *The Crime of Punishment.* New York: The Viking Press, 1968.

Morris, Norval. *The Honest Politician's Guide to Crime Control.* Chicago: University of Chicago Press, 1970.

Mueller, G.O.W. *The Function of Criminology in Criminal Justice Administration.* New York: New York University, 1970.

The National Urban Coalition. *Counterbudget.* New York: Praeger Publishers, 1971.

Niederhoffer, Arthur. *Behind the Shield: The Police in Urban Society.* New York: Doubleday & Company, 1967.

Park, Robert E., Ernest W. Burgess, and Roderick D. McKenzie. *The City.* Chicago: University of Chicago Press, 1925.

Phillipson, Michael. *Sociological Aspects of Crime and Delinquency.* London: Routledge and K. Paul, 1971.

Pursuit, Dan G. *et al.* (ed.). *Police Programs for Preventing Crime and Delinquency.* Springfield, Ill.: Thomas, 1972.

Quinney, Richard. *The Problem of Crime.* New York: Dodd, Mead, 1970.

Quinney, Richard. *The Social Reality of Crime.* Boston: Little, Brown and Co., 1970.

Reasons, Charles E. *Race, Crime, and Justice.* Pacific Palisades, California: Goodyear Pub. Co., 1972.

Remington, F.J., D.J. Newman, M. Melli, E. Kimball, and H. Goldstein. *Criminal Justice Administration.* Indianapolis: Bobbs-Merrill, 1969.

Richardson, James F. *The New York Police: Colonial Times to 1901.* New York: Oxford University Press, 1970.

Roebuck, Julian B. *Criminal Typology: The Legalistic, Physical-Constitutional-Hereditary, Psychological-Psychiatric, and Sociological Approaches.* Springfield: C.C. Thomas, 1967.

Rossi, Peter H. and Walter Williams (ed.). *Evaluating Social Programs: Theory, Practice, and Politics.* New York: Seminar Press, 1972.

Scammon, Richard M. and Ben J. Wattenberg. *The Real Majority.* New York: Coward-McCann, Inc., 1970.

Schafer, Stephen. *Theories of Criminology: Past and Present Philosophies of Crime Problem.* New York: Random House, 1969.

Schar, Edwin M. *Our Criminal Society: The Social and Legal Sources of Crime in America.* Prentice-Hall, 1969.

Scheibla, Shirley. *Poverty Is Where the Money Is.* New Rochelle: Arlington House, 1968.

Sharkansky, Ira. *The Politics of Taxing and Spending.* Indianapolis: Bobbs-Merrill, 1969.

Sharkansky, Ira (ed.). *Policy Analysis in Political Science.* Chicago: Markham Publishing Company, 1970.

Shaw, Clifford R. and Henry D. McKay. *Juvenile Delinquency and Urban Areas,* Revised Edition. Chicago: University of Chicago Press, 1942, 1969.

Sherman, Lawrence W. *et al. Team Policing: Seven Case Studies.* Washington, D.C.: Police Foundation, 1973.

Shevky, Eshref and Wendell Bell. *Social Area Analysis.* Stanford University Press, 1955.

Shoham, Shlomo. *Crime and Social Deviation.* Chicago: H. Regnery Co., 1966.

Stebbins, Robert A. *Commitment to Deviance: The Nonprofessional Criminal in the Community.* Westport, Conn.: Greenwood Pub. Corp., 1971.

Stedman, Murray S. *Urban Politics.* Cambridge, Mass.: Winthrop Publishers, Inc., 1972.

Stratton, John R. and Robert M. Terry (eds.). *Prevention of Delinquency: Problems and Programs.* New York: MacMillan, 1968.

Sutherland, Edwin H. and Donald R. Cressy. *Principles of Criminology,* 7th Edition. Philadelphia: Lippincott Co., 1966.

Tappan, Paul Wilbur. *Crime, Justice and Correction.* New York: McGraw-Hill, 1960.

Taylor, Laurie. *Deviance and Society.* London: Joseph, 1971.

Turk, Austin T. *Criminality and Legal Order.* Chicago: Rand McNally, 1969.

Watt, William and Lloyd A. Free (eds.). *State of the Nation,* A Potomac Associates Book. New York: Universe Books, 1973.

Wildavsky, Aaron. *The Politics of the Budgetary Process.* Boston: Little, Brown and Co., 1964.

William, M.A.P. *Crime and Information Theory.* Edinburgh: University Press, 1970.

Willoughby, W.F. *Principles of Judicial Administration.* Washington, D.C.: The Brookings Institution, 1929.

Wilson, James Q. *Varieties of Police Behavior.* Cambridge, Mass.: Harvard University Press, 1968.

Wilson, James Q. (ed.). *City Politics and Public Policy.* New York: John Wiley & Sons, 1968.

Wolfgang, Marvin E. *Patterns of Criminal Homicide.* Philadelphia: University of Pennsylvania Press, 1958.

Wolfgang, Marvin E. *The Subculture of Violence: Towards an Integrated Theory in Criminology.* London: Tavistock Publications, 1967.

ARTICLES

Barbour, George P. and Stanley M. Wolfson. "Productivity Measurement in Police Crime Control," *Public Management.* April 1973, pp. 16–19.

Bean, Frank D. and Robert G. Cushing. "Criminal Homicide, Punishment, and Deterrence: Methodological and Substantive Reconsideration," *Social Science Quarterly,* 51. November 1971, pp. 277–289.

Bedau, Hugo Adam. "The Issue of Capital Punishment," *Current History.* August 1967, pp. 82–87 and 116.

Bloom, Murray Teigh. "On Trial: Trial by Jury," *National Civic Review.* July 1973, pp. 358–361.

Boggs, Sara. "Urban Crime Patterns," *American Sociological Review,* Vol. 30, No. 6. December 1965, pp. 899–908.

Bordua, David J. "Juvenile Delinquency and 'Anomie': An Attempt at Replication," *Social Problems,* Vol. 6, No. 3. Winter 1958, pp. 230–238.

Bourne, Peter. "Changing Federal Role in Drug Abuse Prevention," *Nation's Cities.* April 1973, pp. 9–11.

Burnham, Walter Dean and John Sprague. "Additive and Multiplicative Models of the Voting Universe: The Case of Pennsylvania, 1960–1968," *American Political Science Review,* 65. June 1970, pp. 471–490.

Campbell, Donald T. "Reforms as Experiments," *American Psychologist,* Vol. 24. April 1969, pp. 409–429.

Campbell, Donald T. "Considering the Case Against Experimental Evaluations of Social Innovations," *Administrative Science Quarterly,* Vol. 15. March 1970, pp. 110–113.

Caputo, David C. "Evaluating Urban Public Policy: A Developmental Model and Some Reservations," *Public Administration Review.* March/April 1973, pp. 113–119.

Casserly, Bernard. "One Issue: L & O," *Commonweal.* July 20, 1969.

Chackerian, Richard and Richard Barrett. "Police Professionalism and Citizen Evaluation," *Urban Affairs Quarterly.* March 1973, pp. 345–349.

Chilton, Ronald J. "Continuity in Delinquency Area Research: A Comparison of Studies for Baltimore, Detroit, and Indianapolis," *American Sociological Review,* 29. February 1964, pp. 71–83.

Cho, Yong Hyo. "A Multiple Regression Model for the Measurement of the Public Policy Impact on Big City Crime," *Policy Sciences,* 3. December 1972, pp. 435–455.

Cho, Yong Hyo. "The Effect of Local Governmental Systems on Local Policy Outcomes in the United States," *Public Administration Review.* March 1967, pp. 31–38.

"City Taxes and Services: Citizens Speak Out—An Urban Observatory Report," *Nation's Cities.* August 1971.

Cowart, Andrew. "Anti-Poverty Expenditures in the American States: A Comparative Analysis," *Midwest Journal of Political Science,* 13. May 1969, pp. 219–236.

Crowther, Carol. "Crime, Penalties, and Legislatures," *The Annals of the American Academy of Political and Social Science.* January 1969, pp. 147–158.

Cultner, Lloyd N. "Thomas Jefferson, Won't You Please Come Home?" *The Annals of the American Academy of Political and Social Science,* Vol. 396. July 1971.

Downes, B.T. "A Critical Examination of Social and Political Characteristics of Riot Cities," *Social Science Quarterly,* 50. September 1970, pp. 349–360.

Downes, B.T. "Social and Political Characteristics of Riot Cities: A Comparative Study," *Social Science Quarterly,* 48. December 1968, pp. 504–520.

Ferdinand, Theodore N. "The Criminal Patterns of Boston Since 1849," *American Journal of Sociology,* 73. July 1967, pp. 84–99.

Finestone, Harold. "Narcotics and Criminality," *Law and Contemporary Problems,* Vol. 22. Winter 1957.

Frisken, Frances. "The Metropolis and the Central City: Can One Government Unite Them?" *Urban Affairs Quarterly.* June 1973, pp. 395–422.

Germann, A.G. "The Police: A Mission and Role," *The Police Chief.* January 1970, pp. 16–19.

Gibbs, Jack P. "Crime, Punishment, and Deterrence," *Social Science Quarterly,* 48. March 1968, pp. 515–530.

Goldstein, Herman. "Police Response to Urban Crisis," *Public Administration Review,* 28. September/October 1968, pp. 417–423.

Graham, Fred P. "Black Crime: The Lawless Image," *Harper's Magazine.* September 1970, pp. 64–71.

Gray, Louis N. and J. David Martin. "Punishment and Deterrence: Another Analysis of Gibb's Data," *Social Science Quarterly,* 50. September 1969, pp. 389–395.

Guthrie, Harold W. "Microanalytic Simulation Modeling for Evaluation of Public Policy," *Urban Affairs Quarterly,* Vol. 7, No. 4. June 1972.

Harman, B. Douglas. "The Challenge of Managing Law Enforcement," *Public Management.* April 1973, pp. 2–5.

Harman, B. Douglas. "The Politics of Law Enforcement Assistance," *The Municipal Year Book, 1970.* Washington, D.C.: The International City Management Association, 1970, pp. 470–478.

Harman, B. Douglas. "Law Enforcement Assistance: Who Gets What, Where, When and How?" *The Municipal Year Book, 1971.* Washington, D.C.: The International City Management Association, 1971, pp. 53–59.

Jeffery, C.R. "Crime Prevention and Control Through Environmental Engineering," *Criminologica,* 7, 3. 1969. pp. 35–58.

Jeffery, C. Ray and Ina A. Jeffery. "Delinquents and Dropouts: An Experimental Program in Behavior Change," *Education and Urban Society,* Vol. 1, No. 3. May 1969, pp. 325–336.

Jones, E. Terrence. "Evaluating Everyday Policies: Police Activity and Crime Incidence," *Urban Affairs Quarterly.* March 1973, pp. 267–280.

Kobrin, Solomon. "The Conflict of Values in Delinquent Areas," *American Sociological Review,* 16. October 1951, pp. 653–661.

Lindblom, Charles E. "The Science of Muddling Through," *Public Administration Review,* Vol. 19. Spring 1959, pp. 79–88.

Mannheim, H. "Comparative Sentencing Practice," *Law and Contemporary Problems,* 23. 1958, pp. 557–582.

Mathis, Frank O. and Martin B. Rayman. "The Ins and Outs of Crime and Corrections," *Criminology,* Vol. 10. November 1972, pp. 366–373.

McElroy, Jerome L. and Singell, Larry D. "Riot and Nonriot Cities: An Examination of Structural Contours," *Urban Affairs Quarterly.* March 1973, pp. 281–302.

McIntyre, Jennie, "Public Attitude Toward Crime and Law Enforcement," *The Annals of the American Academy of Political and Social Science,* Vol. 374. November 1967, pp. 34–46.

Merton, Robert K. "Social Structure and Anomie," *American Sociological Review,* Vol. 3, No. 5. 1938, pp. 672–682.

Meyer (Jr.), John C. "Methodological Issues in Comparative Criminal Justice Research," *Criminology,* Vol. 10, No. 3. November 1972, pp. 295–313.

Miller, Walter B. "The Impact of a Total Community Delinquency Control Project," *Social Problems.* Fall 1962.

Moyer, K.E., "The Physiology of Violence," *Psychology Today,* Vol. 7, No. 2. July 1973, pp. 35–38.

O'Donnell, John A. "Narcotic Addiction and Crime," *Social Problems,* Vol. 13, No. 4. Spring 1966, pp. 374–385.

Ogburn, William F. "Factors in the Variation of Crime Among Cities," *Journal of American Statistical Association,* Vol. 30. March 1935, pp. 12–34.

O'Leary, V. and D. Duffee. "Correctional Policy: A Classification Designed for Change," *Crime and Delinquency.* 1971.

Ostrom, Elinor. "Institutional Arrangements and the Measurement of Policy Consequences: Applications to Evaluating Police Performance," *Urban Affairs Quarterly.* June 1971, pp. 447–476.

Ostrom, Elinor and Gordon Whitaker. "Does Local Community Control of Police Make a Difference? Some Preliminary Findings," *American Journal of Political Science,* Vol. 17, No. 1. February 1973, pp. 48–76.

Parker, Mary Hamil. "A Guide to Federal Drug Programs," *Nation's Cities.* April 1973, pp. 12–26.

Pettigrew, Thomas F. and Rosalind B. Spier. "The Ecological Structure of Negro Homicide," *The American Journal of Sociology,* Vol. 67, No. 6. May 1962, pp. 621–629.

Pittman, David J. and William Handy. "Patterns in Criminal Aggravated Assault," *Journal of Criminal Law, Criminology, and Police Science,* Vol. 55, No. 4. 1964.

Poland, Orville F. "Why Does Public Administration Ignore Evaluation," *Public Administration Review,* Vol. XXXI. March/April 1971, pp. 201–202.

Quinney, Richard. "Crime, Delinquency, and Social Areas," *Journal of Research in Crime and Delinquency,* Vol. 1, No. 2. 1964, pp. 149–154.

Quinney, Richard. "Structural Characteristics, Population Areas, and Crime Rates in the United States," *Journal of Criminal Law, Criminology, and Police Science,* Vol. 57, No. 1. 1966, pp. 45–52.

Reiss, Albert J. "Crime, Law and Order as Election Issues," *Trans-action*. October 1968, pp. 2–4.

Reiss, Jr., Albert J. and Albert Lewis Rhodes, "An Empirical Test of Differential Association Theory," *Journal of Research in Crime and Delinquency*, Vol. 1, No. 1. 1964, pp. 5–18.

Robin, Gerald D. "Anti-Poverty Programs and Delinquency," *Journal of Criminal Law, Criminology, and Police Science*, Vol. 60, No. 3. September 1969, pp. 323–331.

Robinson, Sophia M. "A Critical View of the Uniform Crime Reports," *Michigan Law Review*, 64. April 1966, pp. 1031–1054.

Romine, June and Daniel L. Skoler. "Local Government Financing and Law Enforcement," *The American County*. May 1971, pp. 17–43.

Rudolf, Alvin. "The Soaring Crime Rate—An Etiological View," *The Journal of Criminal Law, Criminology, and Police Science*. December 1971, pp. 543–546.

Savas, E.S. "Municipal Monopoly," *Harper's Magazine*. December 1971, pp. 55–60.

Schmid, Calvin F. "Urban Crime Areas: Part I," *American Sociological Review*, Vol. 25, No. 4. 1960, pp. 527–542.

Schmid, Calvin F. "Urban Crime Areas: Part II," *American Sociological Review*, Vol. 25, No. 5. 1960, pp. 655–678.

Schuessler, Karl. "Components of Variation in City Crime Rates," *Social Problems*, Vol. 9. Spring 1962, pp. 314–327.

Schuessler, Karl and Gerald Slatin. "Sources of Variation in United States City Crime," *Journal of Research in Crime and Delinquency*, Vol. 1, No. 2. 1964, pp. 127–148.

Sharkansky, Ira. "Government Expenditures and Public Services in the American States," *American Political Science Review*, 61, 4. December 1967, pp. 1066–1077.

Shipman, George A. "The Evaluation of Social Innovation," *Public Administration Review*, Vol. XXXI. March/April 1971, pp. 198–200.

Shulman, Harry M. "The Measurement of Crime in the United States," *The Journal of Criminal Law, Criminology, and Police Science*, Vol. 57, No. 4. December 1966, pp. 483–492.

Sykes, Gresham and David Matza. "Techniques of Neutralization: A Theory of Delinquency," *American Journal of Sociology*, 62. December 1957, pp. 664–670.

Tittle, Charles R. "Crime Rates and Legal Sanction," *Social Problems*, 16. Spring 1969, pp. 409–423.

Wanderer, J. "An Index of Riot Severity and Some Correlates," *American Journal of Sociology*. March 1969, pp. 500–505.

Weiss, Robert S. and Rein, Martin. "The Evaluation of Broad Aim Programs: A Cautionary Case and A Moral," *Annals of the American Academy of Political and Social Sciences*, Vol. 385. September 1969, pp. 133–142.

Wheeler, Stanton. "Criminal Statistics: A Reformulation of The Problem," *The Journal of Criminal Law, Criminology, and Police Science*. September 1967, pp. 317–324.

Wilks, Judith A., "Ecological Correlates of Crime and Delinquency," in The President's Commission on Law Enforcement and Administration of Justice, *Task Force Report: Crime and Its Impact—An Assessment.* Washington, D.C.: U.S. Government Printing Office, 1967, pp. 138–156.

Willback, Harry. "The Trend of Crime in New York City," *Journal of Criminal Law, Criminology, and Police Science,* 29. May/June, 1938, pp. 62–75.

Wilson, James Q. "Dilemmas of Police Administration," *Public Administration Review,* 28. September/October, 1968, pp. 407–417.

Wolfgang, Marvin E. "Urban Crime," in James Q. Wilson (ed.), *Metropolitan Enigma.* Garden City: Doubleday & Company, Inc., 1970, pp. 270–311.

GOVERNMENT DOCUMENTS

Advisory Commission on Intergovernmental Relations. *Performance of Urban Functions: Local and Areawide.* Washington, D.C.: U.S. Government Printing Office, 1963.

Advisory Commission on Intergovernmental Relations. *Fiscal Balance in the American Federal System,* Vol. 2, *Metropolitan Fiscal Disparities.* Washington, D.C.: U.S. Government Printing Office, 1967.

Advisory Commission on Intergovernmental Relations. *State–Local Relations in the Criminal Justice System.* Washington: Government Printing Office, August, 1971.

Federal Bureau of Investigation. *Uniform Crime Reports for The United States, 1960.* Washington, D.C.: U.S. Government Printing Office, 1961.

Federal Bureau of Investigation. *Uniform Crime Reports for the United States, 1970.* Washington, D.C.: U.S. Government Printing Office, 1971.

Federal Bureau of Investigation. *Uniform Crime Reports for the United States, 1971.* Washington, D.C.: U.S. Government Printing Office, 1972.

Joint Commission on Correctional Manpower and Training. *A Time to Act: Final Report.* Washington, D.C.: The Joint Commission on Manpower and Training, 1969.

Joint Commission on Correctional Manpower and Training. *Criminology and Corrections Programs,* 1968.

The National Advisory Commission on Civil Disorders. *Report of the National Advisory Commission on Civil Disorders.* New York: A Bantam Book, 1968.

Northeast Ohio Areawide Coordinating Agency. *District 4 1970 Comprehensive Law Enforcement Plan.* Cleveland: NOACA, 1970.

The President's Commission on Law Enforcement and Administration of Justice. *The Challenge of Crime in a Free Society.* Washington, D.C.: U.S. Government Printing Office, 1967.

The President's Commission on Law Enforcement and Administration of Justice. *Task Force Report: Crime and Its Impact—An Assessment.* Washington, D.C.: U.S. Government Printing Office, 1967.

The President's Commission on Law Enforcement and Administration of Justice. *Task Force Report: The Police.* Washington, D.C.: U.S. Government Printing Office, 1967.

The President's Commission on Law Enforcement and Administration of Justice. *Task Force Report: The Courts.* Washington, D.C.: U.S. Government Printing Office, 1967.

The President's Commission on Law Enforcement and Administration of Justice. *Task Force Report: Corrections.* Washington, D.C.: U.S. Government Printing Office, 1967.

U.S. Bureau of the Census, U.S. Census of Population: 1960. Vol. I, *Characteristics of the Population,* Part I, United States Summary. Washington, D.C.: U.S. Government Printing Office, 1964.

U.S. Bureau of the Census. *Area Measurement Reports,* Series GE–20, No. 37. Washington, D.C.: U.S. Government Printing Office, 1967.

U.S. Bureau of the Census, Census of Governments: 1972. Vol. 1, *Governmental Organization.* Washington, D.C.: U.S. Government Printing Office, 1973.

U.S. Bureau of the Census. *Criminal Justice Expenditures and Employment for Selected Governmental Units, 1966–67,* GSS No. 51. Washington, D.C.: U.S. Government Printing Office, 1969.

U.S. Law Enforcement Assistance Administration and U.S. Bureau of the Census. *Expenditure and Employment Data for the Criminal Justice System, 1970–71,* GSS No. 64. Washington, D.C.: U.S. Government Printing Office, 1973.

U.S. Law Enforcement Assistance Administration. *1970 National Jail Census.* Washington, D.C.: U.S. Government Printing Office, 1971.

Index

ACIR (Advisory Commission on Intergovernmental Relations), 68; lower
criminal courts, 54; local police, 48
Alabama: capital punishment, 55
Alaska: expenditure assignment, 88; state-
local costs, 40; state police, 47; total
budget, 92
Amir, M., 167
apportionment, 112
Arkansas: state-local costs, 90
arrests: as criteria of police performance,
18
assault, 169; Ohio control policies, 173; and
social service policy, 186
Austin, R., 35
auto theft, 169, 175; correlation with
services in Ohio, 193; social service policy, 188

Banfield, E., 31, 183
Bedau, H.A., 38
Black Panthers, 10
blacks, 10, 118; concept of law, 205; and
law-and-order, 30; police performance,
28; segregation index, 136
Blakemore, Robert, 37
block-grant system, 42
Bordua, D., 142
BSSR (Bureau of Social Science Research),
25; crime reducers, 27
Bureau of Prisons, 62
Burgess, E., 141
burglary: correlation with services in
Ohio, 193; control policy in Ohio, 173;
and social service policy, 186

California: Banfield's work on Oakland,

31; expenditures, 91; law-and-order in
Los Angeles, 35; local police in Los
Angeles, 47; murder rate in San Jose, 14;
neighborhood safety in San Diego, 27;
safety index in San Diego, 26; spending
on law enforcement in San Diego, 30;
variety in sentences in Los Angeles, 55;
Watts, 32
Campbell, A.K. and Sacks, S., 87
CAP: funds allocation, 197
capital punishment, 36; and variance in
criminal proceedings, 55
centralism, 202
Chilton, R.J., 142
cities: and crime rate, 13; history of
crime, 22
Clark, Ramsey, 31
Cleaver, E., 41
Cloward, R., 140
Cohen, A., 140
Cohen, D., 35
Coles, Robert, 197
Colm, G., 4
Connecticut: expenditure assignment, 89
control: policies, 120
corrections: components, 61; costs, 83,
88, 207; function, 44; NOACA, 99; per
capita local expenditures, 91; policy
and innovation, 201; state-local variance,
62, 63
costs: fiscal assignment system, 87; fiscal
crisis, 73; NOACA, 100; per capital
local, 91; priorities, 80–83, 204, 207;
state-local, 90
counsel: for the poor, 80
crime: categories, 11; concept of deterrence, 112; definitions, 18; distribution,

221

About the Author

Yong Hyo Cho is a Professor at The University of Akron where he teaches urban politics and public policy courses. He has authored numerous scholarly works including monographs, book chapters, journal articles, and research reports. Some of the journals to which he has recently contributed articles include *Public Administration Review, Policy Sciences, Western Political Quarterly,* and *Journal of Black Studies.* He holds Ph.D. and M.P.A. degrees from Syracuse University.